First Year U[ni]
A Survival Guide

MW00682390

by

Kaila Aiello
Michaila Aitcheson
Oluwafikemi Akapo
Emily Allan
Maria Altieri
Jim Armstrong
Ben Atwood
Mike Atwood
Carole Aylward
Andy Baker
Erica Baker
Tamara Banks
Tracey Barker
Adam Bazak
Sandy Benson
Patricia Berkers
Gregory Berlin
Nick Blaise
Shane Bogdan
Isaac Bond
Allison Bowles
Kelly Boyle
Landon Braverman
Scott Buckley
Brent Buechler
Elizabeth Bull
Briana Cacuci
Pat Callahan
Diana Catenaro
Cameron Chambers
Michelle Charles
Courtney Chang
Tammy Chuang
Joanne Colling
T. J. Cooper
Chelsea Cota
Alex Coulombe
Sharie Coutts
Greg Couves
Tracey Cox
Dalal Dahrouj
Barb Daley

John Dallan
Nick Decaro
Bernice Denehan
Brent Dillon
Patricia Doherty
Nathan Downey
Barry Driscoll
Glenda Duff
Bobbi Duncan
Jim Dupuis
Rachelle Dwyer
Yvonne Eefting
Frederick Ezekiel
Gordon Farlie
Cathy Fitzsimmons
Lance Frieburger
Kendra Gaston
Grant Gilchrist
Heather Gill
Samantha Glocking
Christopher
 Goldstein
Kayley Goralczyk
Ryan Goralczyk
Matt Goodman
Cathy Gorman
Lloyd Gough
Anthony Grant
Nancy Gray
Jeffi Groff
Torin Grosso
Gareth Haddock
Kevin Hall
Patricia Harris
Josh Hatt
Jordan Hennessy
Andrea Hewison
Laurier Hnidek
Crystal Hines
Kaitlynn Hodgins
Greg Hoggarth
Kate Hole

Michelle Horan
Devorne Hormeku
Rob Horwood
Ibrahim Husain
Kellie Hutchinson
Jen Imperato
Emily Innes
Anthony Isaac
Riley Jakob
Jennifer Jenkins
Tim Johns
Tom Johns
Timmy Johnson
Bryce Jones
Andrew Judge
Susan Kamula
Danielle Kealey
Eliza Kelley
Karla Kennedy
Maria Khami
Melanie Knott
Noah Kowalski
Vivek Kumar
Kim Kuntz
Dan Labson
Justin Larocque
Diana Lawrie
Michelle LeBreux
James Lee
Nanci Lee
Valérie Lemay
Yichong Li
Kelly Lovelock
Anne Macpherson
Ian MacPherson
Amy Marturana
Jessica Mauer
Angela McCarthy
Shelagh McDonald
Chrissa McFarlane
Jordan McGarry
Casey McIlvenna

Sadie McKenna
Jim McMorine
Christine Meglino
Gustavo Melendez
Ashley Mendelsohn
Greg Milligan
Chris Mills
Trudy Mohrhardt
David Mosher
Meredith Nackley
Nathan Naughton
Tom Nelson
Ian Nicholson
Catherine O'Keeffe
Gary O'Neil
Patti Noble
Flynn Okner
Lindsay Olivette
Bryan Pankow
Kurtis Pankow
Shelby Parenteau
Stephanie Parra
Jocelyn Pender
Amara Pinnock
Alison Plowright
Andrea Poulton
Diane Powell
Ryan Powell
Dave Prime
Kristen Putch
James Quinn
Jen Reile
Philip Reinert
Julie Robinson
Luke Robertson
Brenda Rodd
August Matzko-
 Sangster
Suhayl Santana
Micaela Scully
Tamara Seale
Joe Sgambati

Laurel Simer
Ken Skorenky
James Snowdon
Joel Sparks
Paul St. Antoine
Kyle Steele
Greg Stone
Teri Strain
Allison Stuckless
Jacinta Swift
Lucas Taccardi
Sherry Tellerd
Laurie Tewksbury
Roger Thacher
Anita Thajer
Sonja Tkach
Kevin Touw
Anna Townsend
James Townsend
Lara Traczyk
Emily Traver
Joanne Treidlinger
Cesar Treves
Ben Vescera
Suzanne
 Vandermale
Mary-Jane Van Ness
Nina Volzhanina
Lori Wagenaar
Penny Weber
Kaitlyn Webster
Jourdan Weir
Wendy Wharton
Kelsea Whittle
Whitney Wilson
Arthur Woo
Amanda Woolsley
Payam Yazdan-
 Ashoori
John Young
Monica Zhang

ISBN 978-0-9693137-1-7

Published by CSSP Publishing
(First edition published 1986)

Printed in The United States of America

Editors:

Dennis Field
Nancy Gray

Graphic Design:

nhouse/Nancy Houseknecht
nhouseknecht@gmail.com

Copy Editing:

Kate Hole
Linda Roach
Kathleen Ryan
Len Ryan

Design Consulting:

Linda Myers, lmyers@tdgraham.com

Visit our Website:

www.srvlgd.com

Colleges & Universities represented

Acadia University, Wolfville NS
Algonquin College, Ottawa, ON
Cambrian College, Sudbury ON
Carleton University, Ottawa ON
Cornell University, Ithaca NY
Dalhousie University, Halifax NS
Georgetown University, Washington DC
Harvard University, Cambridge MA
Massachusetts Institute of Technology, Cambridge MA
McDaniel College, Westminster MD
McGill University, Montreal QC
Memorial University, St Johns NF
Mount Allison University, Sackville NB
Pennsylvania State University, Middletown PA
Queen's University, Kingston ON
Simon Fraser University, Burnaby BC
Sir Sandford Fleming College, Peterborough ON
St Lawrence University, Canton NY
SUNY Binghamton, Binghamton NY
Syracuse University, Syracuse NY
Trent University, Peterborough ON
University of Alberta, Edmonton AB
University of British Columbia, Vancouver BC
University of California at Berkeley, Berkeley CA
University of Cambridge, Cambridge UK
University of Central Florida, Orlando FL
University of Guelph, Guelph ON
University of Houston, Houston TX
University of North Carolina, Chapel Hill NC
University of North Dakota, Grand Forks ND
University of Ottawa, Ottawa ON
University of Saskatchewan, Saskatoon SK
University of Texas, Austin TX
University of Toronto, Toronto ON
University of Southampton, Southampton UK
University of Vermont, Burlington VT
University of Waterloo, Waterloo ON
University of Western Ontario, London ON
Utica University, Utica NY
Washington and Lee University, Lexington VA
Wilfrid Laurier University, Waterloo ON
York University, Toronto ON

The Editors acknowledge with thanks contributions from the following Blogs:

ECS Student Blogs, http://www.ecs.soton.ac.uk/blogs
The Freshman, http://dailybreeze.com/news
ULC-PAL Peer Mentor Blog, http://blogs.usask.ca/ulcpal
ZenCollegeLife, http://www.zencollegelife.com

The Online Part of this Book

Many times in this book, you will see a line something like this:

WEB: TIME DRAGS AND TIME FLIES srvlgd.com/TDF

This means there's a story online about this topic. To see it, go to:

http://srvlgd.com/TDF

Normally, if you just type …

srvlgd.com/TDF

… you'll get the same result.

The online section is no better or worse than the printed section. It was difficult to decide which pieces would go there. Often, there were items that were written well but at great length; other pieces were of enormous interest but probably to only a small group of our readers – both were candidates for the online part of the book rather than the printed part. Sometimes, there was near-duplication that we couldn't resolve, and we decided somewhat arbitrarily which piece should go in the printed part.

This book is complete in itself; the online section enriches it most effectively if you follow the links as you come to them. Do not miss out on reading these pieces!

We plan, too, on adding new stories, as people send them in to us.

WEB: srvlgd.com/NEW

Also on the web is an entire chapter on time management; we put it there instead of in the book because it fits better with the online format than it does with the book format. Organizing your time, we heard over and over, is one of the hardest things for most students to do.

WEB: TIME MANAGEMENT srvlgd.com/TM

If there's one thing on our website that we hope you look at, this would be it.

Editors' Foreword

The authors of this book are students who wrote things for us, talked to us, or both.

In the late 1980s, when Dennis was a university prof and Nancy was a university student, we published the original version of this book. A few years ago, we decided to update and republish.

First we took the stories from the original book and removed outdated references. Then we met with some current university students to ensure that our revised material was truly up-to-date.

It turned out that it was, but the students urged us to do two things: add more and newer material to our book, and meet some of their friends who were at other universities. We agreed, and then the scope of our project exploded. Everywhere we went, there were some who wanted to introduce us to their own friends – at another university.

For two years, we visited universities and met with students, almost always in groups. We recorded the discussions, then transcribed them. Usually, we split conversations into several topics; often we put thoughts from one discussion together with what others elsewhere had told us or written for us. As we did all this, we maintained the original student voices.

Two dilemmas confronted us: which spelling to use and what to do about references which once again may seem outdated in a few years. For the first, we chose "US English" since Canadians are used to American spelling, but American readers might find Canadian spelling distracting. For the second, we paraphrased such references. One example: an obsessive and addictive website such as Facebook gave us great difficulty. Perhaps in some years it will seem hopelessly old-fashioned. But as we put this together, it is huge in almost everyone's eyes, and any book about student life has to include it.

Because this book has over two hundred authors, we know very well that there are inconsistencies and even contradictions. Different individuals, different universities, different programs, different times of the year – complete agreement is impossible. However, all that aside, we were struck by the overall similarities between what students told us wherever we went.

Finally, we want to thank everyone who worked with us: authors; students and administrators who organized meetings; people who referred us to acquaintances elsewhere; those who helped us find our way around the university; people who gave us feedback about the book's design as it evolved; our wonderful designer for her patience with us; our respective partners for their patience with us … it's a long list.

We made dozens of visits to dozens of universities over two dozen months. You couldn't possibly have as much fun reading the book as we had putting it together. But we hope you enjoy the result.

"Using the power of storytelling, this book provides truly authentic accounts of the student experience. It captures the voice of real undergraduate students and provides genuine advice that will benefit any future or current university student."

Catherine Mulvihill, University Student Experience Manager

"This book tells it how it is by the people who really know – students! Their advice will help prepare you for college and smooth your path through your first and subsequent years."

Joyce Lewis, University Marketing and Communications Manager

"Too many 'university preparation books' read like textbooks; a clinical and mathematical how-to is not beneficial to students. University is about more than just school: love, friendship, fear, athletics, academia, and most of all, life. This book is so compelling because it is written by university students about their own personal experiences. It is literal (and literary) proof that, in the game of living, anecdote trumps mere advice."

Kate Hole, Varsity Athlete and English Literature Major

"I wish I'd read this book before I did first year the first time."

(Name withheld), Former Student

"Before the university term begins in earnest, I always try to give the students a heads-up about what the year is going to be like. Everything I have in my 'Talking Points' is here and more. I'll have to make some additions for next year."

Alexander Mason, Dean

"Each year, I invite previous-year's students to give presentations to our graduates. I think this book contains everything I've ever heard, and then some. The tone is right too; so much better than a grey-haired adult saying the same things."

Donna Landry, High School Guidance Co-ordinator

"If I'd have gotten together with some of my friends to write a book about first year, this is exactly how I would have wanted it to come out."

Robert Sanier, Second Year University Student

"I gave it to my daughter, and over the following weeks I often saw her with her nose in it. I sometimes noticed her phoning friends to tell them about something. By now she must have read the whole thing at least twice."

Diane Hennessey, Parent

CAUTION

Don't expect this book to be grammatically perfect.

These students have written their stories as if they were telling them to their friends.

They are presented here in all their idiosyncratic glory (or at least as much of it as the editors thought they could get away with).

Don't expect consistency either. 200 people never agree on anything.

I Came, I Saw, I Conquered.

And I had a good time doing it!

The Beginning

No Turning Back

"Have you got everything?" my mother asked as she started the car. I assured her I thought I had, but did I? I ran through the list again in my mind: varsity jacket, laptop, hard hat – you never know what they're going to throw at you – pictures of the gang, my microwave, a corkscrew, and my model cars, of course.

Let's see – what else … oh yes: my toolkit. Now, have I forgotten anything? I've got my favorite beer mug and the bar set Chris gave me for my birthday. That should be everything. Needless to say I will have forgotten something – but my weights couldn't fit in the car …

Dad turned on the radio, and "Don't Forget Me When I'm Gone" blared out at me, interrupting my thoughts. Pictures of high school dances flashed through my mind. The gang sitting in the quad; playing football at the beach; Mark and Tony sheepishly following Mr. Shannon into his office – I forget now what they did that day; the bunch of us going downtown on Glen's boat and then wrapping up in blankets to watch the firecrackers; the last night we all spent together at the local sports bar, talking, laughing, remembering old times, one last time before we all went our separate ways … it all seemed like yesterday.

I didn't want to go. I wanted the car to turn around; I wasn't going. It was all a mistake; I wanted to stay home. Was I crazy? Why leave those memories, leave my friends and home? Who wants to spend four years here? I don't even know where to find it on the map.

Get a grip kiddo, no big deal. It's not as if it's the rest of your life. You'll make new friends and new memories. Besides, you wanted to get away, remember?

Okay – I'm fine now. I glanced out the window as Mom and Dad were discussing pruning the rhododendrons. God, it will be good to get away!

I couldn't help but wonder, though, what I was getting myself into as we finally neared the campus. The last sign we passed said we only had a half hour to go. There was no turning back. What was this first year going to be like? The letter said it was to be an "Introductory Seminar Week" – not an initiation week. Only a small number of upper-years who were organizing the week would be present; otherwise we first-years were on our own. And just what do they mean by "extra-curricular nightly events designed to be informative as well as social"? My friends all got a real kick out of that one.

Suddenly the campus was before us, and I didn't have time to think. We no sooner had the car stopped than a bunch of crazy people, all wearing red, had it unloaded and we were on our way to my room. I could hear my mother commenting that they didn't get treatment like this when she was at university; she loved it. I could tell she thought the place was wonderful already, and nothing she saw or heard from here on in would change her mind.

Dons' receptions, football games, dancing in the pub – it was all a whirl. When was I going to finish unpacking? I still had two suitcases on my bed. Oh well, I didn't want to sleep tonight anyway. Gotta set the alarm: can't miss that early morning swim. This is nuts, swimming in a river at 8:00 in the morning, not that anyone really swam. It was more a case of jumping in and getting out again as fast as you could. After all, all you wanted to do was get your hair wet to prove to your friends that you did it.

Next on to my first (and last) residence breakfast. An interesting beginning for what proved to be an interesting week. I remember sending letters to all my friends telling them about the great country club I was staying at. The fact that we were here for an education hadn't sunk in yet.

Meeting Your Roommate

So you're going to university. Leaving the comforts and security of home to live in a residence you know nothing about with people you've yet to meet. Naturally, you feel excited and eager but also apprehensive and nervous. I know I did when I moved away from home.

One question constantly on my mind was, "Who am I going to be sharing a room with for the next eight months?" I tried to imagine what my roommate would be like. Would she be like the sister I never had, or the person my mother had warned me about?

The day finally came when I was about to find out who I'd be living with. I went into the residence, and was greeted by many friendly girls: the dons of the residence. Each was in charge of a floor. My don took me up to my room and made me feel very welcome. I wondered whether my roommate would be there, but she wasn't – only her luggage.

I met some of the other girls on the floor, but we barely had time to introduce ourselves when we were kindly escorted to a creek that passes behind the residence. When we arrived, there were a bunch of first-year guys wading around in the water. We soon learned that we'd be joining them for a little dip in the creek.

After this strange way of being welcomed into university and residence life, I returned to my room to find my roommate talking on the phone! She just looked at me, sort of stunned, and continued with her conversation. There I was, dripping wet and smelling of putrid creek water, confronted with the person I'd be sharing my room with for the next school year.

I wasn't certain what was going through her head at that moment, but I'm sure she knew how embarrassed I felt! Well, when she got off the phone, we introduced ourselves, and I explained my appearance. We started to laugh about it, and from then on I felt relieved and knew that everything was going to work out between us.

So that's my story of meeting my roommate for the first time. Hopefully, your experience won't be as bizarre as mine was. But be yourself and keep an open mind. Most of all: Relax and Have Fun.

I Couldn't Believe It: The Poor Guy's Mom!

My roommate is a really nice guy. But when I think back to my first experience with him, I still wonder how he ever got that way.

It wasn't him that was so extreme. He just sat there and took it all in, with a resigned look on his face that expressed his familiarity with the bizarre whirlwind going on all round him.

Whirlwind. It was his mom.

She whirled into his room first, with him following behind. I'd just arrived, and was unpacking my stuff. She didn't say hello or anything to me. No, her first words were, "This window needs cleaning. We'll have to make sure it's done." Then she began to unpack all his stuff and decide which of the drawers and cupboards to put it all in. Then she sent him off for more stuff. Only when he returned (for the second time, remember) did she introduce herself to me. She wanted to know all about me, my courses, my sports, my music … and all in a way that made it clear she was interviewing me to see if I'd make a suitable roommate for her son. (Fortunately, I seemed to pass the test.)

Then she went off with him to look at the bathroom, the laundry arrangements, the food in the cafeteria: you name it, she dragged him along with her. When the lectures began, there she was again. She accompanied him to every first one, and gave him sermons about how to handle the subject and the prof.

He knew, of course, that this would all be absolutely amazing for anyone who saw it. But it was obvious that it was nothing new to him. It had all been the same all his life, from kindergarten on. He just had this resigned attitude, and all he ever said about it was, "Well, that's just my mom." And in truth, in other ways, she did seem a nice lady. Slim, young-looking, well turned out, well-spoken, she was good company when she took a bunch of us out to supper at the end of the term when she returned to take him home at Christmas.

I heard during last summer that another university had seen all this as such a problem that they'd felt they had to trick a bunch of parents into leaving their kids alone on the first day. They had a special session for them all, showed them promotional movies about the university, had some profs talk to them, and generally kept them occupied until all the sons and daughters had been whisked away from the campus on a team-building activity that kept them up all night. At the end of the presentation to the parents, they made it clear that they expected the parents to go away and not come back for at least a week.

Naturally, I'd had friends before about whom people had said, "There's only one thing wrong with him: Too Much Mother." Still, at the time, I wondered what the parents must have been doing to make the university think this kind of subterfuge was necessary to get the moms away from their 18 year-olds. Now I know.

A Country Boy Comes to the City

Being from a rural community, I had a few more adventures in the city than some others. I used up the first week trying to figure out how buses work. My roommate had never taken a ride on a city bus either, so both of us were uncertain of ourselves and confused.

We looked at a bus map, but it seemed like another city in a foreign country. After some discussion we were confident that we knew which bus would take us to the mall. The bus stop was just out front of our residence, so we were confident we could be successful. So on the bus we went.

No mall appeared. Then the driver informed us that this was indeed the correct bus, but the mall was in the opposite direction. That would have been the bus stop on the other side of the road, he said. Duh.

The bus went right by the mall. That's when we learned that if you want the bus to stop, there is a cord you have to pull if no one else has. So we did eventually make it to the mall and back. On the same day.

Boy, were we stupid. Were we naive. Here we were, the best and the brightest, and we couldn't even make it to the mall without people laughing at us.

Intro Week was Great!

To sum up Intro Week in one word: Interesting!

I was really confused about what Intro Week was, whether you had to pay for it, what it was about. I went there completely blind. I didn't think it would be interesting. When I looked at the website before I came to university, it looked boring. I was so very wrong. It was probably made to look that way for parents who view the website.

The first night I was there, I found the building very quiet. It wasn't what I expected. I wanted to meet people and get right into university life. Instead, I ended up getting in my pajamas and watching TV. But then my neighbor knocked on the door and invited me to a party. So I got dressed, went out and met a whole bunch of people, which was really cool. And that just kept going on all week.

During the day there were activities organized for us by upper-years. I'd heard that a few years ago, Intro Week had gotten out of hand: people got charged by the cops, and others ended up in the hospital, mostly as a result of alcohol or drugs. So the university decided to get more involved in Intro Week in order to control it a bit more. I don't know if that's true. But I do know that the activities were just what I needed even though I didn't know I needed them at the time.

The first day, there was a 6 am wake-up call – dons marching through the halls banging pots and pans together. You could choose to ignore them, or you could get your butt out of bed and be part of the group. Although I really wanted to sleep in after crashing into bed at 4 am after the party, I didn't want to miss out on anything, so I got my butt out of bed and went to the introductory activity.

We were organized into groups and played countless mind-numbing games that dropped our defenses, exhausted our minds, and relaxed everyone enough to get over being shy in order to get to know one another. Ice-breaker events and things like scavenger hunts that took us all over campus. We stayed up until we dropped from sheer exhaustion. That was the intent of the university actually: to keep everyone busy and overtired all the time, so people who participated had no time or energy left to get into trouble.

Still, to be honest, it was a drunkfest. You could meet someone, and the next day they had no idea they had even met you because they were too drunk, and the same went for you some-times! But on the other hand, you could talk to absolutely anyone without it being awkward or weird. If you struck up a conversation with someone on Frosh Week, it was A-OK! And regardless of the fact that everyone was drunk, I met my best friends from school during that week.

But back to the first morning: everyone was given a shirt to identify us and a package with the week's calendar from which you could pick the activities you wanted to go to. The activities were fun and were worth doing in order to meet all sorts of people. When you go to university, you meet people from all over. Coast to coast, everywhere in between, and

even a few foreign students. So during the first week of school, Intro Week activities and memories are an easy conversation thread! It is amazing what big groups of people and booze can do when combined!

I did read about a few sessions that I wasn't sure I wanted to go to. For example, there was a Sexuality and Sensuality course on the second day. I had heard it was funny so I went with my roommates. It was an hour-long course on sex toys, what they were, how to use them. Eye-opening. I think the university did it for shock value but it brought us first-years closer through participating in the same shocking things. And I now know how to do bondage. But that's another story.

You do need to be careful during Intro Week though. Everyone is in such high spirits that their supposedly-good decision-making skills go down the drain. You are just so excited about this new life you are about to start that you have no problem spending that extra thirty dollars or drinking another drink. During your first week everyone usually drinks more than they thought they ever could and spends more than they would ever have wanted to. Not to say I would want to take any of that back …

As I said, Intro Week sure was interesting!

Frosh Week Sucked!

I thought Frosh Week would be better. What it had been portrayed as was not what it was like at all. It was kind of boring.

I felt that the leaders treated us like we were five. We went to the casino and when we were ready to leave, the leaders informed us that we couldn't go back by taxi instead of waiting for the bus. They would also check our bags every time we got on the bus which annoyed me greatly.

Our move-in date to residence was two days after Frosh Week had started. So we missed two days of meeting people. It made it really hard because everyone had already formed groups of friends. We missed the ice-breaker activities so we didn't even know anybody's name. There were different cheers for different groups; everyone would start yelling cheers and we wouldn't know what to do because we didn't know the cheers. We missed the boat trip which was supposed to be really fun. And our schedule was already picked out for us so we couldn't even choose what we wanted to do.

If I had known it was going to be like this, I would have stayed with my aunt and uncle who live near the university. Then I could have participated in the activities from the start. Frosh Week probably would have been fun if I had done that.

WEB: INTRO WEEK WAS THE BEST! srvlgd.com/IB

WEB: LAUNDRY AND INDEPENDENCE srvlgd.com/LI

WEB: BE BOLD, ACT CONFIDENT srvlgd.com/BC

Hell Must be Like This

I was disappointed when I first saw my residence room: ugly, stained carpet, puke-colored blankets and curtains – and it was tiny! My room at home had been twice as big.

Even then, I hadn't realized how awful residence would be. I knew that some people never get tired of making noise, but this was extreme. I'd figured that at 6:00 pm everyone watched the news, rather than all the mindless TV shows. And honestly, I'd never known any people who dumped ashtrays in the bathroom sinks or threw up in the hall and then just walked away. All these types were represented on my floor. To top it off, my don was one of those eternally (or terminally) cheerful types, and refused to sympathize with people who had real work to do and weren't able to get it done in the zoo she was running.

The worst thing was that my roommate was one of the floor's most popular people. She and her friends made up cute, preppie names for each other and spent their evenings discussing what shoes to wear to class the next day.

They belonged in that place with its shrieking stereos and its hysterical inhabitants while I, sadly, did not.

Best Before September 7th

First year of university was my most traumatic. It was a time of anxiety, shattered dreams, fears, and of facing reality. When I first came to university, I found I had so many hopes and desires. It did not take long for me to realize that I was simply being swept into the cesspool of university life!

I wanted to be that independent adult, out of the clutches of those worried and overprotective parents. No longer would I need to turn to them for guidance. I was on my own. I was going to make something of myself.

Little did I realize that I was going to be alone against life itself. I guess, in essence, that is reality. The harshest of this reality hits about the third week of September. This is when the drawers are empty and the laundry bag is full. Your fridge has begun to emit an overwhelming odor of sour milk marked "Best Before September 7." Then the very thought of eating cafeteria food makes your stomach cringe. The black bags under your half-shut eyes show you haven't had a decent sleep in a week and a half (between the homework and the social life). Finally, apathy sets in, and you no longer worry about the messes scattered around your box-like room. Your mind begins to grind as you realize you must actually live here for seven more months.

This may all seem very discouraging but no need to worry. It always happens, but it goes away, hopefully before you do. Many have survived, and their ambitions have been rekindled. There is a path in life for all. We just have to take our time getting there.

WEB: GROSS! srvlgd.com/GR

First Days in University

FOR A LONGER VERSION,
WEB: FIRST DAYS IN UNIVERSITY srvlgd.com/FD

It happened to me on the first night after I went to bed and things started to quiet down a bit. That's when it dawned on me what had been going on. I was in university. After the music had died, the amigos had left, and my mother as well, I would be alone. Sure I would be constantly surrounded by my peers, my classmates, older people, professors, and everyone else. But in the end, I would be alone.

The onus was on me to make sure that I went to my classes as well as did all the work that I was required to do. It was a scary but exhilarating thought. Not only was all the workload my responsibility, but lots of other things were going to be changing. I myself was going to be changing. I knew that the person I would be in eight months would not be the same as now. I was determined to explore and learn about new things that I hadn't had the opportunity to learn about before.

The promise I made to myself, though, was that however much I changed, I would not change into someone that I would dislike. I would not become fake, and I would stay true to myself. After that heavy philosophical thinking, I decided, "Well, I've got one more week of freedom where I can be completely liberated from worry about all things, so let's not waste it." I then threw myself fully into the Intro Week, and enjoyed it to the max. But when the first day of classes started, I got down to work.

There were glitches along the way. I was late for my very first seminar. Not a good impression. I mumbled something to the prof about getting lost, which in fact I had. The campus was a labyrinth, quite hard to navigate when you're still getting used to it. Luckily, the professor was understanding and told me not to worry about it.

There were distractions: for me it was TV. At home, we only had an antenna on the TV and four or five channels. In residence I had access to hundreds of channels 24/7 and I took full advantage of it. I watched every show that was on, and I did my readings in front of the television. Let me tell you, that doesn't work. It was hard to remind myself that there would be a repeat of that soap I was keeping up with, and that in any case I could always watch it online. Online … more temptations. But everything there today would still be there tomorrow whereas the deadline for that paper would have expired.

Always, something is going on that seems more immediate and interesting than the current work that has to be done. In residence there will inevitably be some sort of drama. Some people are more interested in their sports team. For other people it's going out to clubs and bars. While distractions are necessary and fun, it's easy to get caught up in them. I'm not saying don't go out and have fun. I'm just saying don't let these distractions get so much in the way of your studies that it compromises you. I let this happen to me, and my grades took the punch.

There were fears that were unfounded. I had been worried before I came to university that the classes would be impossible, and I had this image in my head that professors spoke a foreign language that only an elite, esoteric group could understand. I was mistaken. Profs understand that students are new to university, and they try to make the transition as smooth as possible for us. I'm not saying they make the work easy, but they do explain exactly what they want and how we need to do things differently from what we did before.

Do things differently from what we did before. That's what we have to learn too.

New People, New Town, New Life

Well my first time moving away from home was to come here, six hours away from my home town. I was excited and had no worries about moving away from home.

Sounds obvious, but I wasn't thinking about it: you must be prepared to take care of yourself. At home, if something breaks, you always know who to approach to get it fixed. If you don't, you ask around. Now it's different. The second day here, the toilet got plugged and we didn't know what to do. I mean, we're not stupid; we tried to use the plunger but nothing was happening, so we left it for a day thinking if we flushed it, water would start going everywhere. A day later we called someone to come and fix it for us. My laptop battery also acted up and the computer kept shutting down. Then our bathroom light started flickering – something else to fix!

It got worse. My car broke down, and I wanted someone who would do a reasonable repair job and not rip me off. Easy at home: the mechanic my dad has gone to for the last hundred years has known me since I was in diapers. He's straight up. Here, I had no idea who to go to. My friends were new to the city too, and it needed a lot of asking around before I got a recommendation I could trust. And I needed a map to get there.

I mentioned my friends. I hadn't thought of myself as someone who made friends easily. I hadn't needed to do much of it even though I hate being on my own, because I'd already had all the friends I needed. Different here: I made a lot of friends right away (helped by the organized activities designed to do just that for us) because I had to.

My advice to anyone thinking of moving far away: Go for it; it was best experience of my life. New people, new town, new life!

Freedom (1)

Welcome one and all to the great and exciting life of university. By accepting that long-awaited offer that you receive in the spring, you are automatically accepting a dramatic change in your life! This change may be for the better, but yes, it could be for the worse!

Of course, you will expand your mind. That's what university is supposed to be for, and what a feeling it is! But you will also expand your social horizons. That's why, apparently, residence is encouraged the first year – you have a great opportunity to meet people. At the same time, residence may also be the reason why so many people flunk out the first year, so beware!

One of the most common fears of moving away to residence is that you won't meet anyone. "Oh, I know I won't meet one single soul. I will go to my classes, come home, do my homework, and go to bed. The whole year will follow this routine." In fact, these fears prove to be unfounded – almost ludicrously so. You're all thrown so closely together that you'd have to work really hard to avoid meeting people. And you get to know them faster than you ever have before.

Here you find that you have much more freedom than you ever did in high school, both academically and socially. At home you were forced to contend with your parents. At school you were forced to contend with administration, principals, teachers. In university, you are on your own! Nobody is here to make you follow rules. You have the choice to get up when you want, attend classes if you want, and write essays if you want. But if you don't want to, no sweat; no one is going to say a word!

For a while, it's great, this extra freedom, but beware: if you make too many wrong decisions, it will inevitably catch up on you.

Freedom (2)

I have freedom here. I can eat in class; I can get up and leave class whenever I want; I can sleep in and not go to class. No nagging from parents or teachers. No one is going to wake me up to go to class or remind me about what needs to be done and when. I can do whatever I want.

It takes a bit of getting used to, but I like this sense of freedom. But I don't necessarily behave any differently from when I didn't have it. The difference is that now I'm the one who makes all the decisions. The result in terms of my behavior is usually the same, but that is not necessarily relevant to how I feel about it.

In a way, it is more relaxed at this small university than in high school. There seems to be no need for heavy-handed policing systems. Yes, there are people in the residences whose job it is to see that things don't get too far out of hand. But not many, and they don't have a lot to do. Perhaps it's because the place is small and most students know everyone else. If you see people behave in certain ways, you'll see them again tomorrow, and if you don't know who they are, it would be easy to find out. That tames people's wilder sides. I think, too, that the kinds of students who would be attracted to coming here wouldn't be ones whose behavior would stretch other people's tolerances. They'd find it too quiet, too conservative, too constricting, and too boring.

Good. I have all the freedom I want. People who would use their own freedom in ways that would bother me have gone somewhere else. It all suits me just fine in a place like this.

I am in Control of my Own Space and I Like It

I'm a highly-strung kind of person. I always have been, and it was worse in the last couple of years of high school. We only had one computer and my sister was always on it: "Oh, just this one more thing … oh, look what Julie is saying … " It seemed to go on forever, and I could never get my assignment begun. Then there was my dad: "Let me get my mail for a second … oh, I accidentally deleted your assignment." Then of course there were the chores: "Before you begin, you should … " or "I'm going to the cleaners' tomorrow and I need you to … "

None of them seemed to realize that I was serious about my schoolwork and needed to work myself up into the right frame of mind for it. It was impossible for me to organize my life as I had no control over my environment. I have to admit that I made it worse for myself. Whatever it was that happened to me, I could always find a reason why it was my sister's fault, or my mom's, or my dad's. Never mine. My reasons were true, partly, most of the time.

Now life is my responsibility, and only mine. It's a lot more under my control. I live in a house with other people, but I have my own space. We share some of the chores and some of the food. But I can decide for myself when I do my part of the tidying and the cleaning and shopping. I have my own space, my own laundry to do, most of my own food to make, my own desk, my own computer, and my own life to organize. If something goes wrong, there is no one else to blame, just me.

In the first two weeks, it was all completely overwhelming but made better by being so much fun and by hearing that it would settle down once people got into their routines. And that's just what did happen. Now, I feel in control of my schedule and my life more than ever before. I have the power as well as the responsibility for my life.

For one thing I'm not in class for as much of the day, and I can choose where I do my work, sometimes back here in my room, sometimes in the library or some other place. At home, I had to be in bed at 10 pm because to get the bus, I needed to wake up at 6 am into complete chaos caused mostly by my sister. Now I can go to bed at 2 am. If I have a 9 am class I can just get up at 8:50 and go. Shower, hair, breakfast: all can be done at 10.

I can completely time-manage myself. When I get an assignment, I can block it out. Same thing with studying for a test. I put it into that week's timetable along with classes, parties, and other scheduled things. I have to say, "OK, I'm setting my alarm for 8:30. I'm getting in the shower and eating, and I'll take an hour to do my own thing in the morning; then I'm going to the library to study from 10 until 5 with classes in between. Then I'm going to come back and maybe have an early dinner, an hour with my friends, and then get back to studying." Everything goes on my schedule, and each night I look at it so I know what the next day will be like.

If I am disciplined enough to follow it, then I'm not stressed out because the day got away from me. But sometimes it's not so easy to discipline myself – I constantly need to be working at it. It helps to be living in a house with just five other people: from what I've seen, the various floors in the residence can be chaotic, with loud music and people dropping in all the time. I would have to learn to resist all that; I could do it, but it would make life harder for me. For me, here, the computer is the hardest thing to resist. Unless I'm using the internet, I disconnect. And unless I have using the computer in my schedule, I put it under my bed.

I used to stress out all the time because I had no control. Somehow I had to get the four-hour assignment done in two days, but I never knew exactly when I would be doing it, so it stressed me out for the entire two days.

Now I'm in control. I can block it in and not feel stressed out all the time I'm not doing it.

I'm happy with my life, and I'm proud of being able to organize myself so well. Responsibility, power, control: they all go together. Or they should.

WEB: NOT A STRANGER ANYMORE srvlgd.com/NS

WEB: I STILL MISS MY POODLE srvlgd.com/SMP

WEB: I WILL SURVIVE ... I HOPE! srvlgd.com/WS

WEB: FIVE THINGS A STUDENT MUST HAVE srvlgd.com/FT

The Eight Commandments

Coming to university has been very confusing. It's taken a while, but now I have finally sorted out all my experiences in my mind and condensed them into eight rules – kind of like the Eight Commandments. Here they are:

1. Keep an accurate count of your stuffed animals.

2. Always lock your door when you leave your room.

3. Keep your key in the shower with you.

4. If someone comes into the shower room, make sure they don't steal your clothes.

5. Be cautious when answering the door. Watch out for leaners (large garbage bins full of water).

6. When using the phone, check for Vaseline or other substances on the receiver. And check doorknobs for toothpaste and other foreign substances as well.

7. If you have a roommate, good luck. Pranksters now have an ally.

8. Obnoxious loud-mouthed Frosh always get thrown into showers. Are you one?

(Someone once told me that there were actually Ten Commandments, but I guess the others will have to wait until Year 2.)

Classes

Why am I Here?

Why am I here? I am wandering down these stonewalled corridors looking around at the unfamiliar faces as I head towards a large theater-like room filled with hundreds of faces that I do not recognize. I hesitantly look around for a seat and spotting one in a far right corner, I make my way slowly, trying to avoid the masses of people also frantically looking for a place to settle themselves.

"Excuse me," I say, as I make my way through a dozen feet. "Oops, sorry. I didn't see your purse." Two angry eyes look directly into mine, and now I feel really stupid. Finally I sit down, and I don't even have a chance to open my notebook before a voice drones over the microphone. "The objectives of today's lecture are as follows … " Four hundred pens, including my own fly into motion.

Why? Why I am sitting in this room with all these people I will never know? Attentively listening to a prof and finding what is being said so fascinating that I must write it down? Or more specifically, what am I doing in this humongous structure of buildings known as university? Is it because I want to make a lot of money in my life? Is it because I was dying to move away from the house and the street and the city where I'd lived for as long as I can remember?

Well, I know it's not because I wanted to leave my boyfriend. Maybe it's because I wanted a good education and just had to pay thousands of dollars to do it. I just don't know!!! I am eighteen years old. I have my entire life ahead of me and if someone asked me to answer the question of why I am here, I would probably say "I'll tell you when I know. Right now just let me have a good time trying to figure it out."

Course Outlines

At the beginning of every semester of every year in every university you will receive many course outlines. At first they may look like a waste of paper, but they are not. Treat yours well because it's your map, and you need it to navigate through the course. It pays to take the time to read the outline and get to know what your prof expects.

The outline tells you how many projects you will need to finish, when your tests and assignments are due, and how many tests you will be writing throughout the semester. It's a big help in organizing your time. The course outline lets you know what the course is about and what you should be capable of when the course ends.

Course outlines have another use I hadn't known about until a year after the course was over. I'd just kept them as souvenirs really, but I was glad I'd kept them. I was in the process of transferring from one school to another, and wanted to be exempt from three courses. When I first applied, the answer was no. But I'd kept my course outlines from the first school.

What did I need to be able to prove to the professor that I'd covered the material? The course outline.

Teacher Assistants

In most of my courses there are hundreds of students. Obviously, no one prof could deal with us all. To cope, the university uses Teaching Assistants (TAs). These are older students who usually know the course and the profs and the way they think and do things.

There's a study center open at various times of the week, and the TAs are there to help. There is also a writing center where you can go and show TAs your paper and they will give you helpful pointers.

I've been lucky with the ones I've seen so far. If you go at the same time each week, the same TAs are usually there. So you can get one who will remember you from previous weeks, and you can get to know each other. All the TAs seem friendly and want to try to help as much as they can. I've never felt that when I made a mistake, or missed doing something, or got something wrong, that I was in danger of being put down.

They do vary, though. Some seem to know exactly what the prof wants, and others not so much. Most profs hand out introductory booklets at the beginning of the course, where they do their best to explain the requirements. Other times you can find similar things online. But profs are not always as helpful as they might be – one of my TAs explained that a particular prof always says that some things are important but has never found a way to give marks for it. Other times you find out that three quarters of the questions are going to be based on one quarter of the work in the course. Those are the kinds of things that are important to know.

But then you can get a TA who misleads you greatly. One time, a classmate and I were comparing notes. What her TA had told her about the importance of various things was just about opposite from what my TA had said. So we did a bit of investigating and found that one of the TAs had come from another university. He hadn't ever been in any of the prof's classes and only knew what the prof and the other TAs had told him. So it wasn't hard to figure out which TA to believe. One of them, without doing it deliberately or even realizing it, would have been quite misleading.

That brings me to another point. Talking to other people in the course and making friends with them is very important. You talk in the cafeteria or in the residence or on the way from one place to another; a lot of the discussion tends to be about the courses you're taking. The same goes, and maybe even more, for older students who've been in that course in previous years. I feel sorry for students who live at home or off campus and don't have the opportunity to do much of this kind of thing. It must make it a lot harder to know what to concentrate on and what kinds of things to do to get the best marks.

WEB: IT'S NOT ALL TRUE srvlgd.com/NAT

The Inevitable Weeding Out

My major is biology, and in first year I met lots of kids who were in bio courses because they took bio in high school, because it can lead to careers in the health care industry, and because in high school it was easy – at least compared with math and physics. So they thought it would be easy here.

Here's some news for people like that. First Year Biology is Not Easy!

For one thing, the university accepts about twice as many people in first year as they have room for in the years that follow. The first year course is designed to determine which 300 of 600 students are going to be the ones who get to go on, and to get students used to biology as it is here. You need to know all the material, and then to be able to take the pieces apart and put them together in different ways. Apart from 20% labs, the marks are all for multiple-choice tests and exams. Intro psych is the same: they know people will find it interesting and fun (which it is), so they have to make the tests hard to get rid of people who can't or won't do the work.

The challenge is learning how to take these tests and how to make sure you are studying the right things. You could learn that the hard way, which I did, through trial and error. That method results in many bad marks, but by the end, you do know how to handle the various types of questions that appear.

First thing: Almost none of the questions are just memory questions. Some need you to know the work, and then be able to figure something new out from it. Some need you to take something you did in September and put it together with something from a different unit you did in November. To get yourself up to speed for these kinds of questions, you need to know September's work by the time November comes. People who leave all their learning and review to the last minute aren't giving themselves practice for the kind of thinking the questions need, so unless they're geniuses, they can't do them.

Or you can use the services of the TAs who have been through the courses and can tell you how the profs write the questions and any kinds of trick questions that they use. I didn't go to the TAs because I didn't bother to find out who they were and what they were there for; in all honesty, I was intimidated by the thought of going to one. The prof: well, there are hundreds of people in the class, and that's why the TAs are there. And of course, the same thing applies as for anything else in university: if you use TAs at the beginning, you get more benefit from them and save yourself a lot of grief.

I found the different teaching styles of profs challenging. Sometimes I would have a prof who would base an entire exam on his lectures; other profs would test completely from the text. And others would tell us they were going to test from the lectures but used the text instead. That was very frustrating!

I found many profs to be helpful; if they knew a student wasn't good at multiple choice, like me, they would allow an essay exam instead because they wanted to help you get a good grade. But I hated the ones who tried to trip you up to keep you on your toes. They were usually the ones who expected you to be in class each day, to understand every word they said, and who felt obliged to test you on every single word they said.

People complain about it, but this kind of course is specifically designed to be difficult. I graduated fourth in my high school class but from a small school without the kinds of programs offered at other high schools devoted to academic achievement for kids. So it was really hard for me. Yet I wasn't worried about getting weeded out because I knew it was what I wanted to do and that I would do whatever it needed me to.

But the kids who come in not really knowing what they want or who are doing bio just because they thought it would be easy don't do well. I think they would have been better off taking a year off to decide. If you want to be a biology major, you have to start first semester freshman year with these difficult classes, and you will have to take them every year until you graduate. There's no avoiding them. Why go through that if it's not what you want?

WEB: A COMPUTER SCIENCE MAJOR srvlgd.com/CSM
WEB: LEARNING STYLES srvlgd.com/LS
WEB: SHOULD YOU BUY A LAPTOP? srvlgd.com/BL

Distractions in Class

There's no uniform policy around here for using cellphones and laptop computers. Some profs seem to have no rules at all. They seem not to notice them even when the phones go off and even when people talk into them, or when a bunch of people gather around a laptop and start laughing at something – obviously nothing at all to do with the lecture.

Letting this happen is a mistake on the part of … well one prof in particular. She goes fast. You have to work hard throughout the lecture to understand all of what she's saying and make adequate notes from it. Perhaps she is paying so much attention to the material that she really doesn't notice what's happening right in front of her in the class. And these … people with their phones and their laptops first of all make it hard to hear, and second, distract you when your tiny brain tries to process everything. I wonder why they are here if they're not going to pay attention to what's going on, and I find myself getting mad at them for being so distracting and inconsiderate – and at her for not stopping it. It's a vicious circle: being mad makes it even harder to concentrate and that makes the anger even worse. Is it supposed to be some kind of psychology experiment or what?

Then there are the profs who go completely crazy the other way. If they hear a phone ring, they explode, and one even comes around and physically grabs it. One time he even answered someone's phone when he was near it, not too politely either. We all laughed at that, trying to imagine the person at the other end who made the call. He keeps going around the room and disconnecting people from the network as well. He says people can't resist what's there (true), and he needs everyone to pay attention. It's better than just letting chaos develop like in the other class, but it's still really distracting; it takes both his mind and mine off what we're supposed to be there for.

Fortunately, most of the profs are pretty reasonable. If something distracting does develop, they see it and ask the ones who are doing it to consider everyone else and stop. After a couple of times, the problem just goes away. People still do it, but they keep it to themselves and it doesn't disturb anyone else.

Temporary Death

I had a bizarre experience. It was in my English class of about forty, and the prof was handing back the first essay we'd done. My mark was lower than I'd ever seen before, but it didn't bother me that much because I knew the same thing was true of everyone else I knew, not only in that class, but in most others as well. We all had to learn the new way of doing things – you learn pretty quickly that every prof expects different things.

This prof began the lecture by saying he knew what problems there would be with our work, and he was going to spend about half an hour

showing us how to deal with them. So I knew it was going to be a fairly painful learning experience. What I didn't know was how painful.

The prof had a photocopy of one of the essays in front of him to refer to, and slides of parts of it that he projected onto the screen. It was mine! Apparently nearly all the errors you could possibly make were in my essay! He didn't say whose it was, and I had used the same layout and fonts as everyone else, so you couldn't tell from looking at the screen either. But I thought some of my friends in the class would know (not so, it turned out). I also felt that my face had turned into some kind of red and green flashing beacon that would dazzle everyone in the room so that everyone would know whose essay it was. I was all set to slink discreetly out and pretend afterwards that I'd felt sick – not that far from the truth, really. But then I realized that would only serve to identify me even further with these egregious errors.

Then he proceeded to trash pretty well all I'd done. Paragraph after paragraph was gone over in detail, and every conceivable mistake pointed out that anyone could possibly make. It was devastating.

However, some way into the process, he restored my ego somewhat. He said that my essay was actually one of the better ones – clearer than most, which made it the best one for him to use to show how we should correct our approach. He also said that he knew it must be embarrassing for the person who'd done it, and that he felt he now knew us well enough to be confident that whoever the essay belonged to was one of the stronger students in terms of self-image, so only temporary death would result from what he was doing. I don't usually like to boast, but I do think he was right about that. Then at the end, he pointed out one or two things I'd done which he thought were really good. "Better than I usually see at this level" was how he put it. And in fact, although the mark was far lower than I'd ever had before, it was higher than most of the others'.

A learning experience for sure! Learning the hard way! Well, my mother never did promise me that everything would be easy.

Professorly Advice

I've always been a focused and driven student. If I had a goal, I was determined to reach it. I learned a valuable lesson after taking Pathology 240 in my first year. It was a second-year restricted course and the rumor was that it was tough and intense. However, with my high marks I was allowed to enrol in my second term.

After the first class, the professor called me into her office. She was very polite about it, but her message came out loud and clear. "You're only in first year. You don't have the knowledge and I strongly advise you to drop the class." I was shocked at first, then as our conversation continued I realized that she was not trying to kick me out of her class but warning me of how difficult it would be without already having the foundation courses.

I went home and considered my options. I thought long and hard but I rose to the challenge. During the course of the year, I had to work doubly hard to keep up with the older students and at times found the material extremely challenging. The professor had been speaking from experience and now that I've been through it, I completely agree with her. I was not as prepared and experienced as the older students. However, once I'd made the decision, she worked hard to support me. Even when I needed help, she did not once say "I told you so, but you didn't listen … " Instead, she offered me help and encouraged me.

It came close a couple of times to being very different. One night, I went to sleep having decided to quit the course. Something must have happened during the night because I woke up having decided not to. I was at the limit of what I could do, but not beyond.

So I discovered inner strength as well as my limits. It's important to always believe in yourself but it's just as crucial to discover your limits and take advice from those around you. I learned that you need to be smart about which challenges you accept.

Long story short, I loved everything I was learning in that course, and my final mark was an A–.

My Lab Partner

The last couple of days have been extremely frustrating. I just completed a chemistry lab that I have been working on for four days. The reason it was frustrating is that it was a lab that had to be performed with a partner.

To analyze the results, I put in approximately fifteen hours work. My partner neglected to tell me that he was going away and would be unable to help. Being my partner, he had to have the same results as me. So he "borrowed" mine.

It really does bother me that he just used my work, and that in the end he got the same mark as me without actually doing any of the things the assignment was supposed to be about.

Skipping Classes

One of the worst things about university is how easy it is to skip classes. Often you schedule your own timetable, and necessity dictates that you have a block of one or two hours between classes. This time period is too long to just sit around but too short to go back to your room and do any work. I have one set of classes, then a two-hour break, then another class. I find it very tempting to not go back to the last class.

With lectures of at least three hundred students, and usually more, the professor, or so you think, is not going to miss one student. It is especially easy to skip a lecture when the class is in an out-of-the-way place or is particularly dull!

Don't do it!!! I speak from experience.

I had never skipped a class in high school, but university made it all too easy. I have only one class on Mondays, so when I go home for the weekend, I've been skipping that one class and not coming back until Tuesday morning. I then have all the hassles of getting the notes I missed, talking to people about the lecture, and hoping, especially at exam time, that my notes are complete and up-to-date. I found out that it's more work than actually going to the lectures, so now I have decided to stop skipping and try to go to every lecture.

WEB: PROBLEMS WITH STAYING AWAKE srvlgd.com/PSA
WEB: A QUIRKY LEARNING STYLE srvlgd.com/QLS

An Artsie's Guide to Science Majors

Everyone knows that science majors are troubled people – they're overworked. This is rarely due to poor time management or incompetent organization skills alone. It's simply due to the work itself: they have too much of it.

The science major is inflicted with a multitude of readings, class preparations, pre-lab assignments, lengthy laboratory periods, problem sets, and lab write-ups. The list of assignments, the time spent on them, and the frustrations go on and on. It is said that the science major breaks even with his workload on only two occasions during the year: the first and last days of school.

As a result, the science students (already proven mentally unstable because they entered the science program in the first place) become extremely volatile as the pressures of an insurmountable workload reach a peak. When the inevitable psychological breakdown does occur, the typical science major tends to lash out at the people who are more successful and at ease in the university environment. Thus the arts majors become the prime target for abuse, and all because they're in the unfortunate (?) position of having a somewhat lighter workload.

It seems unfair that we, the arts majors, should be persecuted by those jealous of our free spirit – and free time. However, with much creativity and contemplation, I have developed ten ways to avoid the fury of the science major. By following these ten simple steps, we arts students can co-exist peacefully and unscathed amongst the multitude of science majors found at university while maintaining our true artsy heritage.

1. Never get caught sleeping during daylight hours. Science students are always tired due to late-night study sessions. As a result, they highly resent those of us who are well-rested. If you feel you must take a nap, go to a secluded place in the library where no science major is likely to find you. Any section dealing with an artsy subject like philosophy will do – a science major wouldn't be caught dead in a place like that.

2. At the beginning of the year, many students shade in their classes on their course timetable. Because arts students tend to have a limited number of class hours per week, our timetables end up looking somewhat bare: a dead giveaway to a short-tempered science major. To overcome this constant threat, just shade in those time slots where you *don't* have classes. The result is a timetable that is absolutely packed – especially on Fridays!

3. When the science majors are complaining about their busy schedule, be very sympathetic towards their situation while continuing to be rather vague about your own. You don't want to lie to them about your work, so steer the conversation away from your workload back to theirs.

4. Don't go home too often. Science students can never afford the time to go home, and therefore the subjects of home and family are very sensitive spots for their morale. If you are going home, be sure to place a layer of textbooks over your dirty clothes when you leave. That way, science majors assume you'll be doing schoolwork all the time you're away.

5. Never, and I repeat *never*, ask if you can look at the video games on a science major's computer. First of all, it shows the science student just how much time you have on your hands, and secondly, the science major never has any good games anyway.

6. No matter where you are or what you're doing, always be seen carrying textbooks, calculators, and pencils in an effort to maintain the illusion that you're always busy.

7. Never let science majors read your books – especially your philosophy text. Their straightforward, utilitarian minds are in no condition to accept and understand the poetic writings that we arts students relish.

8. If your schedule allows, take an easy introductory science course. That way, you can learn mathematical formulas that will be a perfect undercover technique to escape persecution. Although you'll only have a vague notion of what Heplar's Laws and Deutonium Physics are, spouting a few formulas between bites at dinner will re-establish your integrity in the eyes of the science major.

9. Buy a lab coat. Even if you never wear it in public, it looks impressive hanging in a prominent place in your room. You can always wear it on Halloween – the perfect time for an arts-science role-reversal.

10. Above all, be nice to those troubled science majors. Listen with sympathy to their boring stories of research troubles, their lab accidents, and their dismal social life.

Don't Give Up Too Soon

First term of my first year was not what I expected. Considering the program leads right into what I want to spend my life doing, it was quite alarming to hate it as much as I did.

I like hands-on, but it was completely theory. Hours and hours of it, page after page, diagram after diagram, technical term after technical term, with everything to be precisely memorized. No let-up, no break from it, no variety, just more and more stuff. So I struggled with it and began to second-guess my choice of program.

In second term, though, we got to go to places and practice the things we were learning. I started to see where it was all leading and was now able to see the relevance of things we had studied in first-term.

It would have helped if the profs could have given us some real-world exposure in first term. Maybe they could have brought in guest speakers who had worked in our field of study for years. They could have come into the class and talked to us about their life experiences, ups and downs, successes and failures. That would be a really good way to give first-year students an idea of what it might be like when it comes time to step into the real world.

However, as much as some of us might not like theory, it does give us the necessary knowledge for when we finally get to do the hands-on. So be patient. Well, for a few weeks anyway!

People who Haven't Done the Work

In first year university, you have to take courses right across the academic spectrum. You have to take science type courses and you have to take arts type courses. And what makes a class good is not the same for each kind.

In anatomy, for example, there is very little scope for discussion and class interaction. You just have to learn the parts of whatever is being discussed and how it works and that's all. On the other hand, political science, if done that way with lectures and slides, would be an almost complete waste of time.

I am glad that in this class, I can learn most of what's important through a discussion or argument. But on the other hand, I am irritated when people who have not done the readings state opinions as though they were worth something. They don't know anything about it, so how can they have an opinion? The worst is when there are marks for class participation and people who are completely ignorant of everything spout out stuff that you are supposed to listen to, but there is nothing at all in it. They don't know anything, and they are just talking so that they can get their marks. It's obvious to all of us what's happening, so the prof must realize it too. It's all a complete waste of my time.

Most of all, I hate when people who haven't done the work interrupt the prof. Obviously if you haven't done the necessary work from previous classes, you probably won't understand what's being explained in this one. But don't interrupt the prof; you're just wasting time for the ones who have done the work and are just trying to do the best that they can.

I hope that in discussions, profs recognize the people who haven't done the work (they must, because everyone in the class knows), and score them appropriately when they give participation marks. Of course, they can't accuse people right in front of the whole class. But it would be nice if they said something mild like, "I think that question was dealt with quite well in the readings. Perhaps you missed it … Let me see, yes, pages 1-314." For the rest of us, it would be reassuring that the prof knew what was going on. And maybe it would discourage these people from asking their dumb questions.

Mature Students Waste my Time and I Don't Appreciate It

We are in classes with people who already work in our field of study. So they think they know it all even though they are only in first-year classes. One guy barfs up information at every opportunity. Another one asked if she could use the calculator on her cell phone for an exam. Stuff like this makes me cringe. I don't know if it's because they are older that they are so keen and annoying.

Some of them can never just listen to what the prof says. They have to drag up stuff they've seen that they think has something to do with what he's said, and they tell long and detailed stories about stuff that half the time has nothing to do with anything. Sometimes the prof doesn't mince words: "Look," he

says, "this isn't what this is about; we've got to move on." Yet lots of times they don't accept it, and carry on.

In my criminology class, the prof asked who knew how to roll a joint; the lesson had to do with what we learn in our lives. The only person in the class who raised her hand was this sixty year-old woman who said, "Oh, I know how to roll a joint." Apparently she grows weed on her farm and smokes up with her adult son.

Then there are the times that the prof tells us that he'll let us out of class half an hour early unless there are any questions. And guess who raise their hands? Quit wasting my time people! If you have a question, go up after class.

In my English class, there is a forty-some-old lady who I swear to God is hitting on the prof. She keeps saying that she is going to bring a bottle of wine to the exam and that she wants to go over to his house for dinner.

And then you get this woman who sits in the back and always asks the stupidest questions. You can't help but laugh even though our class is so small that everyone can hear you. Doesn't she realize that we're laughing at her ridiculous question?

They just don't get it though. Just because they are older doesn't mean that they know everything.

Those Eighteen Year-Olds and their Immaturity

One of my classes has about a hundred students in it. Perhaps a quarter of us are mature students, and most of us have already worked in the field that the class is about. The other students are "ordinary" first-year students, which means they're eighteen or so, and right out of high school.

I have to say that the prof is less than perfect. She has lots of academic knowledge, but it's been a long time since she worked in the field herself, and it shows. Some of the situations she describes are ones that wouldn't ever occur now, and other things that happen all the time she knows nothing about. Worse, if one of us has worked in the field (and some continue to work part-time in it), she dismisses our experiences. In one memorable case, she denied that such a situation could ever occur, when from my own recent first-hand experience, she was wrong. When a couple of us questioned her, she said that it wasn't something she wanted to spend time on, and then she went on with the class.

However, this prof does know what she's teaching and gives us excellent information and a valuable perspective on our profession and the wider issues involved in it. She's very organized, and she makes it clear exactly what she wants us to know and to be able to do in the assignments, tests, and (I hope!) the exam as well. So I can forgive her occasional lapses.

Harder to forgive, though, is the attitude of some of the eighteen year-olds. You'd think that if they're going to be members of our profession, they'd be interested in the views and experiences of those of us who actually work in it. But no. If one of us asks a question and dares to mention a real-life situation to put the question into some context, we're met with pronounced shuffling noises, coughing, and hostile-sounding murmurings. Turn around, and you can see them all rolling their eyes at each other in their exaggerated and immature way. Their attitude seems to be: If it's not something the prof brought up, it's not something we need to know about, and we don't want to know it. Just let us out as soon as you can so we can go on with our all-important social lives.

Some of these people might be working as colleagues of mine in a couple of years' time. That scares me. I hope that they grow up before then.

WEB: REVENGE IS BEST SERVED COLD srvlgd.com/BSC

When Will They Learn?

I am sick and tired of jumping through hoops. Completing irrelevant assignments, and meeting unreasonable expectations set by professors who seem to be trying so hard to kill the weak students and maim the rest.

We are given labs in psychology with a hundred more statistics than required; they take more effort and time that way, right?

Class averages are occasionally 42%, and we get back essays with poor marks but no comments on how to improve. C'mon guys, are we here to play games or are we here to learn?

At times, it seems that some profs are trying harder to discourage us than they are to educate us. When I realize I'm paying an exorbitant amount of money to be "educated" (I think my definition varies from theirs), I quickly lose patience with the system.

So what do students do? Some cheat. At the salad bar one day, I was nonchalantly offered a biology paper for twenty dollars. "No thanks … could ya pass the olives?"

Some students tackle every assignment head-on – the hard way. That's what I did until I learned to play the game. I felt that if the profs weren't going to take the time to tell me how they wanted an assignment set up, then they'd have to accept what the students thought was best – until I got the failing paper back. Then I changed the way I did things.

Before I started an assignment, I began to get tips from students who'd had the prof before – or better yet from the profs themselves.

"If in doubt, ask the person who's going to be marking it." That's my motto … that, and "don't eat the meatloaf in the cafeteria."

Profs

Bullshitting

Everyone is familiar with the term. It is an ancient practice that has been learned, refined, and passed down through generations in all types of professions. When it comes to the profession of being a student, it can make or break the grade, the class, the professor-student relationship, and the shape of things to come. But most of all, it can influence how much time you have to focus on other, more important things than research papers or Power Point presentations – like online gaming. It is the age-old and invaluable art … of bullshitting.

If done correctly, bullshitting saves everyone a lot of pain and anguish – in the short term, that is. The student is happy not doing any real work, and the professor is happy because it appears that the student *did* do some real work.

To correctly bullshit a research paper, one must write with flair – with fluff, with big words and lengthy sentences that add to its sophisticated tone. There must be shit, but not too much shit. At the same time, one must remember that crafting the structure and clarity of the shit is an incredibly important part of the process – so that the shit does not, in fact, look like shit. Unless, of course, you have absolutely *no idea* what you're talking about, in which case it's better to generalize the shit as much as possible.

I used to be good at bullshitting. *Very good.* I could bullshit my way through a paper, sure. Papers weren't a big deal. I could even bullshit my knowledge of an assigned reading while speaking in front of the class if I wanted to.

I like to think that I still am a good bullshitter, to some extent, because a little bullshitting here and there can be a useful skill to have in life, but something has changed since I came to college:

Some of the teachers – they *know*.

Allow me to give an example: I'm sitting in my theater and group process class one evening, and I realize that we've been assigned a brief reading from our textbook. It's not that I was being lazy, it's just that it completely slipped my mind.

Well, I think to myself, *you've had practice with this. No problem, you know what you're doing. Just speak with confidence. Don't flinch.*

You'd think I would have known better than to try and out-act an acting professor. We go around in a circle discussing what we found interesting about the reading. *OK*, I think, *all I have to do is repeat something that someone else said but rearrange it so that it sounds different. This is easy.*

My turn comes, and I say something like "I agree. The idea of using extemporaneous improvisation to form fluid sculptures in this context is something I found especially interesting in this section. I guess because I've always felt it would be a difficult thing to do because of all of the mental preparation involved."

My professor watches me as I speak, and I look back at him, confidently. After I'm done, I don't let my eyes go anywhere else. Wandering eyes are a dead give-away. This is what it really comes down to when bullshitting – each person tries to find out how far the other is willing to go before … the shit hits the fan.

"Can you elaborate on that?" my professor suddenly asks.

Uh-oh.

"Well, it seems that I just, um, I don't see how it would be possible for me, personally to … come up with something like that on the spot."

Oh, the irony.

"OK," my professor says, giving me a knowing look. He's grinning. Yup, he knows.

Damn it.

Don't try this at college, kids. This might have worked on your high school English teachers, but it probably won't work on your college professors.

Bullshitting should be a last resort, and by last resort, I mean that it should come even after telling your professor that you didn't actually do the reading, study for the test, or whatever.

Let me stress, however, that guessing and bullshitting are not the same thing. If you think that you might know the answer (and most of the time you'll have at least an inkling of confidence that you just might possibly know what you're talking about), go for it. On the other hand, if you have absolutely no idea what the answer is, and you think that you might try your luck anyway, don't bother.

Bullshitting should be used very sparingly in life. In school, honestly, it can hurt your chances, so please, try to restrain yourselves. The fact is that you can't make up stuff all the time because, let's face it, there's only so much shit to go around.

Profs' Teaching Skills

One of the big life lessons that people learn in college is that they are going to encounter people who might not know exactly how to handle the situation that they're placed into. Professors can be these kinds of people.

Don't get me wrong – some professors are fabulous. But then there are some who make you question why in the hell you're sitting in the lecture hall to begin with.

For instance take my Geology professor. The guy was a seemingly smart guy who probably would have bled iron ore and sediment had you cut him open. His passion clearly was rocks and minerals but choosing to communicate that passion through teaching was probably a poor life decision for him seeing as the only audible

sounds that came from him were grunts and slurs of what my friends and I assumed were supposed to be words. It was no good to look at his slides either because they made no sense! The most that I retained from that class was that it was a very bad fashion choice for Caveman to wear the same red sweater. Every day. Every class. With some other hideous shirt underneath. Fashion fail right there.

But on a serious note – there's no avoiding them. These guys are everywhere, so you need to be able to rely on yourself to study what you think could be relevant to the course at that time. Keep your head about you, and don't get wrapped up in "Ugh, this guy sucks" or you're gonna head down a slippery slope. Just sayin'.

There's going to be more than one of these guys per campus too, ya know. Take Astronomy Guy for one: he couldn't have been any more of your stereotypical dorkwad. Pocket protector and all. He wore his pants too high, he was bowlegged, his glasses had annoying plastic frames, and his poof of light brown hair was always slightly more than frazzled. Oh! And how dare I forget the lisp! This dude was one of like eight astronomers in the country selected by NASA to study the presence of dark matter in the universe … that's intense. As genius as he was, he struggled in the human interaction department – too much work with all those extraterrestrials if you ask me.

Anyhow, Astronomy isn't something that is common knowledge to a lot of people, so it needs a lot of breaking down and baby talk. My guy just kind of assumed that we knew all about G forces and orbital circumferences. Wrong-O. He didn't teach us anything other than that we were all stupid in the galactical department. Such is life I guess.

It's situations like this where you employ the help of that $800 paperback book that you are "required" to have but has never been referenced in class.

The key with guys like this is to just adapt. If they're still teaching, it means they haven't been fired yet, which means that other kids have been in the same seats that all of you now sit in and by some severe stroke of luck, passed. It's feasible, so figure it out. I got B+s in both classes. Just for the record – it's possible.

WEB: WHY DO I HAVE TO PUT UP WITH THIS? srvlgd.com/WP

Boring Profs and How to Deal with Them

If you're lucky, only one class during the term will be extremely boring. (If you're not lucky, you'll have two or three or …) The prof will go on and on, saying nothing really worth writing down. You have to be careful, though, because sometimes even though the prof seems boring and/or confused, he or she actually is saying something that if you think about later, you can actually make some sense of. More: it's probably the same person who teaches the class that writes the exam – another reason to be wary. However, if upon mature reflection you decide you have to play some games to stay awake … here are some ideas.

The first two involve the school paper. Every week during the term, it runs articles known as *Prof Quotes*. If you listen carefully, the prof sometimes says something silly or indicates he's lost. The best one I ever read was, "Let me explain to you why this is obvious." Listening for *Prof Quotes* not only keeps you awake and alert, you might even learn something.

In one issue, there was an article outlining the rules for *Prof Football*. Two pieces of tape or any other convenient markings are placed at either end of the blackboard or the floor. The class is divided in half and each team tries to gain "field position" by asking questions concerning what was written on different areas of the blackboard. If your questions lead the prof across your goal line – touchdown!

Again, you might even learn something.

Another good game is *Prof Obedience School*. This game requires the cooperation of quite a lot of people in the class. Every time the prof performs a selected action, such as nose scratching or foot tapping, everyone leans forward and looks

up encouragingly, pretending to pay attention. After a while, you'll find your prof can be trained to do almost anything.

Prof Obedience School doesn't usually work with psych profs. They tend to know the game already and are capable of telling you all about it. Indeed, some of these cunning people can even operate the game in reverse. (Actually, that's another useful tip. Never trust a psych prof. They're notorious for carrying out experiments on poor unsuspecting students.)

I wouldn't really recommend skipping these lectures, though. Sometimes, a prof can be really boring and confusing just because he or she doesn't know much about some of the topics in the course or isn't interested in them. Then, suddenly, there's an apparent personality transformation – you've come across a topic that your prof knows something about and is interested in. You can't afford to be away for that.

Also, skipping lectures can become a habit. People who do it too often get hooked on it, and as the term goes on it's not just the useless ones that get missed. You can't tell ahead of time which those are going to be. That's why you need *Prof Quotes, Prof Football*, and the like.

WEB: A VERY SPECIAL PROF srvlgd.com/VS

Prof-Rating Website (1)

One of the most useful tools a student has is a website that rates the profs. You might think there would be a lot of students who would put down a prof who gave them a low mark. Sure, some do, but you can tell who those people are. For most profs, there are so many ratings and comments that the general picture that emerges is fairly accurate.

I always look the profs up on this site before I choose my courses. It has saved me from taking a few classes with professors who got rated pretty badly by many students. I've been able to choose a different section of the course or a different course altogether. Once you're in the course, there's actually valuable information about the prof to be found as well – like if they're a hard marker, what their exams are like, if they're willing to help you on an individual basis, if they favor people who participate a lot: all the things you need to know.

Look at the website now! You'll be amazed, fascinated, and enthralled. ike.

WEB: PROF-RATING WEBSITE (2) srvlgd.com/PW

Get to Know Your Profs

Your professors are not like your high school teachers. What you notice first is that most don't know you, will never know you, and can't know you. Especially in first year, classes are much too big for that to ever happen. That doesn't mean that you can never communicate with them though. There are office hours, and there are TAs, whose job it is to work with you. In my courses, I've always been able to find someone who could help me when I needed it.

There was one awful course that I really shouldn't have taken because I didn't have the background. I couldn't understand anything at all about what was going on. Help! I didn't even know what questions to ask. I was going to talk to my academic adviser and drop the course, but then I thought, well, maybe it's worth one more try. So I went and had a talk with the TA; much to my surprise, she seemed to understand exactly what was going on (or not going on) in my brain, and she seemed to want to help and to think she could. She was right; it took a lot of her time and mine, and I never did very well in the course, but my mark ended up being respectable.

Now, from my position of enormous wisdom and experience as a second-year student, I make a point at the beginning of every course to see who there is to talk to about it. Sometimes it's the prof, but most often it's a TA. If I do have questions or problems later on, I have someone who can help. It hasn't happened to me very much, but if I found someone who didn't seem

to know the work or couldn't explain it, I'd look around for someone else. But it's better to find someone at the beginning of the course so that all the way through, you know that there's the prof or a TA who can help with any problems. I also make a point of talking to a TA whenever I get a major piece of work handed back; it's good for them to know you're serious about your marks, and it can be surprising how useful their comments can be. Even if they can tell you that the mark you were upset about is actually quite good for that course, it can make you feel better.

Sure there are vindictive profs, worn-out profs who don't care about their students, profs who don't want assignments based on your opinion but rather on theirs, and profs who are just plain lazy and disorganized. One of mine always seems to jump from one topic to another and to go off on tangents. Either he just reads from his slides, or he just babbles on. You ask him a question about a slide and he doesn't seem to know what to say about it. He contradicts the text and contradicts what he's just said. You think, "How did this guy ever get a PhD? How did he get hired? What were they thinking of when they chose him to teach us this work?"

But here at least, there aren't many bad profs. Most of the ones who seem that way at first are quite different once you get to know them a bit. There was one of mine who seemed very distant and unfriendly, and I got the impression he didn't care about how we did or even maybe was pleased when people didn't do well. It was getting to me; it made it hard to go to the class and hard to concentrate properly on what he was explaining – quite difficult things actually, even on a good day.

One day I went after class to ask him a question; he seemed quite friendly and eager to explain the answer. He even thanked me for asking the question and said that it would help him explain that point better in the future. I also searched out a fourth-year student who had been in some of his smaller upper-year classes. It turned out that this prof was a shy person and found our enormous first-year class quite intimidating. The previous year, a prof-rating website had trashed him which made him feel nervous and insecure. Also, he was depressed about his research which wasn't going well at all. After hearing about this, I began to look at these lectures in a different light; I enjoyed them better and learned more too.

Another advantage of getting to know profs and TAs is that they have contacts that can be useful to you in ways you can't necessarily foresee. One of my profs gave me a reference letter, and a friend of mine got summer work as a lab assistant. The prof wanted someone he was sure could do the job, and he was working closely with the TA my friend knew.

So getting to know your profs, or at least something about them, pays off in many ways. It's well worth the time and effort you put into it.

WEB: KNOW YOUR PROFS srvlgd.com/KYP

WEB: PROFS: DON'T BE SCARED OF THEM srvlgd.com/PD

WEB: PROFS AT A SMALL UNIVERSITY srvlgd.com/SU

A Mistaken Assumption

Profs can be difficult to figure out and adjust to. There are the ones you can't understand because they don't speak English well or because they are great researchers but can't teach. There are ones who want you to write one way and others who want you to write another way. There are ones who seem to give you better marks if you know them and ones who give you bad marks whether you know them or not.

I knew my psych prof really well. He is actually from my home town, so you can imagine my surprise when I got a big fat C on my first essay. In high school, if the teacher likes you, you tend to have a greater possibility of getting a good mark. But here it's different. Even though he knows me and likes me, he is able to separate that from the class.

Besides, in lots of places, the first-year evaluation is almost all done by grad students or even by the computer. So don't assume that getting to know your prof will help with your marks.

Prof's Non-native English

Editors' Note: The first part of this piece was written in September, the second part in November.

I have this prof who doesn't speak English. Well it's supposed to be English, but it's so disjointed and garbled that it's hard to understand anything at all that he says. Even when his slides are on the screen and he seems to be saying the same thing that's written there, it's still hard to get more than about a quarter of it. People ask him to repeat stuff. He does it a bit slower, and then it's possible to kind of get the gist. But then before too long, it's back to the old speed again.

One day someone told him (in a nice way which I thought at the time he didn't deserve) that she was having trouble understanding what he was saying. He told her to look at the slides because everything was there. Well, the slides are online, so if everything's on them, why go to the class? And maybe everything is on them, but you can't understand what it's all about just by looking at them, no matter how hard you try to make sense of them. Once, a group of us from class got together and tried to figure the slides out, but we didn't get far. It all really has to be explained. Even when we ask the TAs, they haven't learned it from the same prof, and it takes them a bit of time to be able to figure it all out and explain to us what's going on. About a quarter of one lecture becomes clear after an hour of explanation, and we have three lectures each week.

It's extremely frustrating, especially because this is a course I need. And from the few parts that I can understand, it's obvious that he's very knowledgeable about it and really cares. It's stuff that matters, and we need to know it. In that way, it's good. But in the other way, it's bad. I want this material. I need it, but I can't find a way to get it. We did ask one of the TAs what we could do, but he said that if we complained to the administration, there wouldn't be anything they could do either. Not hire him next year, maybe, but that doesn't do us any good this year. Besides, he's actually very nice, and if we could only understand what he says, he'd be a really good teacher.

Most people in the course don't seem to be any better off than I am which I suppose makes it better. At least, if I was the only one, it would be worse. But it's very hard to see what to do.

. . . .

In September I wrote a piece about one of my profs and how hard it was to understand his English. Well, now it's November, and the situation has improved a lot. It's still a struggle, but most of us can understand most of the stuff most of the time.

I think he's slowed down substantially, and he certainly puts a lot more on his slides. Maybe his English is better too, or perhaps we've become used to it. Could be, too, that the TAs and other profs have spoken to him and he realized that he had to do things differently. Whatever the reason, it's much better than it was. As I suspected, he's a really good prof, and I'm enjoying his classes a lot. I didn't admit it before, but I had thought of dropping the course and getting the credit at another time or maybe in another way. I'm glad I didn't.

Writing Styles

I well remember my first English class here. I wrote an essay on "Liminality in Sir Gawain and the Green Knight." I looked up the terms and spun off the essay with all the usual flourishes and turns of phrase that had served me so well throughout high school. The result: a 25% mark dip and an admonition to write more simply in the future. Sorry, not an admonition, an instruction. Amateur Victorian Lady Novelist indeed. Bah! Humbug!!

Do you (1) "attempt to dissuade" someone from a course of action, do you (2) "try to persuade him out of it," or do you (3) "say 'Don't do it!'"? It all depends, not only on the subject and the topic as you might expect but also on the individual prof. Should you write, (1) " … an unfortunate shibboleth that, due to my previous

boasting, betrayed them as my own," or (2) "Jeez, I shudda kept my big mouth shut cuz now they'll all know whose it all is."

Yes, I'm exaggerating, but the point is a valid one. What to one might be a suitable literary style would be puffed-up, strained, and artificial bloviation to another. Or what one would accept as straightforward and workmanlike, another would regard as bare-bones adequacy that betrays no familiarity with the subtleties of the language.

How do you find out what the prof wants? Be attentive, very attentive to the way he or she phrases things, especially in writing. Look closely at something that is identified in class as an example of good writing. See if you can find someone who's taken courses from the same person before. Or (and this has taken me a while to learn), you can always ask.

Profs' Higher Expectations

Things here are certainly a lot different from what they were in high school. There you got a reasonable mark most of the time if you were in class, paid attention, read all the articles on the course list, did the work, and then studied hard for the exam.

Not the same now. Last week I got back an assignment that I thought was good for a B+ at least. I'd been to all the lectures and taken full notes. I'd done all the readings. I'd read the textbook and all the articles on the list we got the first day of the course. And I'd studied the assignment instructions very carefully, and I did all of what they said to do. It looked good and felt good when I handed it in, and I was proud to have finished on time and proud that there were no rushed parts in it.

It came back with a C–. I was astounded and extremely upset. If you've done everything you were told to do, what else is there? How could I explain this to my mom, for one thing, and how could it be that perfectly good work got such a low mark? I am here! It's costing me a lot of money to be here – all of what I saved from my various jobs in the past and what I'll be doing in the summer! I'm doing everything I'm supposed to!

At first I thought there must be some mistake, and I was going to complain to the prof. But it's quite hard to get to see him because he has too many students. Then I asked some other people in the course and found that many had experienced the same thing.

There didn't seem to be much written on my assignment in the way of criticism, just the mark and some very lukewarm comments here and there. I knew there was a problem, so I went to the Student Academic Center to see if I could get some idea of what was wrong.

The Counselor looked at my work and said something that, truth be told, I had begun to suspect. She said that she could tell that I'd paid attention in all the lectures and read everything we were supposed to. The assignment was well-constructed too, appropriately broken down into sections, and put together properly. Then she said, "But that's all you've done."

Y-e-e-s-s. And what else could I have done?

She replied with something I've since taken to heart. "You must read for understanding as you've done. And the next stage is that in the writing, you've got to explore the ideas."

And she explained what she meant. Imagine you were in the Student Center with some other people in the course and discussing the work that was in the assignment. Nobody would talk about what was in your work, she said, because it would be boring. People would know it already. If you wanted to get their attention, you'd have to put your own slant on it. Relate it to other things you'd read in the past, or even to some more general ideas about the subject as a whole. For example, if it was anything to do with history (which it was), you could bring in some things that had happened previously or in another place at the same time. Or (rather carefully!), you could explain how it fitted with some political opinions you or other people might have.

Well, it reminded me of what some of my idiot friends did in high school. They hadn't paid attention in class and had skipped over the reading or asked other people at the last minute what it was about. Their writing on tests or assignments was of the kind "In my opinion I think that … ," totally devoid of any sign that they knew anything about the subject. They got mediocre marks, and they deserved even lower ones in my opinion. But none of them are here in this university now. So the solution was not going to be along these lines.

I had to have a view or an angle on the material, and then when I wrote, I had to make it clear that I knew what I was supposed to; then slant some of the things from my own point of view. Only some of the paragraphs in some of the sections had to be written this way; others would just tell what had happened and then what various sides in the war, or whatever, had thought about it, in the way I'd done the first assignment.

At first, I thought it was impossible. But then gradually, I began to see how I could have rewritten my first assignment to include some things like this. Truly, I did have a personal view of the things the assignment was about. And I could back it up, using other things I knew or at least could look up.

Too late for this one. But the next which I'm just beginning now: yes, I can see how I'll need to do all of what I did before, and then some.

But know what? I can feel myself feeling quite strongly about the topics we have to deal with. Some of what the historical people did and said makes me mad! Bringing this in might even make it fun to do the assignment.

Money

How to Score a Scholarship

Most people think scholarships are reserved for the super smart individuals in high school. The truth is that there are more scholarships out there than you think and they are not ridiculously hard to obtain if your marks are good. The trick is that you have to go searching for them. You'd be amazed at how many people just don't seem to bother doing it.

Naive or lazy? Who knows? But you can be the beneficiary.

In my last year of high school, I checked out many resources. I inquired about scholarships at my school and did some online searching for various university scholarships, bursaries, grants, government assistance, company and even foundation scholarships. Great marks are not the only criterion; there are sports and volunteering scholarships, scholarships for minorities, and even ones given by community clubs.

Applying for government tuition assistance is a must. Many universities have a separate bursary application you can fill out to receive extra funding; however, they do take into consideration your government funding to determine your level of financial need.

I found a lot of scholarships through my high school. This is a great place to start because many universities will notify the high schools of the awards and scholarships available ahead of time.

Talk to your guidance counselors. They can point you in the right direction and even nominate you for special scholarships.

Start early. Look everywhere. Talk to everyone.

Scholarship deadlines are spread out throughout the year, and application deadlines can be as early as October or as late as April.

Make a timeline of everything you've ever done. What clubs/sports are you in? Do you volunteer or have a job? Have you won any awards or held any leadership positions? All these factors are taken into account. Another important piece of advice is to make sure you have all necessary documents ready beforehand. Many scholarships will require reference letters, transcripts or written essays. Be prepared and know what is expected of you.

Don't rule out sports scholarships. Some universities aren't supposed to have scholarships for a particular sport because the team isn't in the right division, but in fact they do. Scouts recommend you and, surprise, you're offered an academic scholarship. However, when they disguise their intent in this way, it only binds the student to try out for the team, not necessarily to play all season. I'm sure you get the drift.

There are also scholarships for out-of-country students. Some are sports scholarships, others are – well in this university they're called "diversity scholarships," because the school wants to increase the diversity of the student body. That's an opportunity for someone with an unusual background.

You may think applying for too many scholarships or bursaries will be impossibly time-consuming. But for many, the essay questions are fairly similar. It might take you three hours to apply for the first one, but with the wonders of copying and pasting, it'll take you only one hour to fill out subsequent applications.

Don't get discouraged if you aren't awarded anything or as much as you would have hoped for. Keep in mind that there are others who are also applying. Don't give up. You can do it. Just believe in yourself.

Your First-Year Cash Flow, Yo

Money. The stress a person can gain from worrying about it. But it is an important part of getting to university and enjoying yourself while you are there.

Before you go to university, you should try to research and apply for as many scholarships as possible. The time you spend will be well worth it. The price tag on university is huge and goes way beyond just tuition and housing fees. There are your books which are astronomically costly, going to campus dances or out for dinner, buying what you need at the drug store, and dealing with surprise notices informing you that you owe more money to the university. Any financial support you can get before you go will help you out immensely.

I went into university with a part-time job which I anticipated would help pay for my expenses. I only worked two evenings a week but soon found it too much. I decided to leave my job in order to make time for my friends, myself and most importantly, my grades.

One of the biggest differences I noticed when I made the transition from high school to university is that you become even busier than you ever imagined. The schoolwork just piles up. In high school I could manage a job, but in university it seems almost impossible. I realized having good grades and a degree was more important than a minimum wage part-time job. Leaving my job also freed up time to join a recreational volleyball team, which is a sport I had never played, and gave me time to spend quality time with my new friends.

So how did I manage without a job? I had a little bit of money in my bank account but my "cash flow" was cut off. I was on a meal plan so I tried as hard as I could to only eat at places that took my meal card and I tried not to touch my debit card. I had to stop shopping completely. No more new clothing and no more new toys. I quickly found out how things add up. Needing conditioner or cold medicine was all my responsibility for me to purchase and no longer my parents' responsibility.

I stuck to a weekly budget and tried to use as little money as possible. Soon, I was dreaming of getting shampoo under the Christmas tree. I looked for opportunities to go to free events and for free food – surprisingly, there are lots. The university recognizes that we are students first and we do not have time to work and make a lot of money.

My mom always told me, even if your friends act like they have a lot of money to spend, they really don't. She's right. All university students are just as broke as you are.

WEB: MONEY PROBLEMS srvlgd.com/MP

Student Loans

When I headed off to university, all I could think about was all that money sitting in my bank account that had never existed before. I was really lucky because I got almost $10000 in scholarships and bursaries as well as the maximum possible loan. I was rich. Not so fast, though, kid.

The way the loans were handled was that we paid a certain percentage of the school fees in September and the rest in January. So I figured that if I budgeted really well, I'd have tons of money to play with.

What I didn't realize was that no matter how well you think you've budgeted, you get screwed over in the end. You see, I didn't realize that I should be checking my loan account every month or so to make sure they hadn't changed anything. Because they do. When I returned home in December I was ecstatic to find a letter telling me they had reassessed my financial situation and were giving me $2850 in January. So I thought that I was getting an extra whopping three grand to spend. But sadly, no.

What they had done was fiddle with the numbers and decided that I didn't need the $6000 that they had said I would get in January. Apparently, I only needed $2850. So when I got back to school and dropped a grand to hold my apartment for the summer, I knew nothing of what I still owed the school after the remaining loan was handed to them. Thank God for credit cards. And for Mom.

Textbooks: to Buy or Not to Buy

Textbooks are so expensive. However, there are ways to get around their high costs if you're patient and resourceful. Look first for used texts, of course. There's a better chance of finding one if you begin early. But wait! Read on.

As a general rule, I never buy any books until I have sat through at least one lecture. Only then is it possible to get the true sense of what the profs expect in terms of readings, and if they feel that the textbook is truly a necessity.

For example, if all or most of the information is presented in lectures and on the slides, and the textbook is simply for clarification, I would suggest not making the purchase. Often, profs will put at least one copy "on reserve" at the library. Here, you can sign the text out for a couple of hours at a time.

It's also possible to share texts. My first point, waiting until after the first lecture, is also a good idea because you can see if you know anyone in your class who you might be able share books with. I've never done it myself, but it would be possible to organize a group of three or four people at the end of the lecture to share a book.

Sometimes, though, you should buy the textbook. Even at the ludicrous prices they charge for them. For instance, if you are a biology major like me, a first-year bio text will always

be relevant and serves as a good tool to refresh the basics. Also, if you do your research, you may get lucky and be able to use a text multiple times. I purchased a biochemistry text which ended up being a required text for four additional courses!

With profs putting more and more online, the situation is changing from year to year. Eventually, textbooks may disappear altogether.

But not quite yet. In the meantime, happy hunting.

Money! Money! Money!

Hard to believe July is nearly gone eh? Yup, in just a few short months all of you Pre-Frosh will shed the "Pre" and finally become fully fledged Frosh! Want to eat ice cream on toast for breakfast? Go for it! Don't want to go to class? You won't get in trouble!

Remember, you're adults now, and that means you get to make choices.

Of course that also means you're adults now, and you have to make choices. Some are trivial, like what color sheets you want for your bed; others are important, like where you want to live. Some are easy like "Would you like to go skiing?" and others are hard like deciding if your relationship with a person you said you love is still a healthy one. Yes, in the course of one year at university, you will make exactly 7,873,456,235.834 decisions varying both in magnitude and speed.

And in true university fashion, here comes one of those decision moments before you even have time to comprehend it:

You're going to have to start paying for things.

Now everyone has a different monetary relationship with their parents that I won't even dwell on except to say that personal finance will become more important to you very fast, maybe to different degrees but it will. And it can seem overwhelming when you get an email saying your account was just billed for tuition and you owe four digits before the decimal. But fear not worried Frosh. That's what this entry is truly about: personal finance and some tips to maximize your meager money monthly.

1. *Make a Budget*. It's not really a hard concept, just hard to apply: Spend less than you get. Easier said than done though. Nevertheless, it's a good skill to have and it will serve you all through your life. Your first one doesn't have to be high tech. In fact, to avoid being over-whelmed, I'd recommend just a simple paper and pencil one to start. Some sample categories are things like Entertainment, Food, Clothing, Bills, and Savings. Add up how much you get in a month, subtract out anything you have to pay for, put some in savings, and budget the rest as you feel fit. It's a good feeling knowing that you're spending money you planned on spending instead of just spending wildly on anything that looks shiny and cool, and this way you're constantly making money that you can use later for important things, like investing or buying something like a car or a house.

2. *Cook*. Dining is a hot topic for a lot of students. Some people cook all their meals, some eat on campus for all their meals, and lots of people do some of both. Nevertheless, it is cheaper (and potentially healthier!) to cook for your-self, and it's a useful contrast to your school-work. Most of what you do is intellectually demanding and yields results only in the far distant future – like next week or even further. Cooking is the opposite. Yes there are organi-zational skills, but not the same ones that your schoolwork demands. And the results of your endeavors are pleasantly direct.

   Nearly all dorms have a community kitchen that you can use to cook food in, and if you get a few friends together you can split grocery bills and cook for each other. Not to mention one day you'll have to cook for yourself, and you might as well learn now.

   For the summer, I cook all meals for myself and my two roommates, and I spend about $100 a week on groceries. That's 21 meals for three people, averaging out to $1.58 per meal. Compared to the approximately $8 it costs to eat out for an average meal, I save hundreds of dollars a month. Not bad. You'd have to eat a lot of dollar menu burgers or ramen to beat that.

3. *Buy Re-usable Instead of Disposable*. Buy rags instead of paper towels, real or plastic plates instead of paper. Being able to re-use things will make them pay for themselves super-fast. And it's just good practice to throw less away. Not too long ago, some Business friends of mine went through some number-crunching for how much they'd save investing in rechargeable AA batteries instead of buying them en masse to feed their various electronic addictions. Savings add up.

4. *Re-Use*. Here and in some universities, there are mailing lists where people post things they're getting rid of for people to come and take. Some amazing things show up on ours, called Re-Use; you can get some sweet stuff. Some of the stuff I've received for free include: fridge, couch, road bike, TV (OK, it's about three feet deep, but it works!), hangers, awesome office chairs, skis and ski boots …

   … and that's just what I've received! There are frequently old laptops, computer bits and pieces, furniture, utensils – you name it! I even once contributed half a subway sandwich; I bought a footlong, but only ate half. Re-Use is amazing.

5. *Mint.com*. Alright so now you're saving tons of money. You've got a budget; you're wooing girls with your mad cooking skills and all the free stuff you've acquired from Re-Use. Now to bring it all together, use some kind of finan-cial management software. At the time I wrote this, I used Mint.com, but no doubt it will be obsolete soon.

   It's totally free and a cinch to set up with your banks. You can set up your budget, view your spending habits based on card transac-tions, and even set up alerts to remind you of things like when you're over budget, when your accounts are low, and when bills are due. Mint.com can also suggest bank accounts, investments, and credit cards that can save you money by matching your spending habits. Which brings us to …

6. *Credit Cards*. That's a scary word for a lot of people, and with good reason. Uncontrolled credit card use has made lots of people's lives really difficult. But they are a financial tool that, if used correctly, can give you some great benefits. For one thing, if you're like most people, you're going to have to eventually take

out a loan to buy a house or a car or something like that. When you do, they look at something called your credit score to determine what kind of interest rate you can get (or if you can get the loan at all!). Well the only way to get a credit score is to have had credit history, and one of the easiest ways to do that is to use a credit card. A credit card is a *huge* responsibility though, and all the sort of rules and responsibilities you should be aware of before making the decision is kind of outside the scope of this entry. Nevertheless, some benefits to having a credit card include building a good credit score, rewards for your spending, and flexibility with how much money you have.

If at this point you're sold and rushing off to sign up for the first credit card you get an offer for, slow down. You should find a card that matches your spending, and our good friend Mint.com can help! After doing a bit of research, Mint.com helped me find a student-specific card that offered lower interest and higher rewards on purchases. I also got a bonus for maintaining a high average throughout the school year. It is the perfect card for me, and I use it all the time in place of my debit card, then just pay it off every month. So all in all, I'm not spending more money than I normally do, I'm establishing credit, I'm still not in debt, and I get a percentage of everything I spend back. Works for me!

I have to reiterate though that credit cards are a massive financial responsibility and an advanced financial tool, and you really shouldn't pick one up until you're absolutely positive you can manage its use well. If you find that you are carrying a balance from one month to the next, you probably shouldn't have the card.

7. *Investment*. So the whole point of all this money-saving and budgeting is to start making yourself financially secure. As a reward for not spending it, money you save can earn you interest in your savings account. (You make money … for having money? What's not to like?) and once you collect a fair amount you can invest it in stocks, bonds and the like. Investment is a complicated topic, but the gist of it is that you get compounded interest on what you invest.

So there you go, there's more information than you probably care to know about what it's like managing your income in university. It's intimidating, liberating, exciting, and a host of other "ing" words.

An Easy Way to Save

An easy way to save money – fix things yourself!

It is obvious that in university, people will play sports indoors, wrestle indoors, throw things, and goof off. Along with this comes the unfortunate occurrence of holes in the drywall of your residence.

After a few crazy nights, and three gaping holes in our walls, my roommates and I quickly learned how to patch drywall. The university charges $200 per hole to have them fixed and quite frankly, we as university students could not afford that.

We went to the hardware store and bought a drywall patch kit for under ten dollars. None of us knew anything about drywall, but we heard it was quite simple; all you have to do is spread some filler over the hole, smooth it out, and you are done. That is exactly what we did, and fortunately it looked great. Shortly after, we went around and patched all of our friends' holes, saving ourselves tons of money, and the final count of holes filled that year was sixteen. At $200 per hole, that is a lot of money saved. And you know what, it was kind of fun.

So why are we so excited about saving money by fixing things ourselves? Because everything you get from the university is a rip-off, especially if you live in residence. Parking costs too much; roommate matching costs too much; textbooks cost a fortune. They make you buy the whole pack when you only need one of the books. They change the editions so you can't buy used ones. And often, they require new texts with new authors so you can't use the old ones. The profs told us this on the first day. They said, "Make it easier on yourself and buy the proper text or you won't be able to follow along." Yeah well it's not them paying for it, now is it?

Living away from home is expensive. But you can reduce your cost by sharing an apartment off campus; one of my friends pays $400/month to do just that. Here, it costs $2400 for our three-person unit.

Next year I will live off campus for sure. I know I will have to pay for my own groceries whereas now, I have a meal plan. But I still think it will be a lot cheaper.

So yes, I am happy when I can fix things myself. Maybe I should start a business doing just that.

Disaster with a Happy Ending

When I first went to school, the thought of being given a large lump sum of money from my student loans was a scary thought for me. I didn't want to make the mistake of over-spending and not having enough during the school year. So I made a plan.

First I calculated how much my tuition would be and estimated the price of books. After I found a place to live and figured out all my expenses for each month, I calculated my rent and my car insurance. I deliberately over-estimated my phone bill, laundry expenses, groceries and fuel expenses to make sure I had extra. Then I added up all these monthly costs to see how much money it would be in total just for my living expenses for the two semesters until I went home for the summer.

Only then did I have an idea of how much money I would need to have to make it through the year without worrying about a roof over my head or food in my belly. When I received my large lump sum of money, I took the amount of money for the living expenses for both semesters and put it in a separate bank account. This enabled me to see what I had for spending money, knowing that I would never spend too much and not have enough left.

I found there was only just enough for the necessities of life. So I got a part-time job. Now I could go out with my friends and have a good time. It was a good plan, but it didn't solve everything.

Some things hurt. They nickel and dime you to death: fees for this, deposits for that, and the biggest heartbreak of all – books. Sometimes it seems that they bring out new editions all the time so that everyone has to pay the maximum amount for the very latest and glossiest. When I first came, I'd worked all summer, and then a good chunk of my earnings went straight to the bookshop. Worse: about half the books were ones I didn't like and which were rather useless. Trouble is, you can't tell ahead of time which half that will be.

When you are receiving a loan and working at the same time, you must be very clear about the amount of money you will be making before and during the school year. I was told in February that I had made too much money during my first half of the year, and they attempted to put my money on hold which in turn would not allow me to pay for the second half of the year. I fought the decision, and they gave me the money to pay for the rest of the year. But now I'm not allowed to apply again until I pay back the amount they say I owe them. How can I pay that when I am trying to pay everything else?

I decided to drop from full-time status to part-time when I finished my first semester. The numbers just wouldn't add up unless I stopped doing everything that was fun. It was also hard to admit that my plan was screwed up, and it was partly my own fault. There were things I could have found out but didn't. Fortunately, I already had some education and I had contacts in my field. So it wasn't hard to get a job.

The hardest thing in the end was to say to myself: It's OK to do this, it'll still all work out. It felt like a defeat – well, maybe I can be a little stubborn sometimes. But now I have two lives, each of which I love.

Paid Employment While at University

Most of my friends here have paid employment, usually for about twenty hours a week. Not everyone of course. One girl I know does molecular biology, and with the labs and the rest of the workload, she has no time and neither do most of the people in her program. Another always worked in the past, but this semester he has student teaching which takes him and his classmates out of that game.

Another of my friends has a university-funded job where he gets paid to do things like crowd-control at sporting events. His boss sends him an email that tells him where he has to be and when it begins and ends. A big advantage of these types of university jobs is that your bosses know you have classes and homework and are respectful of that. If you're really overwhelmed, you can usually arrange just not to work that weekend, and when exams are coming up, these kinds of activities wind down a lot anyway.

Other university jobs have science students cleaning up labs and equipment, and senior students acting as residence advisers, dealing with things like unruly students and conflicts between roommates. I think these types of jobs are paid for by the government because not everyone can apply for them; the program appears to be restricted to students whose families can't help them much financially.

Then there are the people who have jobs downtown, in the malls or at fast food restaurants and those kinds of places. Some are hazardous in various ways. I know two who work in fast food on weekend shifts that end after 2 am. If one girl didn't have a black belt in karate, walking home after work wouldn't be very safe. Another friend has a different kind of problem; she works at a high-fashion clothing store. Her original intent was that this job would mean she could depend somewhat less on her parents in order to reduce the flow of extremely annoying inquiries from her mom about what she'd been doing and what had happened to the last batch of money they had sent her. It didn't work out according to plan though, because she gets a big discount on all the clothes she buys at work; she can't resist it and usually ends up spending more than she has made. Of course, she has lots of cool clothes, but that's not really the point of coming to university. Another guy has trapped himself into having to work to make the payments on his car, and insurance, and parking. He needs his car to get to work but doesn't have the time or money to use the car for much else. How stupid is that?

Quite a few people have to start working partway through university because of changes in their family situations. My roommate's younger brother began university this year, so his parents can't afford to help him as much as they did last year. I've seen the same kind of thing happen, but worse, because of parents losing their jobs or separating. One friend even had to quit school at the end of last year because he was the only one in his family who could find work; he had no idea that anything like this could crop up and disrupt his entire life, but he felt he had to do it.

Then there are the rich kids: the ones who wear new clothes every day, breeze around in a new sports car every year, and who boast about all the places they've been in the summer while everyone else had to work two jobs to try to reduce their eventual debt from ridiculous to just stupid. It can be hard to avoid doing physical harm to some of these people – especially with the arrogant attitudes some seem to have.

Having a Part-Time Job

Part-time jobs are a necessary evil. Students who pay their own university costs often find part-time jobs essential, while other students need them for extra spending money, and believe me, there is a lot to spend money on!

In either situation it is important (but often difficult) to remember that too many work hours cause trouble. By checking with upper-year students in my program, I found out that only six to eight hours per week were recommended. I managed to find a job that was six hours per week, one night a week, and paid me enough to help me get by with my expenses.

During exam weeks and when essays are due, it's hard to remember that you are as committed to the job as you are to your courses. Your employer depends on you, and your exams aren't of first importance to him or her. If you don't follow up on your work commitments, then you shouldn't be surprised if the job suddenly isn't yours anymore. But your courses come first, and you must be prepared to sometimes find someone to replace you at work in order to study or finish an essay. The balance is sometimes hard to find.

Take Control of Your Personal Finances

In my completely unofficial and totally informal sociological study of my college friends and peers, I find the most concerning area of irresponsibility to be personal finance. I'm all for having a good time and spending some money to do so. My problem is when there's more money going out than coming in. Also, I don't want to hear about how you have no money and are screwed while in the meantime you zip up your new $750 jacket.

College is the best time to get a grip on your finances and set yourself up for future success.

Take that, You Irresponsible Spender!

Why is university such an awesome time to get a grip on your personal finances? In lieu of rambling on about all the reasons, I'll just touch on the major ones. By the time I'm done, you'll be thinking of reasons on your own.

1. We have more wiggle room for error than we would have in the real world. If we screw up in college, maybe we run up some credit card debt to cover ourselves (which I strongly recommend against). If we screw up in the real world, there's no money for the rent.

2. It's easy to live like a cheap college student. My school shows fairly recent movies for free every weekend, and this weekend I'm going bowling – complete with shuttle to and from, food and drink – for only $10.

   I just picked up tickets to see my favorite basketball team play next week for $20. Your school has a bunch of groups that run cheap events; take advantage of them! Spend less money, and you'll have more to save and invest.

3. Your school wants to help you succeed financially! My school just wrapped up a four-week financial literacy series. Each week, different groups on campus made presentations. Some presentations were by faculty members, but others were by student groups. Look for a similar event on your campus. Because these presenters are usually from on campus, the series doesn't have to end with the last lecture. If you find a particular topic confusing or interesting, get in touch with whoever talked about it. They'll be more than happy to pass along more information or direct you to where you can learn more. If you can't find one, email the appropriate professors and seek their advice.

4. Mom and Dad (or Grandma and Grandpa) are usually there to fall back onto. I'm not advocating that you run for help with every setback, and I'm not saying that someone will subsidize all your wild shenanigans; but in the case of a real, legitimate disaster, those who care about you will be there to help out.

I'm sure by now that you're beginning to see why college is such an ideal time to begin conquering the skills required for effective personal finance.

People We Meet
(Especially Roommates)

A Bad Beginning

I live in a residence on campus that has four rooms around a central kitchen, and a bathroom. The furniture is minimal, so you have to bring some of your own. Then of course there's a TV, a computer, your clothes and everything else. Surprising how much you have to bring with you, really.

Moving in on the first day was a terrible experience. Four sets of stairs to go up, and no elevator. The parking spaces dedicated for arriving students were miles – and two bridges, 34 steps, and a tunnel – away. So my dad decided to pay a fortune for underground parking. Now everything had to be brought up on the elevator everyone else was using at the same time. Then we had to lug it across the road and up the 4 sets of stairs.

Next, a 20-minute wait in a chaotic mass of frustrated people to get the key, and we were ready to begin. We knew it was going to be a zoo, because of course everyone else was moving into the same building at the same time. The real shock, though, came when we opened the door to the apartment that was to be my home.

Stuff in the drawers and the closet. Hair everywhere. Food in the cupboards. Disgusting things just left in the fridge. A heap of garbage in every room. Carpets that were sticky and made your feet black when you walked on them. And the bathroom: Ugh, Ugh, Ugh. The problem was that the previous occupants' moving-out deadline was at noon the same day, and they'd partied the night before and recovered in the morning instead of cleaning up after themselves. You could see that from all the bottles. And from the bathroom.

At least the previous people weren't still there. In one of my friends' apartments, security had to be called to get them out.

My mom cried. At first she refused to bring stuff up, wanting to get the room cleaned up before all my stuff went into it. But of course it was a holiday, and there was nobody to complain to, just a recording when we phoned.

My new flatmates and their families, of course, had the same experience and felt the same way. Things did improve; we worked all night to get rid of most of the filth – especially not fun in the bathroom, I can tell you. A few days later a crew came to steam-clean the carpets – of course, nobody had told us they were coming, and they were mad that they had to wait while we moved stuff off the carpets and out into the hallway. It took a few days for the chemical smells to go away; I figure I've lost a few lung cells and maybe some brain cells as well.

It's OK now. In fact it's great now. We must be the most house-proud people around, because after all we went through, we're absolutely allergic to the slightest trace of garbage or dirt. We're proud of where we live, and we've enjoyed going out together shopping for pictures and lamps and things like that. One thing too: after we'd all been through such a dreadful experience together, we immediately found that we'd become fast friends.

My Life with Biff

I stuck the key in, turned it, and there I was. My room in residence wasn't too cramped, since there was a gaping hole in the wall. All in all, it wasn't too bad, especially since I'd known my roommate from high school – or so I thought.

Soon after I had unpacked, he arrived. The only problem was that he wasn't the person I'd known a couple of months ago. What I mean is that he looked quite different: he was now a "punker."

I wouldn't say that Biff and I didn't get along, but we were far from the best of friends. Biff had this bizarre habit of not doing anything that he believed was a waste of time, such as his laundry. It wasn't too bad, except that he would have to struggle to get his grime-encrusted clothes on every now and then.

Loud music, the stench of dirty clothes, and the mentality of a two year-old were bad enough. But when his behavior began to affect my marks, it was time to end it. Slowly, I began to cut down the size of Biff's room. We had put tape down the middle of the room, and gradually I began to move it, so in the end his half had shrunk to about an eighth. But when it got to zero, then I was happy.

I really don't know what's happened to Biff. After he failed eleven out of twelve first-year courses, the university quietly but quickly expelled him. Rumor is that he is now a DJ somewhere in a small town.

Different When You Live with Them

One of your biggest concerns before heading off to college is probably your roommate. During the summer, the university sends your roommate's contact information, which is good because you can then look each other up, communicate, and learn about each other. Your roommate may seem to be the best person in the world – until you start living in the same room. This happened to me.

Over the summer, my roommate and I became as close as you can be to someone you've never actually seen, and we both became extremely excited to have been matched as roommates. We coordinated what we were both going to

bring, and we planned things that we could do together. I could not have been happier that I was rooming with her.

However after two weeks, my impression of her completely changed. Don't get me wrong; she is probably a great person. But our personalities clashed way too much to be able to room together. My roommate is a passive individual. When she is with her friends and having a good time, she seems like a lot of fun. Not so when you live with her.

My roommate cried numerous times because she was not happy living with me. I'm not one to talk to someone when they're crying, at least not when I don't really know them well and perhaps don't even like them. So I let her cry for the first few times. Then it got really annoying.

Why was she crying? Well, I'm a fairly independent person. I like to be busy all the time and get lots of work done. When I was in my room, I usually had lots of homework to do. She didn't like being ignored and after a couple of months, she said she felt like she couldn't ever be in the room when I was. So she spent most of her time in the floor lounge rather than our room when I was in there.

Sometimes I would accidentally fell asleep with my television on a bit too loud, and that would upset her. Yet she didn't like it when I asked her to be quieter. I had early classes, and she would either come in after I fell asleep or even more often, as I was falling asleep, and then she would open and close her obnoxiously loud and heavy closet doors. I'm an extremely light sleeper so this would wake me up; she would do this in the morning as well.

Oh, and one more thing. I've known people who've come to university with friends from home, and then became roommates. Maybe it can sometimes work, but it can be dangerous to the friendship, and if it doesn't work out, it can even cost you the friendship. And that's what I've seen.

Back to my own experience: I may not have thought about her feelings as much as I should have. I now know that I could have been wrong in that aspect. But sometimes roommates are just not meant to be. And though an experience like that might seem to be the worst match of roommates, you can and should grow from it. Luckily, I moved out after one semester. And lucky her – she got that huge room to herself while I got stuck with someone else who didn't turn out to be too much better.

But I've grown from it, and that is what is most important.

Life with a Roommate

Living in a double room in residence has both good and bad points. Before you make a decision to choose a double room, consider it carefully. Weigh the pros and cons, and think about a few things first.

Nine times out of ten, roommates become best friends for the year. However, it can also happen that things don't work out, and you could be in that 10% that are just simply hopelessly incompatibly mismatched.

Consider that your roommate has different habits, and there will be conflicts. Such as bedtimes, rising times, amount of partying … and believe me, the list of differences can grow quite long. Guess how I know that?

Consider that you will have little or no privacy. What were once "your" things become "our" things: community property. And pray that your roommate has good taste in posters!

Hope for someone about your size who you can borrow clothes from; maybe you'll even have the same taste in music, and you can swap tunes. If you're lucky, your roommate won't even talk on the phone as much as you do.

Maybe you'll have a few subjects in common so you can do homework and assignments together, study for tests and go to classes together. If you're in luck, you'll have the same periods free to eat lunch and dinner together. (University students don't eat breakfast!)

But, most of all, think about what kind of roommate you'd make. Would you want yourself as a roommate?

A Roommate's Nightmare

Let's talk about residence. I don't have many complaints about my residence in first year university: the food was edible, the rooms were nice and comfortable – not your interior decorator's dream, but they were alright, and most of the students were nice … except, can you guess, my roommate.

I hesitate to describe my roommate here as it would not be a very heartwarming description. Let's just say that she and I were not two of the most compatible people. While I smiled now and then, she did not. While I talked now and then (understatement, many would say), she did not. She did moan about her problems – and trust me, she did have problems – while wallowing in a canyon of self-pity, but no, she never talked to me. While I went out for fun (yes, fun and first year university do not have to be a contradiction in terms), she became rooted to her desk.

My roommate would get up in the morning, after sleeping in the same clothes that she had worn for two weeks (although she did change halfway through the term), and plod straight to her desk. She would keep the light on for hours after I went to bed (and I was by no means an early-nighter), working at her desk. She began to look like her desk. I began to talk to her desk. Don't worry, it didn't answer back … but neither did she.

While I took showers, my roommate had discovered that showers were just "not her thing." Neither were baths. I don't think I have to describe in detail the results of this latest incompatibility. Except to say that my days were spent at classes or in the library, and I began a rotation schedule for my nights; 'Whose room will I sleep in tonight?' became my thought for the day.

My roommate did not believe in doing laundry. The first two times that she went against her beliefs (due to severe roomie pressure), she seemed to have the technique. But the third time (and last for that term) she did her laundry, she forgot to read her handbook. My roommate seemed unaware that clothes usually need to be dried, not stored, after being washed. But she will never forget that again. We made sure.

Why am I telling you this? Only to say that my life was hell because of my roommate. I was depressed enough – I didn't need her extra help. But I survived. And I will never forget that term.

It had its good side, actually. My tolerance for roommates has increased drastically, which came in handy later. And because of her, I met a lot of more, shall we say, 'human' students. She was such an interesting conversation piece.

Roommates can be Extreme Too

How many times have you heard, "You had better hope you don't get a crappy roommate freshman year – school will suck!" Well, let me tell you. That's baloney. I had, by far, one of the worst possible roommates my first year at school, and I was by far one of the happiest kids on earth. Not because of my roommate of course, but I learned to make the best of a sticky situation.

Boy, do I have fond memories of that girl – sitting on her bed, all the time, eating the most disgusting foods she could find and as much of it as she could find, all the time, video chatting, having cyber sex with her disgusting boyfriend, all the time; really, it was a great time. Yeah right!

She was absolutely repulsive. She never once washed her sheets. That's nasty right there in and of itself. But the worst part about it was, second semester, the boyfriend would come up every weekend, and you know what happens when boyfriends come to town. I was "sexiled" every weekend from my own room. Sexile is what happens when your roommate brings

someone home and to maintain your sanity you decide to go somewhere else for the night so you don't have to listen to the moaning and groaning. Ewwwww!

I walked in on them a bunch of times because the moron never bothered to lock the door or to tell me when her boyfriend was coming up. Ughhh. I came home once and they weren't there, but their homemade sex dice had made it to my side of the room. Look it up online if you don't understand, but seriously, keep it to yourself.

My best friend lived next door to me on my roommate's side of the wall. I came to her room one day when the boyfriend was up, and she said, "You'll never believe what just happened. See this brush on my bureau? I had to pick it up off the ground because it fell from the banging on the wall from next door." It would be an understatement to say that I was mortified.

Aside from all of that though, my roommate was just an all around unpleasant person. I think we said all of five words to each other all year. She was the most whiny, selfish, stuck-up kid I have ever met. There were several times that I would come home and she would be screaming at whoever was on the phone. Other times she would be telling her older brother that she had been waiting forever for him to write her paper for her. Not a good situation.

She would use the microwave at all hours of the night. Regardless of whether I was sleeping or not. This wouldn't have been so bad had the microwave not been right next to my head. Her making popcorn while I was sleeping made me want to punch her. Argh.

She didn't really shower, ever. The room was absolutely rank. I had three air fresheners on my side of the room, and I always tried to keep the window open. Nothing worked. It was awful.

But, I still stayed strong. To counteract all of this, whenever (on the rare occasion) she wasn't home, I would open the door, turn the music up super loud, and have all my friends on the floor come over to make sure that people knew that my roommate wasn't going to win the battle of the century.

It's tough at times, but you'll pull through. You can't let your roommate make or break your year. My freshman year was one of the most amazing experiences of my life, and I want to thank my roommate for providing me with all these great stories that I can now look back on and laugh about.

But would I want to repeat the experience???

Sharing a Room with a Friend

At university, do not share a room with someone you know, especially a good friend. If you are sharing a small room with this person all the time, it's amazing how fairly small differences in habits can really get to you. Things like how soon clothes are put away, your roommate's stuff spreading over into your half, your roommate borrowing your stuff without asking, different ideas of when there should be other people in the room, when there can be music listened to through earphones so loudly that it can be heard all over the room, the time at which friends need to leave and lights should be put out. Good friendships can be permanently ruined by things like this.

The housing department is supposed to match you and your roommate based on your interests, but it doesn't always work out. What they use to match you is a survey which is not very extensive so you end up getting dumped in a room with someone, and hopefully the two of you will get along. It's not really matching.

For this reason, I chose to room with my best friend from high school. But it didn't work out. It all changed once I started living with her, and I began to see her differently. First, she was a slob, and she didn't care. Sometimes you can talk to people about things that are bothering you so that maybe they can learn to get the dishes done before there is a mountain in the sink and make sure that the place doesn't smell from the chicken juice in the rotting garbage.

Other times you can't. With her, you couldn't. She put dishes in the garbage rather than wash them. Her sloppiness drove me crazy. But at least I wasn't suffering as much as my neighbor: one of his roommates smelled so bad that his friends would not come over, and he even had to put an air freshener on top of his bed. But wait, there's more.

She had guests over constantly and you never knew when you were going to walk in on something. She was shallow. When you live with someone and overhear their conversations on a daily basis, you find out more than you want to. Maybe it was wrong, but I decided to open the door and the window at all times even though she didn't like it, and let my music waft out. Maybe blast out. That way my friends came into the room and I hung out with them and she got mad and left.

Sometimes she became upset that I wasn't home or didn't appear to want her company. That was true. I didn't want to go home because I was sick of all the bullshit and drama. It got to me. I came to the realization that living with my best friend had changed my perception of her. That sucked, but not as much as having to continually put up with her.

Too many times, she didn't tell me that I was upsetting her until afterwards. Or I knew that she was upset but couldn't find out why – she just denied that she was upset. We tried talking about it. But I was always busy with homework when she wanted to talk to me, so I wouldn't be what she called "engaged enough" in the conversation. This would get her even more upset and lead to more crying.

What I'm trying to say is that you may think that you and your roommate will be the best match and that you're going to have a great time, but until you really know your roommate's habits, personality and everything else, don't get too excited.

Know that you both need to work on pleasing the other. If your roommate is a neat freak, please tidy up your side of the room a bit when it gets disastrous. Don't go too far out of your way to please your roommate, but be sure to keep it in mind.

My feeling now is that you should make the most of what you want to do and not worry too much about your roommate. It's your room too. Don't be disrespectful, but you still can make the most of the situation. And you can grow from being put with roommates who you don't have a lot in common with, so use the opportunity. For example, I've realized that I hate living in filth. I wasn't like that before as I was always a messy person. But now I can't stand when people leave their dishes in the sink, and I hate studying in a messy room.

Another lesson: If you share a room with a friend, recognize the risk. You may lose the friendship. Now in my case, it's probably a good thing: she turned out not to be the kind of person I could really be a friend with. But it's true too that sharing a room with someone makes you hypersensitive to any annoyances the person might present to you.

So how did it end? Actually, for me, rather well. I was able to move in with my current roommate who was previously stuck with a truly freaky person. Now the annoying slob has her own room and so does the freak. Both their personalities are so passive that they are afraid to decorate the other side of the room in case they get a roommate who won't like it. Their rooms look like jail cells. No one wants to move in. Maybe that's what they intended!

I'm beyond caring. Now, though, in a room with someone compatible, I can resume my life.

WEB: MORON, MY ROOMMATE srvlgd.com/MMR

WEB: ROOMMATES AND TOILETS srvlgd.com/RT

An Impossible Roommate

I can't believe how finicky my roommate is. You drop a kleenex and he goes into a conniption. Or you've been playing sports and yes, there's sweat; he freaks if you don't shower right away.

If you have used a piece of clothing, he expects you to wash it immediately – if you don't and you accumulate a bagful, it drives him berserk!

Now my mom is a fairly hygienic lady, but she does have a laundry basket that she allows to fill up until there's about a washer-load there; then she washes it. Is she a slob? I think not.

If you should happen to drop a small item such as a pencil and it goes over into my roommate's part of the room, he takes this as a personal violation from which he will never recover. Worst of all: if you happen to leave just one hair in the shower, he becomes apoplectic.

It's really hard to live with a person like that. It won't last, though. One of us will be dead.

Residence or Motel?

My roommate and I had this wonderful relationship: she would bring guys over any time she wanted, and I left the room. Actually, I got along quite well with her, but she did have this problem. It got to the point one time where I left the room to brush my teeth and get ready for bed, and while I was gone, one of her many male acquaintances arrived, and she locked the door! I pounded on it until my fists were black and blue, but they didn't let me in. After this, we had a huge fight, but later resolved the difference. The last month of school was very enjoyable. What I should have done was put my foot down in September rather than March.

Whatever the reason for being upset with your roommate, get it resolved early. She may think you're a bitch at first, but it will save you months of frustration and misery. Your roommate will probably even respect you more for it.

It's your room and your home. Live in it as you like, not only as your roommate likes it. You have to live with each other. These things have to be resolved before they become major problems.

And, to put things in perspective, not everyone has these kinds of problems. Most people get along well with their roommates, with only occasional blowups, which are then quickly and fairly easily sorted out.

Gay Roommates

During my summer holidays, my uncle asked me if there was anything that made me think, uh oh, this is going to be hard to get used to. And yes, there most certainly was.

In my first year, I shared a house with three guys, and I have assigned fictitious names for each for the purpose of this story. I was rooming with Dean, who was straight, as was I. Then there was Dale, who was very theatrical and gay, and Brian: well, would you call him religious? … or conservative? … or redneck? … or homophobic? Each of these sometimes seemed to apply. Neither Dale nor Brian was completely bad. Both had a serious side, a perceptive side, and a considerate side. But they didn't belong together.

Dale clearly wanted to be in college for the "College Experience." He partied every night and came home drunk out of his mind. Even when he was on stage, he was usually half-drunk, and not because that was what the part called for. He always said the booze was the only thing that stopped him from being nervous and self-conscious and let him put his whole self into the part. I'm still not sure how he could pull it off after that much alcohol, but somehow he never fell off the front of the stage, and even managed to avoid sounding slurred – until after the performance.

Brian was a fun-loving guy, but he had grown up in an extremely religious community and could say or do prejudiced things without realizing it. Where he had come from, everyone was like him, so he didn't have a concept of what was offensive. He would do things like post racist posters on the wall, complete with ugly caricatures and offensive names for an entire ethnic group. (I won't repeat any of them here.) Brian would also write homophobic

Bible slogans on the board above where his gay roommate slept, such as: "If a man lies with a male as those who lie with a woman, both of them have committed an abomination and they shall surely be put to death." Brian thought this kind of stuff was funny and okay.

It didn't bother Dean or me that some people are gay. Even so, Dale would sometimes do things with the sole intention of shocking me. Knowing full well that I wasn't gay, he would come in late at night after I was in bed, exhausted after working late. He would shut the door, lock it, look at me and make a completely inappropriate suggestion which I can't write down here. I wasn't worried that he was coming on to me and knew that he was just saying these things to get a rise out of me. The only response was to laugh. Like I say, he was theatrical.

Many of the things he did were with the intention of just having fun and trying to be funny. He was not directly trying to offend us. But he would also do really aggressive things that made Brian uncomfortable. He had taken a particular interest in Brian. He was very suspicious of him, suspected he was most likely gay, and found it completely absurd that Brian wasn't admitting it. So he would specifically do things to offend him, like having sex in his bed with a male partner while Brian was there. He wouldn't have done things like this to Dean or me.

Brian wasn't completely innocent either: he reveled in offending Dale as well. That was a mistake, because Dale was much more creative and could be much more offensive than Brian if he wanted to. And he did want to.

As a result, Brian and Dale developed a really antagonistic relationship. (Yeah, I know, duh.) Brian would post a new homophobic Bible slogan, and Dale would do something new to make Brian feel really uncomfortable. It got so bad that Brian moved out halfway through the year because Dale was getting to him. An interesting twist was that, unbeknownst to Brian, his new roommate, Jason, was bisexual. We all knew, but we didn't tell him, nor did Jason. So I guess it didn't bother him.

Brian ended up coming out as gay three years later but, at that time, you could only suspect what his real orientation was. We did suspect: what made him so emphatic, so obsessed? As the Bard said, he "doth protest too much, methinks" (Hamlet Act 3, Scene 2, in case you were wondering.)

I felt badly for Brian as this was an example of someone having to come and adjust to a new and unexpected situation. It must have been hard for him since he would have been conflicted, knowing he was gay and obsessing over what all of his friends and family back home would have thought. It would have been difficult for someone from a protected environment who was inculcated with lots of things all his life that weren't true, and which would conflict with the reality of certain situations, to come to terms with it.

Apart from that, I don't really know what happened to Brian or Dale. While some of the drama could be pretty amusing, I really don't miss it. But it did teach me lots about how people from different backgrounds can conflict with each other.

Life would certainly be dull if everyone were the same and no one disagreed. And that first year was certainly not dull for me.

WEB: BE CAREFUL, BE SAFE srvlgd.com/BCS

WEB: CRISIS AVERTED srvlgd.com/CA

WEB: A SUICIDAL ROOMMATE srvlgd.com/SR

The Myth of University

There is a myth surrounding universities. I reluctantly admit that I believed this myth as I left high school, possibly out of naivete, or maybe I was too afraid of the reality. Regardless, as my first year of university draws to a close, the fact remains – the myth of university as being a place of higher learning rings of just a bit too much wishful thinking. Like it or not, there are a great many – too many – people here who shouldn't be.

Coming out of high school, having to face challenging (but not insurmountable) entrance qualifications as well as teachers saying, "University is a lot harder than high school, you know," I expected university to be different. I don't mean the living away from home, life on your own, money troubles: they're certainly aspects of life here. No, I assumed (never assume!) that the people in university would be different from those in high school. Not just different, but better. After all, we graduates were supposedly the cream of the crop, the creme-de-la-creme of the public school system, mature, with intellects ready to take the first step into the Big World out there. How was I to know that so many left high school with their shoelaces still untied?

Now, before I go any further, I admit that I'm no angel myself. I occasionally test the mettle of my stereo speakers, but that is extremely mild compared to what the "Hopes of the Future" are doing elsewhere. Usually drug or alcohol induced, vandalism and theft are always good for a few laughs and boasts afterwards. One fine citizen got so drunk that he had to be taken to the hospital to get his stomach pumped, which he undauntedly shrugged off upon his return scant hours later as he gorged himself on pizza with girls foolish enough to give him an audience. Or the girl who discovers "A Guide to Seven-Day Partying" and then wonders why she's failing and why her floormates seem to give her hostile looks all the time.

But what kills me is the time when some lazy oaf, who to everyone (except his "drinking buddies") was little more than a symbol of what a spoiled rich kid with no ambition could fail to accomplish, floundered in his golden opportunity to make something of himself and decided to quit university because of the "pressure." The send-off party he was given would make an old war hero jealous, as pretty girls kissed him goodbye while he tottered drunkenly in an attempt not to spill the drinks that his friends had bought for him. Mind-boggling, and ironic enough to make you want to throw up.

And not just at my school do these things take place, for my old friends tell of being similarly blessed at other universities.

Not everyone at university is a "tool," just those loud, obnoxious and inconsiderate enough to always be in the spotlight. Unfortunately, these few make it difficult and frustrating for one trying to find the people who will remain your friends long after the last beer has gone, as well as provide the intellectual stimulation that this place is supposedly teeming with. I imagine that these people are here either because post-secondary education is "trendy," their parents are paying the whole shot, and/or it's either go here or Get a Job. And we all know how scary that can be. I guess the old-fashioned reason – the reason I'm here – of going to university because of a desire to learn isn't as appealing as it used to be. The first year of university, while for some a period of priority-shuffling, becomes a time of rude-awakening for others like myself.

WEB: THIRD TIME AROUND srvlgd.com/TTA
WEB: TIME FOR ACTION srvlgd.com/TFA
WEB: OH BE QUIET srvlgd.com/OBQ

Students who Waste their Time

I'm in a program that's probably the most demanding one the university offers. In fact, this faculty is almost like a school within a school. There's the rest of the university, then there's us. And we're not the only ones who see it that way. If you ask anyone else in the university, they'll tell you the same thing.

We have to work so hard that there's almost never any time left over. Sometimes it gets to the point where it's even hard to get just a few hours of sleep. And because of the nature of the program, most of the work has to be done at the faculty itself. What they say about us is true: our faces are all so pale because we really don't get out much.

There do seem to be lots of people around though, in other faculties, with far too much time on their hands. It can be hard to take: sometimes people breeze through our working area on their way to the pub. They make a lot of noise, joke around, and then go on their way. We can't go; for us there just isn't the time.

It can be rather deceiving. There was one student I worked with in a theater production who seemed to have a pretty laid-back life. Then later, when her projects came up, she had to work really hard. But if you're not aware of that, it can seem unfair that other people have so much time to goof off. Especially, it's hard to take some of their complaints, their whining. They complain that they have to take amphetamines to get their work done, whereas in fact the real problem is that they've been sleeping most of the time and going out a lot.

They're disorganized as well. In our program, we stay up late working. But these students exaggerate; they claim to be working all evening and into the night, but in fact they are mostly chatting, singing and socializing. They complain about having to stay up, but they don't actually do very much work. They go to their profs for extensions, "Poor me; I'm just so stressed out with the workload," whereas the truth is that they wasted time all month and then spent the last couple of days getting over their hangovers. My feeling is that you shouldn't get to say you worked all evening and into the night if you didn't actually do it. It's hard to have a lot of patience with people like that.

But then I think, they're getting back about what they're putting in. Our program leads to a professional life, but theirs doesn't lead anywhere much unless they make it happen, which they're not doing. During their years here, they're just wasting their time and their considerable tuition dollars. I wonder what they are doing with their lives. When I remind myself of that, I'm not jealous of their life at all.

WEB: SUPPORT FROM ALUMNI srvlgd.com/SA

Family and Friends,
Old and New

Missing You

Wow! Isn't this exciting? You're going off to school, away from home, to make new friends, learn new things, and experience life. But, you're upset because you and your boyfriend/girlfriend are going to different universities or are going to be separated for other reasons. You'll hardly ever be able to see one another.

Just remember, "absence makes the heart grow fonder," and this is very true, believe it or not. By not seeing each other all the time, you often ponder over all the good times and the fun you had together, and then you come to deeply appreciate the person and realize how special he or she is to you. It makes the times that you do spend together all the more special and exciting to look forward to. Often, being apart from one another helps to strengthen the relationship and add a special quality to it.

Moving On

One of the most important things you need to keep in mind when coming to college is the idea of moving on versus holding on. You need to find a balance. Don't let go of everything you had back home, but don't hold on to it too much.

I came to college with a boyfriend. I was happy that I would have someone who I already knew when I arrived on campus, just to make the transition a little bit easier. In the beginning of the year, everything was just fine. But that began to change.

During my first term, I pledged a co-ed fraternity so I could meet new people and get involved. This bugged my boyfriend because I would spend a lot of time with my new friends and I was extremely busy with the pledging process. I was ready to move on from high school, find new friends and make the most of my first year of college. My boyfriend, on the other hand, wasn't getting involved and spent much of his time in his room. He also kept going home to hang out with his high school friends while I definitely wanted to stay on campus, get involved and make new friends. He was upset that I had a new life and he didn't.

After a while I didn't want to spend as much time with my boyfriend because he was getting on my nerves. He did not like the fact that I was spending the majority of my free time with other people, and he was constantly telling me that I had changed. I know I changed. I'm glad I've changed. College changes people, usually for the better.

I have had so many amazing experiences and already have the best friends I could ever imagine. My boyfriend on the other hand was extremely lonely and continued to talk to his high school friends all the time.

So in case you didn't figure this out already, I broke up with my boyfriend and after a period of being upset, I have had a much better time here. I didn't feel like I needed to check in with him anymore, or see if he would approve of what I would do every night. Since I broke up with him, college has been even more of an amazing experience.

So remember, hold on to things that are close to your heart, but it is important to let some things go. Allow yourself to grow and change, but don't forget to keep in touch with your best friends and your family often.

WEB: I THOUGHT I KNEW MY BOYFRIEND srvlgd.com/TKB

University, the Ultimate Breaker-Upper

August 13th: "We're just going to see how things go and stay together even though we are at opposite ends of the country."

August 31st: "Yeah ... we're breaking up."

When people go to a university far away, many are left with the question of what to do about the relationship with their boyfriend or girlfriend.

What do you do when you're going to school and he or she isn't? Do you allow the long distance factor to break you up? Is it fair to your second half that you're moving far away and they are just supposed to wait for you to come home? Can you have a relationship without seeing each other until Christmas? Can you ever date someone who is so far away and make it work? What is needed for a "true" relationship?

Is geography always the deciding factor in who we love? If there truly is just one person in this entire world that is our true love, then how can we expect that this one and only person will exist within city limits? So what do we do when we are faced with the challenge of university? Do we all just break up with our boyfriends/girlfriends of nine months ... two years ... five years? Five years ... that's me ... long story... .

How can you get over someone when you don't want to break up with them but you have to? You still have feelings for them, but common sense tells you that staying together without ever seeing each other can't work. Or should you try to make it work? Is "making it work" even possible?

Should we be putting this much thought into a high school relationship? When our parents were our age, they were getting married at eighteen, nineteen, twenty and they already knew their true loves, so why can't we? Why do our parents say that we are too young? So in the end, what do we do? Are there even any right answers in these situations?

Myself? My boyfriend and I broke up a month before I went to university because I was moving across the country and he was going to attend the university in our home city. We knew five years would be too long a time to remain together from a distance. But still to this day, I miss him a lot. But as much as I love him, I think about the famous quote, "If you love something, set it free. If it comes back to you it's yours to keep." The timing just wasn't right. Maybe if we had met once we were older and had finished our post-secondary education, then we could have stayed together forever with no interruptions.

We'd started dating in elementary school and we experienced lots of things together. We went to Paris for spring break with our high school, to Disney World one summer with his family, and to various theme parks across the country where I tried to get him on a roller coaster with me but he was just too scared.

Our last year of high school, when spring came and we had to decide which university we would each attend, we started thinking seriously about whether we would stay together. I had never wanted to go to university in our home city but I could have stayed within an hour's drive; then we could have stayed together. But when I got my acceptance and a scholarship from this university, it was too good an opportunity to pass up. When it became clear that I was moving across the country, we both decided that staying together wasn't going to be an option.

We both felt that it would be impossible to feel like we were in a true relationship with each other since we would be so busy with homework and could only see each other once or twice a year. Young, free, we both wanted to experience university life to its fullest, without restricting ourselves from meeting new people.

Even though we knew in the spring that our relationship would come to a close at the end of the summer, I missed him more than ever when he went away that summer on a family vacation.

When he came home, I couldn't picture how hard it would be to be apart from him for good. No more watching movies together, no more sharing rides to school, no more ball hockey in the driveway and I could no longer see his adorable kitten, Philly.

Now that I've survived the transition, it wasn't as hard as I thought it would be. I send him a "hey" almost every single day, and that gets the feelings of how far away he is and how much I miss him out of my system. Even so, I still feel I would be jealous of any girl that he is around. Our mutual decision that we would go our separate ways was sad because our five year adventure had to come to an end solely because of geography. But I did find once I made the move to university, being in a different city helped me get over the breakup much easier.

I dated another guy for the first three months that I was in first year. I met him in the first week of classes and we hit it off from the start. He taught me to snowboard and shared his entire music collection of 7000 songs with me. I absolutely loved sharing my world with him just as much as he did with me.

So here I was, at a new university: new friends, new boyfriend, new clothes and a new life. But that relationship ended as well: he wanted us to move too far too fast, and I was hesitant even though I was falling for him. He didn't know how to communicate how he felt about issues in our relationship, so his feelings built up until he became very unhappy. And most importantly, he wanted Sex and I didn't. His feeling was that Sex makes or breaks a relationship; my feeling went back to something my mom once told me about having pride in yourself. I'm like that. I want my pride. I couldn't be all the things he wanted me to be.

So the relationship came and the relationship went. While it was interesting to be with someone fresh and new, this boyfriend and my ex were very different. My ex-boyfriend from back at home was captain of the hockey team and my university boyfriend hated the sound of skates on ice.

Even though my ex-boyfriend and I continued to communicate throughout this relationship, I never told him about this new guy because he had made it clear that he didn't want to know about anyone I was seeing because he would become jealous. He was happier not knowing. He knew that I was most likely out living my life but didn't want to think about it.

I wasn't tempted to get back with him because we couldn't deal with the physical distance between us. We continued to stay in touch, and we still do. I still miss being his girlfriend, and I wish that our long term relationship hadn't had to come to an end. We both wanted to be with each other, but it just wasn't the time. If he was in the same city as me, I would still be going with him for sure. Even though I had those feelings and I probably always will, dating new people is just as exciting.

When it comes to the question of whether you break up or not because of school, I do not see a breakup as a bad thing. In university, you are supposed to meet new people, and I believe you will find absolutely extraordinary people that you will want to share your world with, no matter what. The ex-boyfriend from back at home is still my friend, and I never want him out of my life. The recent boyfriend and I are not good friends at all.

My ex-boyfriend from back home and I promised each other that if we end up living in the same city again after we are done our Undergrads, we will give dating a shot again. I can't help but look forward to that time.

In the end, it's all positive. I gained new insights into relationships, and into the way I react to new situations. And I gained a new music collection.

A Turn for the Better

My life has taken a turn for the better. My first month here was extremely hard for me because I had to leave behind a beautiful family with loving parents and my cat, and I had to leave behind my boyfriend. This is the part that hurt the most. He is the first guy I have ever really loved, and I have never felt anything like the feeling I had when I left him. We are still going out, and I see him on the weekends sometimes, but my thoughts are with him almost all of the time. I feel like he is closer when I write about him or talk about him, but none of this compares with being with him.

I have been adjusting, finally, to the awful workload and the homesickness, and I am truly grateful to my roommate and the girls on my floor. Without them I would feel lost and alone; they are the ones that make me laugh and make me feel like university could be my second home. Right now, I don't feel I'll ever have another boyfriend or feel anything at all for any other guy (yeah yeah, lotsa people have told me that'll change). However, I do feel I've made plenty of new friends, and amazingly quickly.

WEB: WEEKENDS srvlgd.com/WK

WEB: A SECOND FAMILY srvlgd.com/SF

WEB: FRIENDS OLD AND NEW srvlgd.com/FON

WEB: FRED IS MY MOST RELIABLE FRIEND srvlgd.com/FF

Going Back Home

Living conditions when you're attending university perhaps come as no surprise. You have been forewarned and advised about residence life or living on your own. But no one can prepare you for the first trip back home to "visit."

You walk into the house and you feel as if you've just walked into your grandparents' home. Everything is familiar yet somehow very distant. The place is exceptionally clean and the food tastes better than it ever has.

You feel like a visitor, acting formally, minding your manners. Your home seems different, even unfamiliar, because none of your things are around.

But suddenly it all comes back, and you begin to feel more like yourself. Things begin to look as they always have; you feel at home.

Relationships with People Back Home

My roommate doesn't feel that her relationship with friends back home is any different now that she has gone on to university and they have stayed back for another year of Grade 12 – the victory lap, as they call it. When she goes home, she says she still feels like she is in high school. Her friends are talking about the same old teachers and the same old stuff, but it doesn't feel like that long ago that she was part of it. So she can still relate.

But I feel the total opposite. I get frustrated with friends who are calling all stressed out about something. I think, seriously, you call that stress? They are complaining about having to do an English assignment, and all I can think is that they have an extra year to do all the courses that I shoved into one year. So they would be having an easier year than I did, and still they are complaining. And I have two midterms tomorrow and an essay due the next day. Really! Get real, people!

I have moved on from that stuff but they are still there. And when I'm on the phone with them, I am thankful I got away. But you never really get completely away from the drama: people angry with each other, feeling left out or betrayed, misunderstandings, mistaken attribution of motive, seeing someone upset and wanting to help.

High school, university: just a different level of drama. But it's still drama.

Fed Up!

Sometimes, it seems that there just aren't enough hours in the day!! This is one of them. It always seems that everything is due in the same week. I write everything down on a calendar and try to manage my time accordingly, but I still end up cramming and burning the midnight oil. This confusion leads to the big question, "Why am I here?" and "Should I be out working like my friends?"

Don't get me wrong: I like school. But … sometimes I just get really depressed and discouraged.

My three closest friends throughout high school are now all out in the workforce. One is presently a secretary in a legal firm. She is doing quite well for herself and owns her own car. Another close friend works as a real estate secretary. And a third, who went to college after Grade 12, is currently working in her chosen field as well: she's a dental assistant. She has just purchased a brand new car.

Well, sometimes I can't help being a tiny bit jealous because they all have 9-5 jobs with weekends off, money in the bank, and even a means of transportation. I know personally I wouldn't be satisfied with a secretarial job, but I envy their freedom. For instance, I usually go out with them every weekend, but lately I've had to refuse because I have an essay or assignment due. Other times I visit them, and they show me the new clothes they've recently bought on a shopping spree; it seems that I haven't gone shopping for ages. But of course, I'm not bitter towards them. I just say, "Well, I'll have to borrow that sometime. You know how student funds are."

I've often talked to my mother about how my friends are full-time workers, and she keeps telling me, "You'll be better off in the long run." I am confident still that this is true, and I'll just have to remember that all this hard work will pay off once I begin my career. I might as well work towards a career which I know I will be happy in. One thing about the future: that's where you're going to spend the rest of your life.

Seven Hours Away

I just arrived at my room from an evening lecture. I am feeling quite frustrated right now since I am worried about the workload for the month ahead. Even though I have done a lot of work in advance of the upcoming break, I still feel enormous pressure.

Today I received a letter from a friend of mine who attends another university, and she has expressed how much fun she is having. I feel that the excitement here has died down. I still want to get to know more people, yet it seems as if everyone has already chosen their selected group of friends and therefore aren't as easy to approach. It doesn't seem like they want to expand and meet more people; they may feel secure enough with the friends they have. Actually, I think that is too bad. I guess I will just have to work harder at getting to know more people. At times it is pretty hard to get to know someone really well since you are really busy doing other things. This makes socializing pretty impossible.

I really miss the close relationships that I had at home with family and friends. People usually say that you make real lasting friends at university but that hasn't been the case so far for me.

It probably will take time. It just seems to me that time is moving quite slowly; I hope it begins to go faster soon.

I don't know whether or not living so far away from home makes me feel more homesick and lonelier than other people I know. Most people go home on weekends and they feel great afterwards. They feel like they are starting over again, and they have a good positive attitude. There are so many times that I would like to go home for the weekends. But since I live seven hours away, I really can't just get up and go. So far, I've only been home once.

I thought that I was adjusting to university life and being away from home, yet the same lonely feelings come back.

These thoughts were in my mind this afternoon when I was reading an article for our history class about the immigrants to our country a century ago. These people left home and permanently lost touch almost completely with friends and relatives back home. The only communication was by mail and that took over a week, with the same for the reply.

That insight has helped me quite a lot. With today's technology, I can be virtually at home any time I want despite the distance. I don't always need it – in fact I don't actually spend much time doing it. But having it available all the time makes me feel very lucky compared to my ancestors.

WEB: KEEPING IN TOUCH WITH HOME srvlgd.com/KH

The Importance of Friends

When I was in high school, I had friends, but I never thought of myself as needing them. Not that I thought I didn't need them – I just didn't think about it.

When I went to university, I was lucky to move into the same residence as a former schoolmate of mine. I say I was lucky only because in the initial terror of foreign surroundings, it was nice to go through it with someone. However, after the first day, it didn't really matter since we met many new people anyway.

After the first few weeks of classes, I slowly began to descend into hell. First, I began to feel bogged down with work. "Who doesn't?" you probably ask, but I didn't know that then. Then I began to worry about my work. Then I began to panic over my work. And then, of course, I couldn't do my work. As this was happening, I was losing more and more confidence in myself (if ever I had much to lose in the first place).

I can honestly say that I'm not sure if I could have stuck it out without friends. I don't think I have ever needed them as much as then. In the past when I'd had problems, I found it hard to share them with people because I thought I'd burden them or bore them, or that they just wouldn't care. So I tried keeping it in. This didn't work. The more I kept it in, the more isolated I felt. I hung around with people every day: I went to meals with them, shopped with them, played squash with them, partied with them. Yet I felt so alone.

Finally, one day I burst into tears at supper and ran to my room with about five people trailing. I learned a lot that day: I learned that keeping things inside you does not make you tough or confident or unselfish. It makes you lonely as hell. Because I let it all out, I became closer to my friends, and they began to let their problems out too. We helped each other. And in first year, you need that.

Share your problems. Friends learn so much from each other and can help each other so much through sharing. Don't keep it in and don't lie. Oh, was I a sucker! I saw so many people who seemed so confident and smart, and I felt like such a loser. These people were going through the same things as I. Some couldn't or wouldn't admit it. Some didn't realize it. And many lied. But they were all going through it.

WEB: WE'RE IN THIS TOGETHER srvlgd.com/ITT

WEB: NEW FRIENDS srvlgd.com/NF

WEB: FRIENDSHIPS AND THE PRESSURE OF WORK srvlgd.com/FPW

WEB: TO ALL MY FRIENDS srvlgd.com/TAF

Understanding and Accepting

Recently, I was having a heart-to-heart discussion with friends at 4 am and one of the girls was describing a problem that she had encountered in university. This girl has strong beliefs which are not considered to be "normal" by university standards and she finds herself ridiculed or looked down upon because of her values and beliefs.

I find it somewhat ironic that in a university, where people are supposed to develop open minds and tolerance, many people feel it is their duty to change other people who are perfectly happy the way they are.

This girl is somewhat different from me. She doesn't believe in drinking, doesn't enjoy dancing, and believes very deeply in her religion. Still, we are able to get along. She doesn't try to change me and I don't try to get her to do things that she doesn't want to do. For the months that we have been here, she has managed to survive university life by standing by her values, and I don't see any reason why she should change. I also don't see why people can't just accept her as she is. If she did what everyone else wanted her to, she wouldn't be happy with herself anyway. I resent the fact that people take it upon themselves to try to change others.

I think that some of the most important things that people learn at university are social skills. Clearly something is lacking when people are not accepted because of their personal beliefs. There is room for all types of people in this world and nobody should ever have to justify their right to do what they believe.

Actually, I have to amend that last thought. People have a right to do what they believe as long as it doesn't get in the way of other people's lives. The ones who torment my friend do get in the way of her life. And some of them make other people's lives worse too, by coming in drunk and noisy and waking us all up, and leaving their puke on the floor for the rest of us to clean up. She does nobody any harm; they do.

WEB: A CHANGING VIEW OF YOUR PARENTS srvlgd.com/CVP

WEB: MOM AND DAD ARE STILL THERE srvlgd.com/MDT

Relationships with Moms

I am closer to my mom than ever before. Part of it is because I control the relationship more. She knows she can't nag – I can always put the phone down. Also, there are things I can say by email or phone that I wouldn't say if she were actually in the room.

My mom is a genius at figuring out what's in my brain. She's had 18 years of practice. But since I was about 12, it's often meant that unless I want to tell her absolutely everything about something, I don't say anything at all. She can look at my face and say something like, "You're really upset about that, aren't you?" Or even worse, "Sounds like you might be getting a bit serious about this person."

Now usually, I just want to give her a bit of an idea about something and not spend all evening talking about it. When she and I are in the same room, though, I don't control what happens once I say something; she does. I'm apprehensive about that, so I don't mention anything at all about the subject.

But now, things are better. During a phone call or in an email, the person who's in control of how much I say isn't her anymore – it's me. I can just say there was a paper I did that got a poor mark, or someone I met who I expect to see more of. She knows that if she wants to go further into it, and I don't, I can just change the topic, end the phone conversation, or ignore the email. Also, she can't see my face: I think that's the key. She only finds out the exact things I want to tell her, not all the other things that come out on my face and that she can read like a book.

Now I can decide in advance whether to say something and what to say. I control it. I have the power to "limit the number of dimensions of the interaction" which is the way I heard it described once. But in any case, I end up telling her more about my life than she has heard for quite a few years before I moved away from home. Really too, I love my mom a lot, so that feels pretty good.

Relationships with Parents

One of the more complex times of my first year of college was coming home for winter break. I spent the first term getting used to the freedom and newly gained independence I had living on my own.

When I returned home, I felt confined and caged in. I had to deal with curfews again, I wasn't always allowed out, and I had to clean my room on the same schedule (Mom's) as I'd had for at least the previous twelve years. I remember getting into more fights than ever before with my parents and wanting nothing more than to go back to school.

It is really hard to find the balance between upsetting parents versus establishing the rules. It's important to sit down with them early on, perhaps even the first night you get home. Tell them about your life at college and the independence you have. Express concerns you have about coming back home and living in their house. Remember that they love you and that they want to keep you safe. Don't get angry with them for parenting you; it's their job. They are going to be overprotective, and it will be hard for them to let go of certain rules. You might find that at first you have to take baby steps.

The rules that previously applied in their house have to be altered radically. No longer is it appropriate to have rules whose reason for existing is to protect you from dangerous situations or from the consequences of your lack of experience with things. And if your morality is to be protected, then it's you that has to do it. They're no longer in the position of being able to do much about any of that, but hopefully they'll respect your decisions.

But more than new rules, there also has to be a new way of setting rules. Now the responsibility for your welfare is yours. Part of what you need to do, though, is respect the fact that it's their house, and you're now living there, in a way, as a guest. For example, my mom can't go to sleep until I've come back. Appropriate when I was sixteen, but not now. However I can't change it, and neither can she. So if there's to be a curfew, this is now the reason for it as opposed to the need to protect or control me.

It might be too much for them to take in at once, so take small steps, accept compromises, and always make sure you are on the same page. That way, you will survive your first winter break of college. And more important, you'll preserve a relationship that has always been, and hopefully will continue to be, one of the most important ones in your life.

WEB: CHRISTMAS CAN'T COME SOON ENOUGH srvlgd.com/CSE
WEB: LIVING FAR AWAY srvlgd.com/LFA

People Change

One thing that very few people expect as they leave high school and enter university is the inevitable change that occurs among their old friends. It seems that we expect those friendships and people to remain constant ... but as the old saying goes: People Change. As high school friends are separated by distance and immersed in vastly different environments with different types of people, personalities and characters are bound to change, and we must learn to accept it.

I can remember when "the old gang" got back together again for a party at Christmas, I found some of the changes in people really surprising. Some had taken the freedom of the university lifestyle to an extreme by excessive drinking and drug use while others were deeply depressed and introverted because of the academic or social failures that they were facing at university. Not all the changes were negative, I am pleased to announce. Some of the people who were once shy and withdrawn were now outgoing with a greater self-esteem as they developed self-confidence in the independent lifestyle of university.

But I think what took us all by surprise was the fact that we found we actually had very little in common now. We were no longer on the same sports team, or student council, or in the same classes. The constants that we had shared in high school and that had once supported our friendships were now gone. Our friendships were deteriorating. If you think about it, it makes complete sense ... hard to accept but makes sense. Now one person was studying physics, another history, while another had quit school altogether and was stocking shelves at the local supermarket. Some were enjoying school while others weren't. Some were getting married while others were on their way to Europe.

We were all changing; some for the better, some for the worse.

It would have been nice to remember those people as I had known them during high school – those friendships that you could always depend on – but I soon discovered this wasn't the case anymore. We all felt awkward and distressed with the changes … needless to say, I've been to better parties.

WEB: POST-CHRISTMAS BLUES srvlgd.com/PCB

WEB: LOOKING FORWARD TO THE BREAK srvlgd.com/LFB

WEB: OLD FRIENDS srvlgd.com/OF

WEB: THE BREAK srvlgd.com/TB

WEB: NOT A LITTLE KID ANYMORE srvlgd.com/NLK

Gained: New Friends, Lost: One Sister

When I came here, I only had to move an hour away. My home was just a short drive to my dorm. However, even that small distance gave me the room I needed to grow. I've changed a lot since my first day on campus.

Before, I was a little more reserved and definitely less outgoing. After getting into the swing of things at the university, I met a lot of people and was able to put myself out there a little more. I've definitely become, as many would say, a "social whore." The social aspect of my life has begun to strongly outweigh the academic aspect, something that I would have never let happen in high school.

Partying is a part of college that I've begun to embrace. I love going out with my friends and just having a good time. It's my way to unwind after a stressful week of frantically trying to get everything done. This is one of the biggest changes that I have experienced. Before entering college, I was against drinking altogether. I never went to parties, and I refused to drink at all. Now, things are a little different. I enjoy the partying and the drinking!

As a result of many of these changes, I lost touch with my younger sister. She's only two years younger, and we had been very close.

We did most of the same activities in high school. Everyone knew us as "Big Sister" and "Little Sister." It was so hard leaving her when I packed my things for college. We cried a lot and talked to each other very frequently for the first few weeks.

However, after a couple of months passed, our chats grew further and further apart. Now, we only talk when I go home to visit. Why? She claims that I'm not the same person who left for the university nine months ago, and she has trouble accepting that. I feel abandoned by her, like she doesn't care about me anymore. Because I am more outgoing, and more social than I was before, I'm not worthy of her attention. She has not been the supportive sister that I thought she would be.

It's funny how I finally have the social life that I had always wanted in high school, and in the process of getting it, have lost the person I was closest to. My parents always told me to hold close to my sister because she and I will be friends longer than anyone else we have ever met.

I feel like things will eventually work out between us. Right now, it feels like the kind of interaction two business partners would engage in; there is no depth to our conversations. When I go back home to visit, there is definitely a difference in the way we interact with each other. There's a curious and unfamiliar distance between us. My bet is that when she ventures off to college she will encounter very similar situations and begin to understand the other side of the story a little better.

Now, there's nothing I can do to salvage our relationship until she can learn to accept me for who I am. But I want my real sister back!

WEB: CHANGED RELATIONSHIPS srvlgd.com/CR

WEB: FULL CIRCLE srvlgd.com/FC

WEB: NEW PHILOSOPHY, NEW PERSON srvlgd.com/NPP

Different
from What I Expected

Homesickness

University was my first time away from home, and I had never been homesick before. I didn't expect to cry when my parents left for good. It was a feeling I'd never experienced and was not expecting.

At the end of last year I was really looking forward to moving away to university and having a ball! I'd been waiting for this for years. Well now I was finally here, and it was not quite what I had anticipated. Yes, a lot of work, and yes of course, new people, but absolutely not to miss my family and old friends so much.

I just wasn't used to all the partying, all the running around from event to event, being surrounded by new people all the time, all the late late nights and early mornings. I even had thoughts about transferring to a school closer to home. I also thought that I was the only person feeling this way. It helped to be open to the friends I had just made; they were really supportive, and being with them made the feelings go away somewhat. Lots of them were feeling the same, and I wouldn't have made it if it weren't for them.

But still, I couldn't wait to go home that first weekend and be with the friends I'd known all my life. To go home, I even missed a huge concert here with one of my fave bands. I was scared, though, that I wouldn't want to come back.

My parents came to pick me up, and as soon as we turned down the familiar roads leading to my house, I suddenly wasn't homesick anymore. I thought, "Why did I miss this so much? I was so excited to get away." And from then on I was never homesick again, even though I did call my mom every day at first and kept in contact with my friends from home. But by the end of the year, those daily phone calls had turned into weekly ones.

So, the moral of the story is that homesickness is a normal feeling that everyone will experience at some point and that you may be scared and uncertain. But trust me, by the end of the year when it's time to move out of residence and go back home, you're not going to want to go, and you'll miss it.

A City I Now Call Home

This is the condensed introduction, rehearsed to perfection, that has brought me great success in making acquaintances in the self-contained city that this university really is. I say acquaintances instead of friends because only three weeks have gone by and I haven't had the time to share life stories, experience the hysteria of finals, or suffer stomach-aches from the dining hall food (because suffering together always brings people closer) – all necessary to establishing lifelong friendships. And because I've always had the best friends back home, it has been a bit lonely.

I live in a dormitory area located on the north side of the campus. The north side is quiet and dormant; crickets sing their mating songs without disturbance; horses and carriages are still the primary mode of transportation; aliens drop by to kidnap earthlings only to leave discouraged and empty-handed; and the city lights in the distance are a solemn reminder that we are more than a little isolated.

This area is on a hill. To bike enthusiasts, the hill presents an opportunity to break the sound barrier as they ride down texting and sipping coffee. But to the ill-advised, ignorant first-years, equipped with nothing but flabby limbs, it is a problem – especially on the way back. So for even the most ambitious first-year looking for a social life, the thirty to forty-minute walk to the south side of campus and back is a non-trivial endeavor.

In addition to the distance and incline, this isn't exactly the safest campus in the world. In fact, the first words from our lovely residential director and advisers were about the possible dangers that lurk outside. So while most people continue to enjoy themselves through the night, others do retreat to the dorms when the sun goes down to avoid a potential attack by a homeless person.

But contrary to the warning, the homeless have done more good for me than harm. They sing songs in front of the giant block many classes are held in, and they acknowledge my existence – something most of my fellow students do not. To me, the homeless people are an addition to the campus that makes it vibrant and different.

Apart from the homeless, this university has many types of people that I've never met before: communists, socialists, folks who sit on poles, protesters, a 7-foot-6-inch Chinese man, and people talking to themselves. Everything has been new to me, a happy-go-lucky kid from suburbia. The sights, sounds and tastes have all been different, some for the good, some not.

Even though I complain about our dorm's hilltop location, I recently saw a sunset in super high definition quality without any smog to alter its beauty. The next day, I ran around a forest glade at midnight with a hundred people playing Capture the Flag.

Two Saturdays ago, I was part of an entire city in unity as we destroyed our traditional first-game football rivals 52-13. At the stadium, I was able to partake in the loud shouting. Looking up at the crowd and the sea of our colors, I realized I'm part of something special.

And although every day has something new, some things are starting to become consistent. I've found where I can avoid starvation, which road leads me to my desired destination without endangering my life, and which bathroom stalls accommodate my needs without endangering my stomach's equilibrium. But more significantly, I'm starting to see more of the same people instead of constantly meeting new people only to have them go MIA.

I think this means I'm on the path to making friends and not just acquaintances. I think the loneliness is going to disappear. And I think I'm starting to call this place home.

What I Wish I'd Known as a Freshman

As most schools are now back in session for the fall semester, I find this to be the opportune time to share my list of things I wish I knew this time last year when I first set foot on a college campus. So, without further ado:

1. *Professors do **Not** Bite (at least most of them don't)*

   This was one of the tougher things for me to get over. I'm an athlete and fairly big guy: 6 feet tall and about 200 lbs. Nonetheless, my biblical literature professor – all 5'5" of him – intimidated the living daylights out of me, at least for the first few weeks. It wasn't that he was a mean or condescending man; rather, it was his intelligence and complete mastery of the subject that I found so intimidating.

   Finally, I worked up the courage to meet with him during office hours to discuss my term paper and was blown away by how friendly and helpful he was. I even found myself nonchalantly making a few biblical jokes! Another of my professors willingly stayed late into the evening on several occasions to help me understand the subject material. As a straight A student my whole academic career, I've never been as proud as when I aced that final to earn a B for the course.

   Lesson learned: most of your profs want to share their knowledge with you. They were once undergrads just like you and me.

2. *You do **Not** Have to do all the Readings*

Most of your professors will make it clear during that first class meeting that their class is the most important class you'll ever take and that you'll need to closely study each and every word of each and every reading in order to pass. It very well may be that that class turns out to be the most important one of your life, but your professor could be exaggerating a bit when it comes to the reading.

I'm not suggesting that your prof is deliberately misleading you. Nor am I suggesting that you slack off and not even bother to open the textbook. What I am saying is that after the first couple of weeks of class you'll get a feel for which of the readings you'll need to do in order to do well in the class.

Oftentimes, the syllabus has both primary and supplemental readings. Find out which sources provide the meat and potatoes and get to know those ones well. As for the others, skim them if you're interested in the topic, but you should be able to get by without knowing them inside and out. Talk to your professor, the other students in the course, and people who've done the course before. Find out what you'll need to know for the exam and save yourself the time and effort of doing the work that turns out to be of marginal interest or use.

3. *The Goal of each Class is **Not** to get an A*

Yes, I said it: The goal of college isn't to come out with a squeaky clean 4.0. Yes, grades are important but no potential employer wants to see a student who spent their past four years cooped up in the library to get a 4.0 and ignored all the opportunities afforded them to gain real world skills. Note: This isn't just me trying to justify my not having a 4.0, but rather what I've learned from talking to recruiters who come and visit my campus to look for prospective employees.

What is the goal then? In a word: Learning. As I previously mentioned, the grade I'm most proud of is the "B" I received in managerial accounting. I struggled a lot with a few early quizzes and found myself needing to ace the final in order to pull off a decent grade. I spent many hours meeting with the professor to go over concepts I didn't understand. In the end, I aced the final and earned a "B" for the semester. Obviously I didn't get an "A" but does that mean that I didn't know the material? Not so. I wound up learning the material well enough to ace the final and, more importantly, I learned a lot more about myself and what I could achieve when I put in the work. I know that I'll recount this experience to interviewers in the future, and that they'll be impressed too.

4. *Just Because Everyone Else is Doing it does **Not** Mean You Have to*

This applies to so many aspects of college. For one, just because everyone else seems to be on one schedule doesn't mean you have to follow the same one. I noticed a lot of people lounging around between classes and then spending many late hours studying and doing homework. Instead, I preferred to get up early and do my work in the morning before class, in between classes, and in the afternoon before dinner. That way, I'd minimize the time I had to spend on schoolwork after dinner and could instead spend my time doing something I enjoyed. Instead of passing out each night from brain overload, I could have the relaxation time I needed and get to bed at a decent hour.

In another regard, just because everyone else seems to be out partying all weekend, that doesn't mean that you have to. (And here's a secret: not everyone really is partying all weekend. Not even all the ones who say they are.) I limit my nights out to a few times a month. The first few weeks of school, it was fun experiencing the freedom of staying out into the early hours of the morning, but it got to the point where I suffered from the after-effects. Staying out late meant that I'd sleep away most of the next day and, when I did wake up, I'd feel sluggish. My campus hosts many activities on the weekends that I can go to, have a good time, and still be in bed at a decent hour.

These are my big four things. Look back over the headings. Note that each of the four has the word "*Not*" in it. I wish I'd known those *Nots* last September.

An Unpleasant Surprise

When I came to university, I figured that it wouldn't be much harder than high school. Boy, was I in for a surprise.

The work really isn't harder or more difficult to understand; it is just more detailed and therefore more time-consuming. With labs and tutorials, class time averages about four hours a day. I know there are people who miss classes, but I don't know how they ever catch up on what they miss.

All professors expect you to have read the assigned readings before class, and if you haven't, you are totally lost. For my six classes, I find myself reading three to five hours of new material each day. In addition, there are about three essays, reports, or labs to hand in each week. There just doesn't seem to be enough time for all of it.

WEB: UNIVERSITY WORKLOAD srvlgd.com/UW

Learning How to Learn

When I arrived here at university, I expected two things: first that the work would be a little more difficult, and second that there would be more of it than there was at high school. Boy, was I right! But I didn't know the half of it.

In high school, I could remember getting an assignment, taking the time to do the best I could, and still getting it finished with a week to spare before I had to hand it in. You had time to do the best you could. This isn't the case at university. Sometimes you have to compromise and say, "I just don't have the time to go for an A." You've got five assignments due in one week and you have to be pleased that you got the assignments handed in at all.

Needless to say, it's discouraging when you're working as hard as you can, and your marks still fall precipitously from what you're used to and what you expect of yourself. Sometimes, you're tempted to just say forget it (that's putting it mildly), get up from your desk, and go out to the pub to drown your sorrows. But

you soon find that this really doesn't solve any of your problems … in fact it complicates matters because now you have to do your chemistry with a hangover, and I have enough problems doing chemistry when I'm sober.

So, what do you do when you've got a pile of work in front of you and it's all due at once? Don't panic. Have confidence in yourself and relax. The first step is to find out how much each assignment and test is worth and estimate how long each assignment will take to complete so that you can prioritize what work is most important. Before I begin studying for a test, for example, I quickly flip through my notes and text book to get a rough idea of how long I should spend on each section, and I then devote my time accordingly. Always try to keep in mind that you should prioritize your workload so that you get the maximum number of marks for the minimum time and effort. I'm not suggesting that you put the least possible effort into your work; rather, make sure that the time and work that you do put in produces maximum results in terms of marks.

To avoid the "all-nighters," don't procrastinate. I know that at the beginning of the year some of my friends said that they "worked best under pressure" so they left things to the last minute. They soon discovered, however, that at university the pressure is always on and that procrastination only made things go from bad to worse. They found themselves in a position where everything was due at once, and they realized too late that they had passed the point where they could avoid handing in work that was second-rate and/or late.

I remember at the beginning of the year I'd be given an essay assignment with a two-week deadline; I'd put it off because I figured I had all the time in the world to get it done. But then, a test in another course, a big essay in yet another with a tighter deadline, and the story goes on until the first one was completely gone from my mind. Suddenly, an all-nighter, whipping off some jargon (counting the words as I went) to hand in the next morning. After all that hard work and effort, I couldn't figure out why I only got a D+. I guess the primary reason was simply that the essay was a piece of garbage and only worth a D+. One day it finally dawned on me that if the profs gave you two weeks for an assignment, they expected to see two weeks worth of research, thought, and insight within your essay … something that can't be done overnight, I'm afraid.

So instead of procrastinating, start thinking about the essay right away so that you're the first one to the books. But more important, if you get a good start on the assignment, you allow yourself time to overcome unexpected problems that might arise.

Stress

I have always been a person who stresses about things, but up to this year my stress has always revolved around school. But since I came to university, stress has somehow embodied itself in almost every aspect of my life.

There was the stress of choosing and paying for school, the stress of dealing with a worried and sentimental mom, the stress of moving in, the stress of Intro Week since some kids were partying all the time and constantly knocking at your door not to mention the beer and piss and puke all over the halls. Even though it was tons of fun, there was stress – on my body. Lack of sleep, getting sick …

Then there was the stress about marks and not knowing where you stood: whether you would get 84% or 48%. There was the stress about living on a campus where you could not walk around alone safely at night. And the stress of being completely on your own. Funny thing, with all those people so close by, how can you feel so completely on your own? But you do – at least sometimes.

In high school I was always an 80s and 90s student. So when my first work came back in the 60s, it totally freaked me out. But everything is relative, and it is something you just learn to deal with: the expectations are higher, good marks are harder to come by and as long as you are doing your best, that is all you can

do. You can seek out all the resources you want on campus (and you should), but essentially it comes down to you and how much work you're willing to put in.

Living downtown in a big city was a huge adjustment. Having moved from a city where I could safely walk alone at any time of night, I wasn't used to seeing homeless shelters and druggies and suspicious guys hanging around; it was disconcerting because it's all just next door. Here, we always need a buddy to walk home with.

I was scared about stress and so very over-whelmed, but I had to develop strategies to deal with it. Sports was one strategy for me. Networking was another.

Here are the lessons I learned: Be smart. Don't let people change you unless it is for the better. Work hard. Be sociable. Then you will be fine.

An Overachiever's Emancipation

I walked slowly into the behemoth-sized, modern building with my parents. This is where it's going to begin – course registration. I've worked hard to get here; this was it.

"Hey! You're an incoming student?" I nodded, as I was looking around at the hundreds of other students, being ushered around by various overly enthusiastic upper-year students. "Okay, be right back – just gotta get the name list," he said as he disappeared into the crowd.

These were the big leagues. No more small towns for me – in the middle of a large city was the campus, a smaller city all in itself! As excited as I was, I was also scared. I graduated from high school as the top student and made it here with the highest entrance scholarship there was.

"This is university," we heard a representative say on the microphone, addressing mainly parents. "In many cases, your children may be exposed to unprecedented liberty. This may be advantageous for the students, especially socially. However, nobody will force them to do their homework, assignments or studies. Nobody will remind them of their quizzes, tests, and examinations. As you can imagine, this independence may lead to academic difficulties."

He continued: "Your children may be, actually, certainly are, used to A or A+ averages – they wouldn't be here if they weren't. Despite this, most freshman students' averages drop, and statistically, 43% of our students experience a 16.4% drop in their grades; this is sometimes traumatic for them."

I turned to my parents, surprised, as they listened on. "We know that as parents, you function as an integral component to their success and … " It just became a blur after that. What?! Drop by 16-point-what?! You've got to be kidding me. The upper-year student returned: "Alright, follow me!"

This is how my career at university began: with fear. I had a lot to live up to, with a lot of weight on my shoulders. This was certainly not from my parents, since they never pressured me, but from myself. Throughout high school I was an overachiever. It didn't really help that most of the other students around me thought of themselves in the same way. It also didn't help that a single class here had more people in it than the entire student body of my high school. At this point it wasn't really an issue of getting your mid-to-high 90s, but a question of even getting above average!

It was with this mind-set that I began my journeys to the library. It was an act of necessity, really. The residence was impossible to study in, thanks to perpetual partying and never-ending noise. I remember the first time I went to the library on the second day of school, during orientation. Understandably, it was pretty empty, but I wanted to get a head start. Time was certainly not to be wasted now that I was in university. Then came assignments, tests, and exams. Every single half mark required my fullest effort, 2 am library adventures, constant undue stress, and a lack of most intrinsic happiness, all at the expense of any meaningful social fun: the experience of an chronic overachiever.

My extraordinary effort didn't lack for results. In fact, it got results even better than high school. I realized, however, that the method of obtaining such results was counterproductive. I began to consider questions of balance and cost-benefit ratio.

Some were living in extreme ways: always partying, not attending class, and living a life only afforded by way too much freedom. Really, I was no better off, but simply at the other extreme. What was needed was a fine balance, a middle ground that would result in a life outside of academics, but without putting success in the classroom on the back burner. For me, balance consisted of getting involved in volunteering, community work, and rediscovering passions in life, like dance.

Achieving balance is easy to urge yourself to do, harder to achieve. You can say it can't be done, but that's an excuse, a cop-out. A high-mark junkie like I was can be rehabilitated, but it would all have been easier to do if I'd realized the need for it at the beginning. For the record, balance doesn't necessarily have to be incompatible with high grades – after all, I still manage to maintain the marks I had in high school.

But the incentive is simple: a true university life, with emphasis on the word "life." That's something that everyone should have.

The Pressure Cooker

During my first year of university I chose to live on a Res floor that was designated, "Special Interest for High Achieving Students." My hope was that I would be able to connect with students with similar interests. While I did share some interests with my floormates, I found that there was a lot of competition and stress as well.

It was as though school was supposed to be easy for us. If it wasn't, then clearly we were doing something wrong, or maybe it was that we were just not good enough. For example, after a physics test or a calculus exam, everyone would compare answers, and if you were not in the majority, then you were looked down upon. I'm not sure whether this attitude was intended, whether it just happened, or whether it just seemed to happen. In any case, I did not like it.

I did learn to escape from this particular source of tension by doing my work in my room or off residence. So the university's intention when they put us all together didn't work out in my case. The idea must be that the competition inspires everyone to ever-greater heights of achievement. For me, it only underscored all my fears and uncertainties. I had to get away before I could function efficiently again.

Exam time was worse. The levels of stress became unbearable. It got to the point that if certain people came into a room, I would leave because they would be so frustrated with themselves that they would start to infect me too. There were people I studied in groups with for exams, but I preferred to avoid those whose affliction was most extreme.

For next year, I've arranged to live with more normal kinds of students. Some aren't in the same program as me. They don't have labs, and their work seems to go at a much less frantic pace than ours does. I've enjoyed sometimes being with these more relaxed students, and I'm looking forward to broadening my horizons with them next year.

Maybe the pressure cooker suits some people. But I've learned that it doesn't suit me. At all.

One for All and All for One

People think that we are very competitive at this university and that this competition can often be destructive. They think we hide our work or things that others need, that we screw up stuff on others' computers, and tear out pages from textbooks so that others can't use them. Things like that. I know it can be true. I have an older friend who goes to another university and does Meds. It seems that there, it can be really aggressive and vicious.

Some have cars, but when they have to go to a hospital in the suburbs, they don't seem to want to give each other rides.

People put each other down all the time; my friend was scorned because he did part of an internship in a very rural area, mostly with First Nations people. "Passport Country" was what the others called it. These people always did whatever would make them look good, whether there was any actual achievement there or not. They did just enough of something to make it look good on a resume; then they quit. Worse: they did whatever they could to make the people they didn't like look bad – diminish their achievements and their work, and spread rumors about them that they knew would get back to profs and supervisors. Of course, not everyone is like this. But some are, and these incidents certainly stick in people's minds.

But it doesn't happen here. I think many people believe this myth about us, but it's just not true. I don't know if it used to be like that, but I have to say that I've never seen it or heard of it, and trust me, if it did happen, it would be all over the place at once. People leave laptops lying around, and anyone can walk right into the building off the street and steal them. But they don't. We have competitions with monetary prizes, and still people help each other. In the beginning, maybe some do hide their work because they think they are doing something very great and special, and they want to hand in work that will prove how good they really are. But it doesn't take long for everyone to realize that they won't come up with anything that someone hasn't done before and that we are all struggling and we are all on the same page. If you ask someone for help, people will be glad to assist. Of course everyone would like to get a better grade and be near the top of the class. But I've never seen anything vicious.

I'm not saying that we're not competitive at all and that people don't sometimes play games. Some students, when they go to the TAs, try to make it seem that they're not going because they need help. You look at them, and they're trying to look like they know more about the work than the TA. They compete with each other to impress the prof. And they talk smart with each other; they have to convince each other that they are the best. I definitely see that a lot. Scary really, because most of these people intend to go into medicine. I often wonder if they'll make the best doctors with attitudes like that.

Another thing that I really don't care for is group projects. Some people complain that they end up doing most of the work because others know that they can do good work and the group wants to get the best possible mark. So one person often gets pressured to do most of it and then the others just check it over when it's done and put their name on it as if everyone worked the same on the project.

But my most unpleasant experience was different. Last year I had a group project with a few other students who assumed that I didn't know much. Two members of the group knew each other, and they assumed I wasn't up to being trusted to do any of the stuff that was difficult or interesting. If I asked a question, they would look at me in disbelief that I didn't know the answer. So they tried to give me the most tedious and boring parts of the assignment and keep the interesting parts for themselves. I kept asking for more and telling them I could do the work and questioning them as to why they wouldn't give me anything substantial. But they were determined to do it themselves. I felt they completely pushed me out of the creative part of the project. My feeling was that we were all in this class together and we all needed to do well so I didn't understand why they were trying to keep me out of it. I didn't even get to see the whole thing before it was handed in.

And when we made our presentation, they had actually done something wrong (I saw it right away), and the teacher corrected them, which of course meant a lower mark for all of us. If I had seen their part of the work, I could have corrected the mistake, but no, they were just going to do it by themselves and leave me with the menial stuff.

I know I'm a loner, and I don't really like group assignments. But I'm always doing work with other students. We work together on reviewing lectures later in the day or the next day, we read each other's work before it gets handed in, and we review together for exams. And it's not always with the same people because not all classes have the same people in them. You really can't work except in groups with at least one other person because it would get too tedious and boring, and only your brain would be working on it, instead of two, or four, or six. But for me, it's important to know that it's my own work that I'm responsible for and that even when I've worked closely with other people, I'm not responsible for their work; they are.

WEB: MILITANCY srvlgd.com/MT
WEB: PRIDE srvlgd.com/PR
WEB: DISAPPOINTMENT (1) and (2) srvlgd.com/DSP

University is not the Sex Show I Thought it Would Be

Going into first year, I had been dating a girl for about a year. The last weeks of summer were stressful because I was worried about what would happen to our relationship when university started since we were going to different universities. Troubled thoughts of co-ed dorms, partying, sex, and the infamous "turkey dump" overflowed my thoughts. Other friends of mine were in relationships too, but ours felt more serious. University was approaching, and I did not want our relationship to end.

Once Frosh Week got underway, I wanted to make sure that I made as many friends as possible and yet still make time for Jane. We talked – even if only for a bit – every night.

Frosh Week was much different than I had imagined. Going in, I pictured my girlfriend being the only attached girl in her residence, and at parties I assumed she would be surrounded by 27 horny guys at all times trying to get her to have sex. However, university was not the "sex show" I deemed it to be. Sure, there are other guys and girls available if you are interested, but there are tons of other first-years with girlfriends and boyfriends too. There is no pressure to hook up. The only stress caused by the relationship was that created by my thoughts and assumptions.

I talked to Jane often and visited her when I could even though my program was a very time-consuming and intense one. I was still able to have fun and go to the bars. What made it even easier was that we trusted each other.

A lot of people are unsure whether they should continue with their relationship going into university. All I say is, "Be true to yourself." If you both want it to work, then try it; you will be surprised that it's quite possible to make a relationship work if you both want it to.

One thing I took from the experience was that I should not worry about the unknown. I spent the whole summer and the first part of first year agonizing. Then I realized that university wasn't the sex show I thought it would be. And now three years have passed and my girlfriend and I are still dating.

WEB: MY HIGH SCHOOL BOYFRIEND srvlgd.com/HB
WEB: OVERHEARD IN THE SHOWER srvlgd.com/OS

First-Year Relationships

So I had my first college relationship three months into my first year, with a popular senior on campus. Looking back, it's kind of funny that I managed to catch the eye of a senior, but it was an overall good relationship. Owen and I became friends quickly. Pretty soon we were talking on the phone every night, and I began to develop feelings for him. Not too long after, he asked me to be his girlfriend.

It surprised me that I could click so well with someone three years older than myself. That was the nice surprise.

Our relationship was a great one for the most part. Every relationship has its issues, but we honestly did not have many at all. We spent a lot of time together, and our relationship was very public.

I had previously thought that college was a "live and let live" kind of place, and that people would be quite tolerant of others' lifestyles unless they intruded upon their own. I was wrong about that, and that was the nasty surprise. Other people on campus, particularly girls, did not like the fact that I was a freshman and he was a senior. They said and wrote mean things, for example that he was "only after one thing," how well did I really know him, our relationship wasn't going to last, etc. At first, and even a little bit now, it really bothered me that people were saying these things. Since when was my relationship anyone else's business? Owen comforted me, and we both decided to brush it off. At the end of the day, we knew we cared about each other, so nothing else mattered.

If I were a different person, I think I would have felt more pressure. Perhaps we would have broken up because of the mean things people said or were rumored to have said. There was a clique of first-year girls called the "Core" who, I heard, did not like me at all because they wanted "first dibs" on all the hot guys on campus. If I were a different person again, I would probably have avoided public places with my boyfriend, like the dining hall, and I wouldn't have walked hand-in-hand with him on campus or anything like that. We never kissed in public because I am not a fan of PDA (Public Displays of Affection, in case you don't know). However, at the time, I had no doubts about our relationship, and I genuinely cared for him. We had a truly great, communicative, caring relationship while it lasted, (for over a year,) and I have no regrets.

We continued to date for most of my second year until we broke up this past April, and all in all, the relationship was very good. We did have a bad breakup and unfortunately don't talk anymore, but it was great while it lasted, and I hope that eventually we will be able to be friends again.

Your life is too short to let others dictate how it should be run. If you believe in something, believe in it wholeheartedly, and don't let anyone undermine your belief, regardless of what it's about. College is a place of learning, growing, and maturing into the man or woman you will become, so don't allow other people's opinions to influence you. Be yourself. Those who mind don't matter, and those who matter don't mind (that's a quote from Dr. Seuss).

Finally Adapting

Now that half a year has passed, I find that I am finally adapting to the environment here. The workload is much heavier than high school, and expectations are high, but university life also has its benefits, such as the social life and the friendships that develop in residence.

Oh yeah, yeah, I know. You've heard that dozens of times before. So had I. But it was still a surprise when it turned out to be true.

When I first came to university, I expected that most people would be very involved with their studies. All through high school, teachers warned us of the work that would be required of us in university. I ignored a lot of what they said because in public school, teachers warned us of the pressures of high school, and I had managed to adapt to that change quite well. University is a different matter altogether. I've had to make major changes in work habits and attitude.

Students are left on their own to do assignments and to complete readings. There is much independence in the schedule; one can choose to do essays and assignments ahead of time or at the last minute. I find organization to be of great importance at university. Finding time to complete work is a must because it is difficult to do a good job on assignments if they are done the night before. Finding a balance between social and academic life is more of a challenge than I first thought it would be, especially living in residence. One constantly finds things that are more tempting than schoolwork.

Although my marks so far are not up to where I would like, I feel I have learned much about people and life in general – and that information is truly valuable to have. It's hard to say exactly what the insights are. It's more that now I somehow seem to be able to handle it as long as I understand what it is that I'm supposed to do. I guess I can describe it best as a learned intuition, except for the contradiction in terms. Maybe it's a mysterious combination of improved confidence and unconsciously-acquired street smarts.

Even though I can't really explain what it is, I do like it, and I appreciate the results: I can handle things now which just a very few months ago would have thrown me into a complete panic.

It's not as Good as People Say; It's Better

I cannot count how many times I have heard someone say, "College is the best time in a young person's life." And for me, that has turned out to be an understatement.

If there were any advice I could give to somebody about deciding on college, it would be to choose the school that's right for you. I can't stress it enough. Listen to what other people say (maybe!), but don't let anyone else decide where you should go. It's you who'll be living with whatever you decide.

I wanted to make sure I got the true "College Experience." Leaving home, being on my own, making a whole new group of friends. So I traveled 1100 miles away from home to get that experience. At times I miss home but not as much as I miss school when I'm on break.

When you arrive, be adventurous. Step out of your comfort zone. Get involved in a club or team. You won't regret it. I'm involved in extracurricular activities which helps make friends quickly. The friends I have made here will be my friends for the rest of my life. They will most likely be at my wedding someday.

As far as classes are concerned, well, I know not everyone would agree, but for me they're about the same as what I was used to before.

The weirdest thing to get used to was the freedom. Not only did boys live in the same dorm, they could be in our rooms! I'd been to a single-sex school with quite strict rules – actually very strict rules. Now I really felt like I was finally able to be myself. I could make my own decisions. I didn't have to go to bed at a certain time. I didn't have a curfew. I didn't even have to come home at night.

And I found my own way of managing my time. I'm not sure if I manage it well, but I always find time for everything. Procrastination has a bad name in lots of places, but I think you can use it to your advantage. You just have to be smart about it. For me, procrastinating has become a way of life. I don't think I could write a paper now without procrastinating. I guess I like the pressure because even when I try to start early, I end up working at the last minute. The work has to have time to kind of fester away in my mind. I know it's living somewhere there in the far recesses of my brain because I find myself making notes for myself as an insight occurs or inspiration strikes.

One time last semester I had a 10-page paper due. It was about 4 o'clock the afternoon before it was due. I hadn't done anything really, except for looking up and printing off all the information I needed. At 6, my friend came into my room and asked if I wanted to go to a hockey game. I couldn't refuse the offer and decided to take my information with me. During breaks in the game, I highlighted facts I needed and wrote down anything I could use. After the game I was happy. I had been able to hang out with my friends, but I was still in a good position to finish the paper, though a bit later in the night than I'd planned. I got about four hours of sleep, but I finished the paper and that's all that matters.

Anyway, a lot has happened, and I've learned a lot. Not only about the things I've done in class but also about myself and how I handle things in a way that works for me.

And it's better than anything I could have ever imagined. Yes there are the occasional stressful times, but all in all it has been amazing.

Rehab: Just in Time

Profs aren't going to keep telling you to stay off your phone or out of the online world. They're not going to remind you about what needs to be done. Their job is to teach you, not to be your parent. They won't normally even tell you you're at risk of failing. If you don't pay attention, fail to hand things in, or hand in mediocre work because you didn't give it the time it needed, it's not their problem. It's yours. The decisions are all yours to make. You just have to plan well enough, and control yourself well enough to decide what's more important (easy), and then to do it (not easy at all).

Of course, you'll have learned by now that almost everything needs more time than you expected, never less. Maybe previously in your life, you had someone to help you make decisions like this, or some routine that you were used to and could stick to. Now you don't.

First term, I fell into all the traps. I had a lot of hangovers. I missed a lot of lectures, and even when I went, I didn't make proper notes. I didn't begin my papers soon enough, and I didn't spend nearly enough time on them. I was never prepared for classes, or seminars, or tests. Or the December exams.

Rehab was hard for me. Christmas meant feeling humiliated and sorry for myself. Then I realized that university is all about learning to take responsibility for yourself, to manage your time, and to improve your self control. It's about learning not to need crutches to keep you on the road and out of the gutter. Do that and the rest follows.

Now it's almost the end of the year, and I feel great! But I look back a few months, and it scares me to think how close I came to losing everything.

Advice to my Little Sister

I have a sister in Grade 10 who no doubt will be going to university before too long. Here are some of the things I've learned this year which I wish I'd known before:

1. You think you're the only one that's homesick. You're not. But especially guys: they will never admit to it. Only later, when it has died down, will people tell you just how miserable they were.

2. You often can't work in your room in residence. It's just too noisy, and too many people come round distracting you. If you really want to work, you often have to hide away somewhere. Fortunately, here at least, there are places to do that.

3. Even though in high school you might have done everything as perfectly as you could, you often do have to compromise your standards here. Sometimes, with the best will in the world, you just can't find the time for everything. When you compromise, do it with your eyes open. Take time to plan and to decide what things are going to be only adequate. When you do this, pay close attention to how many marks the various things are worth. That's being smart.

4. There are always people who seem to know it all, who find that obscure topic oh so easy to understand, who have done the assignment in no time straight that you've slaved over for hours and still can't get right, who got all the notes from their cousin … and who are better than you in almost every way that counts. After Christmas, most of these people seem much quieter and more restrained; others can't be found at all.

   Don't be fooled. (There are genuine geniuses, but they're usually rather quiet, and you might not get to find out that they always get an A unless you know them really well.)

5. Weeks go by when nothing is due to be handed in. You can go pubbing and partying as much as you want, secure in the knowledge that no work is due for the time being. Then, just as the deadline approaches, you get several profs who pile the work on – all due at the very same time that the things assigned last month are due. Then you have to pull some all-nighters, hand stuff in late, or hand in mediocre work. There's a way around it: get some of the work done as soon as it's assigned. Space the work out as much as you can, and make sure there will be time next week and the week after to deal with these unpleasant surprises.

6. Lots of things take much more time than you expected they would. Nearly everything, in fact.

7. You do need time to yourself and time for your personal and social life. Take it, use it wisely, and do your best to avoid feeling guilty about it.

8. To succeed, you really have to believe in whatever you're going for. If you're at university (or are in the program you're in) because of what your parents or others think you ought to be doing, then take advantage of first year to think over what's really right for you. Your friends can be a big help.

9. Exams are hell.

10. Despite everything, at the end of the year, you look back at it all and realize that it was the best year you've ever had. You've gone through a lot of tough times with people you just got to know in September, and by April, with the help of these people, you've come through. These people are now really good friends, and you realize that none of you are the same people that you were just eight months before.

    It's a great feeling.

WEB: MAYBE I CAN MAKE IT AFTER ALL srvlgd.com/MI
WEB: PLANS CHANGE srvlgd.com/PC

Marks

C Rather than A

Low marks in university are not necessarily a sign of low intelligence. Low grades in your first year don't necessarily mean that you're not good enough to be in university. It is expected that your marks will drop in first year. It's rare to find someone whose marks increase.

You have to understand the situation you are in. Firstly, if you achieved 80% in high school, when you reach university you'll have to adjust to the fact that you are now an average student as opposed to being above average. Secondly, you're going to find the workload in university greater than that in high school.

Don't let being average in university get you down. You have to understand that achieving an A or A+ in university is much harder than doing it in high school. So if you get a C+ or B, don't despair. You're doing OK. It's your first year. Give yourself time to adjust. Achieving a B average in university is comparable to getting an A in high school.

Lastly, don't think you're the only one getting low marks. I made the mistake of thinking that, and I let it get to me. I soon found myself competing with others. That was a bad move. It's a mistake to put yourself in competition with others. They're in the same position as you are and thinking exactly the same things. Do what you can do.

Frustration

I'm so mad, I just want to scream. Today, I was handed back a psychology lab that I worked very hard on. I received only 45%! I must have put at least 35-45 hours of work into that lab. And for what? Nothing!

A friend and I did the whole thing together (which we were allowed to do), calculations and write-up: the only difference was that she printed hers in color while my printer has only black ink. She received 65%. Even that mark does not seem worth the effort we put into it.

We have the professor of the course teach our labs, where others have only TAs. We checked some of those people's labs and from what we saw, almost the same work had received 70-80s compared to our 45-60s. Something seems fishy. Perhaps I should have confronted my prof, but I didn't for fear that the mistake may well have been my own.

It's just so frustrating to have done so much work and to get little or no reward at all for it.

WEB: MAKING THE GRADE srvlgd.com/MG

Coping

I'm finding that at university, I'm having trouble getting the high marks I used to. This is very frustrating because I hand in something I think I did really well on, but instead I get back a great big fat C. I've never gotten a C in high school. Now, I'm surrounded by them, and I'm struggling to keep my head above water.

One thing I have done to correct my situation is this: every Monday morning I write down everything I have to do during the week and group it all into categories so that I can do a bit of everything each day during the week. To discipline myself into making sure it gets done, I can't go out or go to bed until what I wanted to accomplish for that day is completed. So far I have found this very effective, and I feel much more organized and happy about what I am doing. There's something very rewarding about crossing things off lists. It feels great!

Another thing I plan to do from now on is to check with my professors or TAs before I start any of my essays or assignments to find out if I'm on the right track. This way, I'll know what direction to head in; hopefully the mark on the paper will be an improvement and reflect the effort I've put into it.

I hope this new approach will help me improve my marks and reach that goal of straight Bs. I know I've got it in me and if I stick to my schedules, work hard and keep a positive attitude, then maybe at the end of the year I'll be pleasantly surprised.

If at First You Don't Succeed, Lower Your Expectations

Engineering is based on perfection. How do you see yourself compared to those around you?

For my first term I got some of the lowest marks ever in my life and yet I was working my hardest. I thought: I must have the lowest marks in the history of the university. What catastrophic event happened over the summer that made me so dumb? I shouldn't be here at university. I cannot do the work.

However, things are not always as they seem including the marks in these courses. What they don't tell you is that in Engineering, it's all relative. If half the class got 30% and you got 31%, you're above the median; you know they can't fail half the class. Believe it or not, the university does want graduates.

It will be very difficult for you to get the same marks that you had in high school. But there is a saying, "If at first you don't succeed … then lower your expectations." In terms of marks, it could very well be that 30% here is harder to get than 80% was where you came from. The work is such that no one expects you to catch on completely to everything right away. So lower

the mark you expect of yourself. Compare what you get, not with 100%, but with what everyone around you is getting.

Doing this will not only allow you to keep your sanity but will also allow you to enjoy other aspects of university life instead of worrying about marks all the time.

Putting Things into Perspective

Low marks are one of the most discouraging things for the hardworking student. In my case, it seems that if I get a bad mark for something I really worked hard on, I might as well not even have put a worthwhile effort into it. For this mark, what's the use of trying?

On the other hand, if the low mark was accompanied by some constructive criticism, that wouldn't be too bad – not as discouraging. One thing I keep in my mind when I get a bad mark back is not to take it to heart. You have to realize that school is only part of your life, and that the bad mark is from only one assignment in one course. Basically I have learned to try at least to get things in perspective.

Whatever you do, don't let school get you down. Just say to yourself, "I screwed up this time, but I am going to show that prof just how good I am next time." Be aggressive with your studies. It helps.

Multiple-Choice

It surprised me quite a bit to find out how different profs are from each other and how requirements vary from one to the other. In some courses, everything seems to be done by multiple-choice tests. And they're not like the multiple-choice I'm used to from high school, when if you knew the work, you could see the answer right away and just check it off. No, these are different; there's a skill to doing them, and it varies from subject to subject and even from question to question.

MARKS

Often, for example, you'll have a mathematical problem to do that takes maybe five minutes and maybe a whole page of calculations. At the end, you see if any of the answers (a)-(e) on the test matches what you got when you did the problem. If none match, you're in a lot of trouble. Of course, this raises your level of stress as you come near to the end of the problem. There are no marks for getting it nearly all right. Maybe in the problem there are ten things you have to do, but if you get nine right and one wrong, you get zero. Like, 90% = 0%. The same mark as someone who's goofed off and done none of the work at all. And just because of one stupid mistake on my part. But that's the way it's set up, and I guess there's no other way when there are so many students.

What do I do when my answer doesn't match any of the ones in the question? Do I look over my work to see if I can see a mistake? Do I redo the thing and hope it comes out to one of the answers that at least could be right? Or maybe skip it and try the next one, then come back to it if there's time? There's a technique to this, and I haven't caught on to it yet.

In other courses, like biology, you can often do the question by eliminating some of the wrong alternatives. Each question needs you to read four fairly long sentences or even paragraphs, one of which is the right alternative. It's not often you see any ridiculous ones that you'd know were wrong even if you hadn't done the work, but still there are skills in screening out the wrong alternatives. It's hard to describe because it's actually different from one question to the next. Sometimes you have to recognize the right answer; other times you have to go through them all and eliminate the wrong ones one at a time. Or maybe a combination of each. The only way to develop the know-how is to have done a lot of them; you get better at it as you do more of it.

Another thing: I soon found out the hard way that the prof who sets the questions knows the kinds of mistakes people will likely make and puts them in for the alternatives. They're diabolical, some of these guys.

Something else you have to watch out for is timing. Lots of the questions take a long time to figure out, either because there's a lot of reading or because there's a mathematical problem that takes time to solve. With either kind, under the stressed condition you're in, you can get absolutely confused and completely screwed-up. You've already invested several minutes on the question. So it's hard to do, but you absolutely have to: give up and move on. Now occasionally, inspiration strikes you later on and you can come back to it and see what to do. In my experience though, that mostly happens after the test is over, especially when you're discussing it with others. Once, I suddenly woke up in the night, understanding exactly what to do. Yeah, it's all sick. But it's part of life here.

Actually, the way the profs construct the questions is very clever. Once you've mastered the method, you can see that only someone who understands the work thoroughly can do the question. If you haven't done the work, or only understand part of it, you won't be able to do the question. At best, you might see that two of the alternatives are wrong but then have to guess from the other two. There are no marks off for wrong answers, so if you find yourself in that position, you're best off to guess. Your chances of hitting it right are better than if you didn't know anything. So over a lot of questions, it works out about right.

There are over a thousand people in these courses, so I can see why the departments use multiple choice. One good thing, though, is this: we all get our results pretty well right away, with all the stats about medians and things. We can see how well we've done compared with everyone else. And they give us the right answers for the ones we got wrong, so we can take it away and see if we can figure out our mistakes. That's useful. It would be even more useful if we ever had time to actually do any of it.

WEB: COMPUTERS MAKE MISTAKES TOO srvlgd.com/CM

I was Cheated

Too many students are cheated because they are afraid to speak up against a situation which they believe is not right. For example, unfair marks. With hundreds of papers to correct, many teachers hire graduate students to mark papers, and it's easy for a marker to give an inaccurate grade. I discovered this the hard way.

During my first year of university, I was very nervous when I was about to receive my first graded university assignment because it was worth 10% of my mark for that course and it would be the first reflection of my progress in university. Not to mention, I had put in an incredible amount of effort and uncountable hours into this assignment. When the paper was handed back to me, I desperately flipped through the pages until I came across my mark. I was not happy. Very unhappy, in fact. The mark that I received for the assignment did not reflect the amount of agonizing work that I had put into the assignment. I was convinced that university was going to be impossible.

I was so distraught that I decided to confront my professor due to the fact that the assignment lacked corrections. I figured that if I didn't know where I went wrong, I couldn't improve for future assignments. Surprisingly, my initiative paid off. My professor was stunned at some of the inexplicable, unjustified marks that I'd received. He decided to have the paper regraded. When the time came for me to pick up my newly graded paper, I was curious as to how my mark would change. Would the professor find a lot of corrections and significantly increase my mark, or would he find that it had been correctly graded, be insulted that I'd even asked, and drastically lower my mark out of spite?

When I picked up my paper, I was ecstatic. My mark increased by 32% and was now sitting at a 92. I informed my friend who was taking the same class; she did the same thing, and her mark increased nearly 30% as well. This was not the only time that going over corrected assignments paid off. In fact, after examining a sociology exam, I was able to get the entire class's marks increased by 2% because of a mistake that the professor made on a multiple choice test.

After this incident, I realized how important it is to check over corrected assignments. If you feel that a mark is not justified, don't be afraid to confront a professor about it. However, I do advise that you have good rationale behind why you believe the mark is not what it should be. I also recommend that you be polite to the professor about the situation. Confronting the prof and angrily demanding he raise your marks will just result in antagonism. Your mark could well be changed, but chances are that it will not be in your favor.

Grading

Grading in our program is different from most others. There's no right and wrong, just good, better, best … and sometimes not good enough! Grading has to be subjective which of course means that there are times when people don't agree with it.

A disappointing grade is frustrating when you've handed something in after staying up late to do it and you've given it everything you've got. You have a sense of ownership of it, even an emotional attachment to it. That makes it easy to want to defend or explain your work when someone offers criticism, when they have things to say other than what a wonderful thing it is and how it couldn't be improved upon. Even if something is said that could be construed as an additional point, it can come across as a criticism of you for not having thought to put it in. You do have to get used to that. But you have to take these criticisms courteously and realize that engaging your critics creates a dialogue that can actually benefit you and your work, that not every comment is a criticism, and that the prof is showing you respect by listening to what you have to say and reacting thoughtfully to it.

I'm not the kind of person who says that the prof must be wrong because I didn't get a mark as high as I would have liked. But what I don't like is that sometimes a person who I don't feel is qualified gets to grade my work.

A lot of grading is done by grad students who are TAs. Some have graduated from programs less demanding than ours. Others have specialized in an area dissimilar to our program. In both cases, the TA is no more informed about our work than we are. So there are times when they have difficulties reviewing our assignments, causing a lack in credibility on their part.

I can think of one instance when my TA was just plain lazy and simple-minded. He had received his undergraduate degree in something much less rigorous than this program. His ideas were uninspiring, and he spent more time discussing his years as a party animal frat boy than anything else. It was frustrating to take criticism from someone who was never given such assignments in his program. He was just grading according to how our prof had instructed him and even some of that he didn't follow properly. In this program, we put everything we have into our work, and we can be resentful when someone like this has so much influence over our grades.

Fortunately, the prof is responsible for the content taught and the final say in the grading process. That's good because all our profs are people we respect. In the end, I'm confident that my grade will reflect my ability and the work I've done and that it will be as fair as it could be.

These Marks

And I thought I did badly in the calculus exam! Yet here it is right on the Official University Report. No way can I have scored so well.

About 67% going into the exam, then the dreaded exam itself which seemed to zero in on exactly what I was shaky on.

Now this mark. They really must have made a mistake. NO WAY could I have done this well.

There is a possible explanation. Rumors are always going around that they bell the marks, and I really think they must have done it with ours. I kind of thought it might happen because some upper-year students were talking about it during the year, and they said the same thing had happened to them.

The other thing I've heard is that some departments deliberately make the work hard in the first-year courses. Then the students weed themselves out. There may be a few who really don't have the brains. There are certainly a lot who either don't want to do the work or can't control themselves enough to get down to it. Procrastination is the name of their game. Geography, sociology, and psychology seem to be the most common weeding-out courses as far as my friends here and at other universities tell me.

You can usually find these things out if you ask around. It's just a question of smarts, I guess.

WEB: GOOD MARKS srvlgd.com/GM

Exams for Science Students

In my first-year engineering course I learned first-off: don't expect to walk in unprepared, plug numbers into equations, and walk out. No, you've got to prove yourself.

You rarely see questions on the exam that you've already done in your problem sets. Instead, you've got to work harder than ever to understand the question. You've got to think on your feet (or rather your seat!). And you've got to be fast. No exam you'll ever write will have extra time planned into it. The prof who wrote the exam is assuming, rightly or wrongly, that you know your stuff inside out. Even then, you won't get everything, and not all of what you do get done will be right. For those of us who don't know it all (and that's all of us), there's a strategy to writing exams, a way to "cut your losses," if you will.

Usually, your prof will put at least one near-impossible question on the exam, just to make sure no one gets 100% on *his* exam. Accept that, and even look for that question on the paper. Try it near the end if you've time, but don't waste time on it. As for the "normal" questions, look for the easiest one. Do as much as possible, and then move on. *Do not waste any time.* If you sit and think too much, you'll lose that nervous edge that keeps you on top of things.

When you get stuck, start making assumptions and writing them down. Then get on with your question. If you change something, don't erase it; rewrite it beside the old version. If your old version was right, you might still get marks for it. In any case, let the marker figure it out; it's not your problem.

To summarize: exams will be hard and will make you think. Don't waste time. But above all else, *be prepared.*

WEB: FINAL EVALUATIONS srvlgd.com/FE

Next Year Will be Better

I'm feeling rather down about the marks I got on my exams. I knew I didn't do well when I wrote them, but the realization still hurts. Going from nothing less than A all through high school to all C and B, and only one A hurts. The philosophy exam mark really bothered me too. I didn't expect to go as low as 67%.

It seems impossible to prepare for eight exams and write two essays all in the same week. There are just not enough hours in a day. I wonder how any professor could expect students to do so much. Besides the lack of time, how is any student expected to study when everyone else in residence is partying and having a good time? Sometimes it seems impossible to find peace and quiet.

Sure, I could blame residence life or the lack of study time for causing the barrier between myself, my books, and good marks. But these are just excuses. Time is valuable, but there's enough of it to enjoy residence social life, and

to get the work done too. The key is to organize it. Right now, I'm just at the point where I can't wait to get this year over with and start a new one, with a better awareness of what's expected in university.

Standing Out

For the first time in my life, I do stand out!

Going into first year, my confidence was low. Throughout high school, I had heard stories about the geniuses my teachers went to school with, and it seemed to me like the whole world would do better than me at everything. I heard rumors of how, "your average drops yada-yada percent in post-secondary" and, like most people, I assumed these rules applied to me. My average was eighty-something in high school; pretty good, but I figured it was definitely not good enough to compete in a "great" place like university.

At the beginning of first year, I signed up for a program that asked me to fill out surveys once a month for the entire year. I remember one of the questions on my first one was, "What do you expect your average to be at the end of the year?" At this point, I expected 70s in university – pretty good, but still "average." However, after getting back my first midterm, I did better than I thought I could. But, of course, I thought it was a fluke. I got another midterm back and did okay, so now I was not really sure where I stood. When the next set of surveys came, I remember thinking that maybe I could actually pull off an 80 average in university. For the next few midterms, I started studying with confidence, and I did even better.

I'm happy to say that my marks are as high as they've ever been. It took me a very long time to realize that it is possible to stand out in university.

Going into first year, I had assumed that all great things were done by "geniuses." But it took me a while to realize that great things can also be done by regular people.

Can I Do It?

It Used to be So Easy

I used to be so organized. I never really did anything, but I was always so organized it looked like I did. Being organized, I just didn't have to spend as much time actually working. I had a good memory then, and putting organization and memory together, I was laughing.

Unfortunately, over the years, I've let both slide. I started tuning out at some point, and now I have to really work at getting back to that level of achievement. I've made feeble attempts to get organized, but they haven't really worked. I think it's because I get too distracted. Or maybe I don't really want to work (which is true).

This week, I'm going to have to force myself to get down to things. Actually, it's not so much organizing myself, it's sticking to what I organized. That's definitely what I'm going to work at … next month.

WEB: ONE PERSON'S GUIDE TO SURVIVAL srvlgd.com/OPG
WEB: UNIVERSITY WILL CHANGE YOU srvlgd.com/CY

Overwhelmed

Today can only be described in one word: overwhelming! I awoke to realize I had a pile of reading to accomplish in three short hours before my classes began.

While walking to psychology, I remembered that I still had two chapters yet to read for this particular course. I also began to realize that there were ninety-eight pages of history to finish by Monday, a whole book of sociology that was to be read for the same day, an English poem, and a philosophy test to study for. Lord help me! If I ever get through my first year of university, I will celebrate for a month.

This university is seriously into brutality. I sometimes feel like a zombie because of all the work I have to do. I lie awake at night because I can't sleep knowing that I have so much to do and wondering when I will get it done and of what quality it will be.

Profs seem to think that their course is the only one being taught in the whole university. By putting together all of the chapters I have to read for all of my courses, I figured out that I must have twelve chapters read by next week!

This is going to kill me. I haven't gone out at all this week because I have been cooped up in my room reading. One thing that bothers me is that my neighbors go out every night and party their heads off. Do they not have chapters and chapters to read like me or do they just not care?

Well, back to the books.

WEB: CAN I MAKE IT? srvlgd.com/CIM
WEB: A TERRIBLE DAY srvlgd.com/TD

My First Skipped Classes

This morning when I woke up I felt sick. My initial thought was that I had the flu, but soon I realized it was nerves. All weekend my boyfriend said to me: relax. I was uptight, and it seemed my mind was constantly on the two English essays, one accounting assignment, three exams, one test, and preparations for classes. My stomach is in a constant knot, and I go to sleep thinking about how to plan my time and what I'm going to do tomorrow.

So I stayed home today and skipped my two classes. Although I felt an initial pang of guilt, they were not the most crucial classes, and they were the first two I missed. I didn't feel up to going, so I sat at the desk for most of the day and completed one of my English essays.

I can't believe I'm so worked up, really. I'm usually pretty calm about such things. I know I can get all the work done, and I think it's psychological. I wasn't like this last year.

I do feel better now that I have accomplished something today, and as I complete each exam or essay, I will feel even better. Today's snowstorm has put me more in the Christmas mood, and I can't wait until my nerves can settle.

Guilty

Lately I have been feeling very guilty due to the minimal amount of work that I do. For some reason I can't motivate myself, which is unfortunate.

Unlike high school, university teachers are not here to motivate me and make sure I'm doing all my work. This responsibility, at the university level, is the student's burden, with little or no encouragement from the teacher.

It is essential that I get organized and try to set all personal problems aside so that I can concentrate very hard; exams are less than a month away. I have learned a lot about how things are structured here, and I feel that the experience will help me strive to become a better student in my second year.

I still have a lot of growing up to do.

Desperate for Time

I'm ashamed to admit that I've skipped a lot of the reading my profs have assigned. Why? Because most of my massive workload consists of reading. So reading which does not directly result in a better mark becomes slotted down into the category called "non-essential reading." This reading is obviously of a lesser mark-related importance and therefore gets saved for last and done only if time permits (which time rarely does!).

I feel badly because it's not that this reading isn't interesting or valuable to me; but in terms of marks, it has little immediate value, and I have to prioritize my time somehow.

I know it will be argued that this reading is just as important in the long run, which is true, and I regret losing these opportunities for intellectual enrichment. It could be argued also (and justly so) that this is what university is all about: the acquisition of knowledge.

True. But unfortunately, the only way that such knowledge is measured here is by marks. Catch 22.

Not my Week

Okay, I think I have had enough of university and I'll go home now. Everything is going W-R-O-N-G .

First, I was very pleased I had my psych lab done a whole week early. It was all finished (ten pages long) and stored on my computer. On Monday night I thought I would print it out. I watched with satisfaction as the clean pages filled with neat print from my new printer. I felt good when I pushed the stapler through the pages. There, all done. Or so I thought.

Now on Tuesday night I found a wee little mistake near the beginning, that became squared, becoming bigger and **bigger** and **BIGGER** until it ate up my whole report. Every calculation, every table, every conclusion: all have this mistake embedded in them in multiple places. Now the pages are unstapled and wrinkled, and I'm at my computer doing my lab the night before like everyone else – except I'm doing it over again. So what does it matter? Tomorrow is a new day.

I wake up on Wednesday and remember I have a meeting with my English professor. She is going to help me with the development of my essays so they can become B– work. I catch the bus an hour earlier, and I wait in the deep caverns near her office. I wait. I drift.

I'm almost asleep when a voice says, "Are you waiting for professor … ?" "Yes," I respond.

"Well she has the flu today and will see you next Wednesday morning at 9:30."

Oh great. Here I am, stuck in the middle of a grey building for an hour with nothing to do. Even better, my essay is due in two weeks, and now she can't help me this week. I can't work on it this weekend. I'm going to go crazy.

But instead, I find a dimly lit corner in one of the murky buildings, try to catch my breath, and realize: residence food can't kill you, my friends give me hugs, I can go home any weekend I want, and my boyfriend is coming up in a week and a half. I'll live.

WEB: CHEER UP! srvlgd.com/CU

University, a Worrier's Dream

A lot of people drift through life, taking it as it comes and not worrying about much. Others don't seem to be able to. I am writing this for the latter.

University is a worrier's dream. Where else can you find so many interesting things to concern yourself with? You worry about your courses, your professors, your finances – you worry about worrying! Or maybe you don't, and I'm just crazy.

So here are some things that applied to me:

1. Once I got to know my professors, I worried less because I realized that most of them were not out to get me but to help me. All of them are human (well, almost all …) and once you know them as people, they seem a lot less intimidating.

2. Getting to know my classmates helped me too (which is why I recommend residence to every first-year student). I discovered that we were all in the same boat and had the same problems. I worried less about my courses once I

realized that many people come to university not knowing what they want to do any more than I did, and they just drift for a while until they find a direction. You're not alone in feeling this way.

3. And your finances: well, tell me a better time to be broke. Now, at least, you can spend the little money you do have without guilt because you know you're already broke and a few less dollars won't make a difference. Later, when and if you enter the dreaded world of responsibility, you may not find it quite so easy as this year has been.

How am I Doing and How Do I Know How I'm Doing?

One of the problems I have is not knowing how I'm doing in the various courses. Some courses have tests, so we can bring them home and compare how we did with others who are taking the same course. But what about the other hundreds of people who are there? There's no real way to know.

Worse, though, are the courses that don't have tests. The first thing we do that the profs will see is a paper that has to be handed in sometime in October. Of course, with all the other things we have to do and all the other things that are going on like people coming by and saying, "Come on, let's go out and … ," it's hard to find time to even begin it. For me, I neglect it for a while, and I wake up in the night and go into a panic attack because I haven't done it. Well, actually, haven't begun it. Then the next morning I get up and put what I'll need on the computer screen before I go to breakfast. Then when I get back home, it's there, and it's hard not to notice it or to do anything else at my desk or even on the computer – I'm too afraid that if I do start something else, it'll crash the computer and everything I've opened up will be lost. Then I might not be able to remember everything that was there or what I was about to do with it all.

So I have a strong incentive to begin it, then I get into it, and with any luck I get interested in it and actually want to continue doing it. Actually, I've done this twice now, and one of the papers I've actually finished! In September. And the deadline was October 29th! Feels really good.

But then there's still the original problem: I don't know whether it's the kind of thing that will get good marks. How do I know what the prof wants? I've read all the instructions and guidelines over and over again; they look quite clear, and my paper fits into them quite well. But rumors keep going around, seemingly originating with people who were in the same course last year, that he's a really harsh marker and that he trashes people's work to the point that they're in tears. The paper looks good to me, and to a couple of people I've shown it to. (But then they would say that, wouldn't they? And there are some I wouldn't show it to because I don't want my ideas stolen.)

So I still have the uncertain feeling. People I've talked to in second and third years say it's normal, and that I should get used to it or get over it. Yeah right. Maybe I should try to get one of the TAs to help me; they're not really supposed to do your work for you or even to help you with the papers, but I might get some insights about what the prof really wants. Or maybe I could find some second-year students who I could talk to about this prof. Then again, they've all got their own stuff to deal with, so why should they worry about someone like me? Still, I'll be on the lookout for the opportunity.

A Paradox

Obviously, one would expect that success comes for the person that is ambitious and hard-working. Well, surprise, this is not necessarily true! I am beginning to think that success comes easier to the unambitious and lazy people.

Ambitious, hardworking people automatically have more stress. They always find three times as much to worry about. They are constantly under pressure because they begin worrying about due dates months before the average person does. In contrast, the easy-going, care-free people are just that: relaxed and seemingly unconcerned about school pressures. They work better because they start their papers refreshed rather than exhausted.

Work often seems to be of better quality if done with no pressure. The evidence for this hypothesis has come from the analysis of the characteristics of one person: Me!

Taking Advantage of What's Available

One difference between high school and university is that here, no one really seems to care about how you do. It's hard, actually, to see how the profs really could. With hundreds of students, there's no way that they could keep track of everyone like high school teachers do. It's easy to get depressed and to feel you're left here all on your own, not knowing what to do. But if you take that view, you're lost. Instead, take control again. If you're not sure of something in a course or if you have problems with something in it, it's really important that you take some action before it's too late.

First, there are the TAs – Teacher Assistants, who are mostly grad students who are there to make a bit of extra money. There are times and places posted where they'll be available, and most of them seem to know the prof quite well: what he wants and how he likes things done. Not all are useful. Some aren't interested in you and just seem to brush you off. If that happens, you just have to find another one, maybe at a different time. On the other hand, if you're really nice to some of the TAs, they'll maybe end up giving you more help than they really should.

It took me longer than it should have to realize that it's all about learning what your profs want. It's not about how you want to write but how they want you to write. They each have their own personal preferences. You just have to figure them out, and do it their way. So it helps to talk to TAs who know the prof and to people who have taken the course before with that prof. They can tell you the real rules which are often different from what the prof says at the start of the year.

Next, there is something called the Writing Center. You can take a paper there that you've worked on, and someone will look at it and tell you if it's any good and make suggestions about how to improve it and how you could go on from what you've done.

These are the ones I've used. Looking back, I'm not sure they've actually improved my work all that much. But what they have done, though, is made me feel better and given me confidence. I'll probably continue to use the TAs, but I don't really need the Writing Center that much anymore.

I've looked around a bit more since I started writing this, and I've discovered that the university has quite a few offices to help people who need it. In fact, there's a special office for students who are transferring here from somewhere else. Another special office deals with people with disabilities of various kinds, including learning disabilities. Counselors there help them work around some of the things they can't do easily and also contact the profs and ask, for example, for extra time for the student on tests and maybe a quieter place to do them. For people whose problems go a bit deeper than mine, there's a Study and Tutoring Center. I talked to someone who went there, and he said that they helped him organize his time so that he could get down to work and not waste time worrying about not being able to even begin to do his work. Also, there's an Office of Student Support which helps people who are ill or depressed.

Those are just the places I've found out about so far; there are probably more. This university makes a real effort to keep you in school. I'm sure other universities have the same kinds of services as well. But nothing is any use to you if you don't take the initiative to go wherever it is and use whatever is there. I'm glad I found out about all these other places. I don't expect to need them myself, but maybe there'll be friends who are having trouble that I can send to the right place for some help. And, knowing that these things are there makes me feel a lot better about myself and my time here than I was feeling in September, when everything seemed so big and impersonal.

Midterms: the Most Brutal

I find midterm exams much more difficult to handle than the finals. For one thing, classes don't stop during midterm time, and your midterm often includes what was taught in the last class, maybe even the class before. That is brutal. If you have to go back and study things from weeks earlier, then you won't have nearly enough time. Even with as much as possible already done, you still fall behind in your other classes. Or when you have two midterms on the same day, you obviously will study for both, but closer to the date you have to make a decision. If you try to study for both equally, you either just won't do it, or you won't retain anything for either one. So you learn that you have to focus on one that you will study more for.

The first midterms I did were the hardest because I hadn't learned to figure out what the prof really wanted on the exam. I can do that better now, but it still is the hardest thing in most of my courses. Finals were much less frightening than I'd expected in September. At least for finals, you can focus on them completely because your classes are over. The finals are based on what you have learned throughout the term. You have already studied half the stuff for midterms, and only half is new.

The worst problem with finals was the bone-head profs who were so slow throughout the term and then zipped through the material like lightning during the last few classes. One told us, as he raced through the classes, what we had to know for the final and what we didn't have to know, which was great. But another just said, "Know Everything," and that wasn't so great. Gee, thanks for narrowing it down! In another class, the exam was full of stuff that the prof had barely even talked about in class. If I hadn't been taking two other courses where some of that same material was covered, I wouldn't even have known what the questions were about. You never know what you are going to learn in one class that will help you in another.

A Whole 100 Seconds in Hand

Let me set the scene for you:

Midterm season.

Group lab report due to be "handed in" online at 11:59:00 pm today.

Group has 3 members.

10:00:	Get home from night class, knowing that I have to help the group finish the lab. The discussion section needs to be completed. The lab needs to be edited. I need to eat a sandwich.
10:15:	Finish jam sandwich and start searching for references for the lab.
10:20:	Group Member 1 calls. He says he is having trouble with his girlfriend and will not be able to help us complete the lab.
10:22:	I find Group Member 2, and we decide how to split up the rest of the work.
11:15:	I send off my half of the work to Group Member 2.
11:35:	I receive Member 2's half of the work.
11:40:	We begin to edit the lab together on the computer and over the phone.
11:50:	We decide that the lab is complete and that it is time to "hand it in" online.

11:51:	My internet browser has frozen … moment of silence on the phone.
11:52:	While panicking, I open a new browser, and then the website to send the lab attachment.
11:53:	I attempt to click on the "add attachment" button … nothing. It doesn't seem to work. We are now desperate for ideas.
11:54:	Over the phone, Member 2 and I agree that I should send the file to him as an email attachment.
11:56:	Email is sent.
11:56:	Member 2 saves the file to his computer.
11:57:40:	File is attached, sent and handed in from Member 2's computer.
11:57:45:	Relief.

WEB: MIDTERMS SUCK srvlgd.com/MS
WEB: HELP! srvlgd.com/HLP

'Tis the Season to be …

a) Excited?
b) Depressed?
c) Who cares?

I just feel like crying. The tension and pressures of university knock me to my knees. There is so much work to be done and so few days until Christmas that it literally depresses me. Nothing upsets me more than this feeling of incompetence.

I often wonder if I'll make it through the year. Sometimes I just feel like giving up; my goal almost seems unreachable. Maybe I'm just not university material. Perhaps I shouldn't be here. But then I think of all the other students here who seem to have no worries or fears. I know of friends from high school who went on to post-secondary education with lower grades than me. So how come they can do it?

All I can think about are the endless assignments and readings that must be completed for certain dates. Maybe my expectations are too high. Last year in high school, it seemed quite easy to complete assignments in a short period of time, but now I find myself constantly working in order to keep on top of things.

Perhaps I should first relax, and take things as they come instead of trying to get ahead. I've never failed a course or anything that matters before, so why should I start now? All I can do is put my best effort forward and hope to be successful!

Christmas Exams

It feels like only a few days ago I was unpacking the last of my clothes and books, laying out my binders for the following morning, and preparing for the first 8 am class of the year. And now, it's the night before the end of the last full week of fall classes, and I'm thinking, geez … was I asleep or what? When did all of that stuff happen?

Even though classes will soon be finished, academic demands certainly will not – and far from having an excess of free time, I will now be filling the majority of my waking hours studying, reviewing, rewriting notes, and otherwise cramming my head full of every minute scrap of information that I can stockpile from each of my classes. Caffeine will become a good friend of mine, and I can almost guarantee you that, if I'm not in the gym, in bed, or in that five-minute transitional period that I've allotted myself for food, I'll have my nose in a book or a page of notes and a pencil clamped tightly between my teeth (it's to prevent the grinding). That's right, guys and gals, while the semester may technically be over, there is no rest for the wicked – or the university student, for that matter – and it will take a lot more than an absence of classes for me to completely de-stress.

Just ask my current roommate – we're like mirror images of one another, stress-wise. Or ask last year's roommate – he got to see me at my best last year, strung out on caffeine in the midst of exams, with my fingers permanently glued to my laptop and bags under my eyes big enough to hold groceries.

So, while the rest of my family is back home, listening to "a Charlie Brown Christmas" and relaxing in front of the fire with homemade cookies and cappuccinos, I'll be here at school, thinking to myself, why am I back in this head-space again? Why, after a focused, proactive school semester, am I still feeling this anxiety? Why, after promising myself that I would plan a precise study schedule – and doing so – am I still so bloody freakin' nervous?

If I asked my mom for help, in all likelihood she'd spend an hour on the phone with me, calming me down, before express-mailing me a care package with all sorts of homemade food to help combat the homesickness until final exams have passed.

If I asked my dad, he'd probably chalk the whole thing up to some mental defect of mine ("You always stress yourself out. Just stop worrying; you'll do fine!"), and then he would get my mom to express-mail me a care package with all sorts of homemade food. And if I called my grandma for comfort, she'd probably tell me that I'm strong, capable and young, that I've managed thus far and I can do so again, and then ask what kind of homemade food my mom sent me in my care package.

And in essence, they're right – I can handle this. I've done two rounds of exams already, and I've managed. I just need to stop causing myself undue distress and just de-stress right from the start. I need to recognize that I'm spazzing out and need to calm down and take care of it now before it escalates to something bigger. I need to vent my frustrations, then put them aside and just take everything step by step. If I focus on the little things, and not the big picture, then everything will fall into place – I'll just study every day, take it one exam at a time, and roll with the punches wherever they come.

So, for now, I guess this is goodbye. I need time to focus on my schoolwork and really put my nose to the grindstone. I won't stress out, though – I promise – I'll just take everything piece by piece, and let the chips fall where they may.

At least, that's the plan.

WEB: TIME DRAGS AND TIME FLIES srvlgd.com/TDF

WEB: AFTER CHRISTMAS srvlgd.com/AC

WEB: NEED A MARCH BREAK srvlgd.com/NMB

I'm Done for; This is the End

Well, it's the end of the second term, and this is it for me.

At first it was a great time: the freedom, no attendance taken at classes, the absence of anyone to tell you to do stuff, the far-in-the-future deadlines, the booze, the parties …

I survived, barely, until Christmas. Sweet-talking the profs, deadline extensions, minor revisions and paraphrases of others' already-marked work. Warnings, but nothing that couldn't be shrugged off.

Second term not so good. Procrastination was about the same. But less fun, more hangovers, more guilt. More people looking funny at me. More rolling of eyes on the part of the profs.

The same last-minute scramble as in December: to get stuff in, to make excuses, to have dead-lines extended. Profs not so understanding. Fewer people to get work from to make altera-tions to and then to hand in. A couple of really negative letters from the administration.

And now, the exams. Not a good scene for me because I really don't know anything at all. Everyone else seems to be doing all-nighters – amphetamines but no recreational drugs, and no parties, that's for sure. But I'm so far out of it that nothing will do me any good. I just don't seem to know where to begin. One person emailed me a summary of all her notes for the exam; I couldn't understand anything she had written.

So as far as further education is concerned, that's it for me. A wasted year. Worse. All my savings consumed. My parents' contributions gone. They don't know much about what's been going on; I've been able to be optimistic with them up to now. But now they're soon going to get a big shock.

And the future. Will anyone hire me? Will I ever be able to afford to go to school again? Will I ever get accepted anywhere else anyway? Will anyone want to be friends with a person like me?

Doubtful. I'm done for.

WEB: WORKLOAD srvlgd.com/WL

Exams Are Over

I feel like I am in heaven. No, I didn't just meet the most gorgeous guy at the university, but I did survive my first set of university exams! What a total relief. It feels like a hundred pounds has just been lifted off me. What a feeling!

For the last two weeks I have done nothing but read, write and study. I think I was one of the luckier ones; I had quite a few of my essays due earlier than the exam dates. I'd hate to have the pressure of exams and essays both at the same time. I'd probably go nuts!

I really hope my exams went okay. It was an awful lot of work to do. I'd hate it if it turned out that things didn't go so hot. But realisti-cally, by the middle of the week all I wanted to do was get my exams over with and get home so I could relax!

I think I'm pretty lucky to have a roommate who is taking a lot of the same courses as me. Often we studied together. We read things to each other, quizzed each other, made each other write things down – all things that helped us pick up things we'd missed. Some-times at night when it was getting late, we'd start getting our tongues tied up while reading a sentence or make really stupid mistakes. By then, we knew it was time to shut our books.

Confidence: Fake it if You Have To

When I first started university, I was the least confident person you have ever met. You name it, I was scared of it. And I showed it. I thought about my fears and worries constantly. I admired those who seemed more confident than me. And many times I felt like I didn't belong at university at all.

I had a rough first term which resulted in my almost dropping out. I had done well mark-wise in high school and knew how to work hard for what I wanted. We hadn't even gotten many marks back yet, only some assignments, and my marks were respectable. But I doubted myself. So much so that I made arrangements to switch into a different, less demanding program. And I dropped a course, a course that was necessary for my major.

Then I got my midterm marks back and found I had done much better than I had feared. What was crazy is that I had no idea. I thought I had bombed, but I hadn't. Shows you the power of the mind. Needless to say, I didn't switch to the less strenuous program. I made up the dropped course the next year, and I realized a few things.

I should have tried to be and act confident even if I didn't feel it. I should have faked it. People treat you based on how you present yourself to them. If you seem unsure of yourself, they will relate to you that way. It is a vicious circle.

You are going to meet people who are smarter than you and people who are going to make you wonder, "How in the world did they get into this school?" The key is for you to do some self-reflecting and not get caught in the trap of thinking you are the dumbest person there. The truth of it is that there is always going to be someone who is better than you in something. But this also works in reverse: there is always going to be someone who you are better than with respect to a subject or a sport.

By self-reflecting, you will have a chance to truly realize your strengths and your weaknesses; this recognition can be empowering, and you can learn to use both to your advantage.

And in the end, who cares whether you're smarter than the next person or not as smart, or better looking or worse looking, or lighter or darker, or … ? We're all what we are, and all we can do is have the most fun or make the most of our abilities or excel in whatever we decide to do, or (and this is most of us) some combination of these things and a few others. But that insight, for me, came later. At the time, my conclusions were:

You gain nothing and lose a lot if you let people intimidate you, professors included. It is okay to assert yourself and have opinions that are different from someone else's. Stick to your guns, and if you don't feel confident but still feel you are right, fake confidence, because eventually, it is going to become real confidence. People are attracted to a confident person, and a lot of people cannot tell real confidence from fake.

So Go For It! Have you ever heard of a Self-fulfilling Prophecy?

Pitfalls
and Bad Situations

Mistakes:
Your Own can be Hard to See

I failed my first year of university. So I packed my bags and went home.

Looking back, I realize my mistakes.

I had too much free time. My bus ride home from campus was two hours, so in between classes I had to find ways to fill my time. Instead of staying on campus and doing my work, I would go to the mall and just hang out. Because I had so much free time, I figured there was always tomorrow, or the next day, or the weekend, to get things done. If a due date was two weeks away, I thought that was a lot of time, so procrastinating did not seem like a bad thing. Then due dates began to pile up, test dates started to come quickly, and what was previously a lot of time was suddenly no time at all. Even after some failed first semester courses, I couldn't seem to work between my classes. I guess I figured that what worked in high school would work in college.

I didn't pay enough attention to my poor math entrance test results. Because I didn't do well enough on these tests, I had to take prerequisite courses for the math courses required for my major. In effect, they were prerequisites for prerequisites. So not only did I figure that they didn't count for anything (a mistake which cost me dearly), I didn't think about perhaps changing my major to something that involved fewer math courses. In retrospect, I should have paid attention to the reason for these low marks and the reason for these entrance tests: I sucked at math and was nuts to take a major which involved so many math courses.

When I received a letter telling me that my grades were too low to continue my studies, I didn't go and talk to anyone to figure out where I could go from there. I can't exactly say what my mind-set was at the time. It could have been school burnout. By the time I got the letter, I didn't spend time looking into my options because I figured I could be done with school and just get a job. I was young and wasn't thinking of the long term.

A year of working in a dead-end job that I didn't like reminded me of why I wanted a degree in the first place. So I decided to move on. I chose to go to community college instead of back to the university. But this time, I switched my major to something with less math and with more core classes than electives. Each semester I could check another three or four courses off my checklist, so it felt like progress was happening faster.

At the community college, the first few semesters didn't seem much different from high school. But as time went on, classes became harder and the work more time-consuming. Taking courses at a community college was helpful because it helped me ease into my next step: re-enrollment at the university I had gone to before. But this time I made some changes:

I took advantage of some of the gaps in time between classes to get involved in some clubs. I started with just one but in my second term, joined another as well. Having less spare time between classes helped me make better use of the time I did have, so I got more work done. If there was no meeting on a given day, but I had some time, I'd hang out in a computer lab or cafeteria and read my textbooks or try to knock off some homework.

On club meeting days, I'd go to the meeting room early and do something for a class before the meeting started. I learned that figuring out the time management thing when you don't have a lot of time available is easier than when you have big chunks of time.

I took a different major than I had when I was there before, more along the lines of what I took at community college. I found the new courses related to each other and related to my end goal. I enjoyed many of the profs because they taught using their real-life experiences for the course material; this gave us better insight about how the content of the text could be used in the work force. Since I had struggled with math in the past, I took some of the necessary math courses online. The advantage was that when you did your homework online, you would immediately know if you got it right. The website would tell you. Of course wrong answers were just wrong and there was no hint as to how or why, so it took a little longer to figure it out, but I think that was the point of doing it that way. I think having to go back and figure it out helped a lot come test time. I liked having immediate results and not having to wait to know what I needed to do.

I had reached my maximum semesters of financial aid so I needed to finish in May. This was my first and last chance to succeed. All of the classes I had scheduled that year were "must pass" classes. I had no wiggle room.

Looking back at my previous awful first-year experience at university, I could have avoided my mistakes by actually going to the learning center and meeting with advisers. Maybe they could have helped me to understand that failing these courses wasn't the end of the world and helped me to develop a new plan. I could have also gotten involved in extracurriculars right from the start and given myself a reason to stay on campus rather than wander off. A little more focus on time management would have been helpful although I've got to say, it took me a while to figure out the secret to managing time, that being having less of it to deal with.

Choosing Courses

I made this mistake once and never again. Don't do it. Do not choose courses based on their title alone!

I am in science and had to take a number of arts electives. I thought that "Couple and Family Relationships" would be an interesting course. Was I wrong! It was deadly boring; going to that class was more painful than having teeth pulled.

I quickly learned to do research before picking a course which consisted of either bugging profs for course outlines or asking others who had taken the course. This gave me a much better idea of the content of the course, how hard it would be, and what was expected assignment-wise. And, most important of all, if it was any good.

Moderation

The thing I struggled with most during my freshman year was time management. In high school, after a day of classes, you do your extra-curriculars, go home, eat dinner, and work on homework. You have parents and teachers to check up on you. Your life is mostly dictated by outside forces.

When you get to college, you have complete freedom over your life. You make your own choices and create your own experience. And if you come from a very strict household as I did, you might have a lot of trouble adjusting to the freedom.

My newfound freedom in college caused me problems when it came to the party scene. Since I came from a very uptight household, I never partied in high school. My parents kept tabs on me at all times: I had to call when I arrived no matter where I was going, and my parents waited up for me to come home.

Coming here, I could do whatever I wanted, wherever and whenever I wanted. It's really easy to go out every weekend and go wild. Soon you realize that nothing is stopping you from drinking during the week too. Before you know it, you will have established some pretty bad habits like drinking on a Monday or skipping your first morning class.

I'm not by any means saying don't party. Partying is fun, different from the workload stress and a great way to meet people on campus. Older friends (not necessarily friends of my parents!) have told me that this time in your life doesn't last for ever; once you're older, you won't usually have this instant bond with people you meet.

So yes, by all means, go ahead. Don't waste the opportunity. All I'm saying is that it's important to take things slowly. Ease yourself into your newfound freedom. It's all about moderation.

If you are in Res, you are living with your friends 24/7. It's insanely easy to spend all your non-class time hanging out with your friends. So it's really important to get into the habit early on of taking a little time for yourself. Studying with friends can be great sometimes, but other times you need to take time to get things done by yourself. Study, do laundry, call your parents, or just listen to music: do it by yourself. If you don't start taking time out for you right from the beginning, you'll get stuck in the habit of spending all your time with your friends and really getting nothing accomplished.

Another thing I ran into trouble with was money management. My parents gave me a debit card which had the 2000 dollars on it that I had earned over the summer. The same things I mentioned earlier apply to money. Just be aware of what you are spending. It doesn't seem like you are spending a lot of money when you go to McDonald's or Denny's, but it adds up fast.

A good idea is to set a limit for the money you can spend for fun every month and the money you need to spend on the essentials. I never checked my account during the year because I just figured there was no way I was going to spend 2000 dollars in eight months. So at the end of the year, I discovered I had spent a lot

more than I'd imagined possible. Use online banking; if you can actually see how much you are spending, you can be more careful. Another temptation: at the beginning of the year, banks are all over you trying to sign you up for their credit cards. Several of my friends fell into this trap. Some got behind and didn't pay the bills off monthly. Others though – in fact everyone – found that using the card made it harder for them to know exactly how much money had gone and how much was left.

I loved every minute of my freshman year but if there is one lesson I learned, it was definitely to take things in moderation, and that it's OK to say no sometimes (okay, I guess that's two lessons, but they are related). Succumb to some temptations, but not all. Have fun though! People know what they are talking about when they tell you that these will be the best years of your life.

Procrastination (1)

I want everyone to know that this article was written by someone who made procrastination an art. In other words, I perfected it!

During the first month, I kept all of my assignments up to date and I had most of them done before the due date. However, one day early in the second month, I was visited by the ugly gremlin we all call "Mr. Procrastination." After that brief visit, I found I had become a different person. It now seemed that anything was more important than schoolwork. I would take a gamble on calculating how long I would need to do an assignment; needless to say, I'll never make a living in Vegas!

I saw the light one day when I accidentally left an "insignificant" (or so I thought) psychology assignment until two days before it was due.

Well, after many grueling hours of work, that little insignificant project turned out to be 52 pages long. When I realized how long I had spent on this project, and it still wasn't the way I wanted it, I became very depressed.

So the next time that sneaky little gremlin came to visit me, I told him it was over and I didn't want to see him anymore … and I haven't! I can honestly say that I have never since had to take classes off or to pull an all-nighter to get an assignment done.

Every now and then I still catch a glimpse of Mr. Procrastination whenever a pub or a movie comes up and I'm doing homework. This I know will never change.

Procrastination (2)

Procrastination … I decided to write about it right now because I realized I've been doing it for the past couple of hours! I ate dinner and came back to my room at 7 pm, planning on a quick phone call to my boyfriend, checking my email briefly and then starting homework. Then all of a sudden I looked at the clock – oops! I didn't get anything done before my 10 pm water polo practice. I usually realize what's happening but not how much time I am actually taking out of a potentially productive day.

Procrastination is a whole new game these days. Not only are we distracted by the tons of activities we could be doing that do not involve classes and homework but also by the computer that can become a prison. There is a never-ending world of discovery, information, and contact with friends and family to partake in every day. I do not even have a TV in my room, nor do I play video games; but I know plenty of kids who spend too much time on that as well. In high school, I found myself on the computer a lot, and that carried over into college. The addiction has gotten worse.

There is one simple aspect of college that you must follow if you want to do well, and that is planning. Plan out your week day by day and hour by hour. Figure out when you will have time to do work and how much time you know you need to complete each assignment. Though you may think it seems simple to just find the time to get your work done, procrastination is often tempting – no, irresistible.

Although allowing yourself to take breaks is healthy, if done for too long and too often, you will fall behind. When you're taking a break and you're getting to the end, it's so easy to reply to just that one more text or email. That leads to your having to check various sites, go onto chat … and the evening is over.

Another problem for me arises for an odd reason: I actually am interested in most of my courses. So sometimes I'm working on a specific piece of research and get sidetracked into a topic which seems fascinating and intriguing. It's an odd thing, but when something is not actually of any immediate use, working on it results in a lowering of stress, and that's tempting as well. Like the stress is reduced, but you can still tell yourself you're still working. Close enough to the topic that you don't feel that you're goofing off, but far enough away that you don't feel the stress.

Falling behind in college is not fun. Once you are behind on one reading assignment, it is very difficult to catch up. There have been times when I have never completely caught up in a class. It's all about buckling down and getting work done. If you can't avoid your computer, go to the library without it until you get your work done. Disconnect from the internet? Turn off the computer? Sounds good, but can anyone actually do it?

It's sad how we have become so addicted to technology. But cold turkey: impossible. It all just has to be controlled.

WEB: PROCRASTINATION (3) srvlgd.com/P3
WEB: I CAN ALWAYS DO IT TOMORROW srvlgd.com/DIT

Under Pressure

Procrastination has become a way of life at university with the overriding motto of "Never do today what you can put off 'til tomorrow." I have learned through experience that procrastination is one of the best ways to gain insight into troublesome assignments and exams. This is the way it works:

When you are given an assignment and you try to complete it early, you'll spend many hours staring at the paper and pondering how to solve the questions. You probably won't get the right answers.

On the other hand, if you leave the assignment to the last minute, you no longer have the time to think about the answers, and a panic instinct is triggered. All of a sudden, you will start writing down solutions to the questions although at the time you may not realize just what it is you're doing. This carries on until the end of the assignment, at which time you suddenly feel exhausted and wiped out and usually sleep through your next class. But the assignment is finished.

So remember, if you have time to do an assignment today, put that time to constructive use: watch television or go to the movies, or anything. But don't do that assignment!

Two small problems: the magic doesn't always work. And for some, it doesn't ever work.

Being Obsessed with Work

During your first year of university, it's very easy to fall into a rut. I mean being obsessed with homework. You have to remember that the years at university are supposed to be the best years of your life. Do you want only memories of assignments, classes, and exams? No, of course not!

However, some first-year students are very gung-ho about schoolwork, and consequently they devote all of their time to it. But if you don't take a break from studying to relax and enjoy yourself, you will become a victim of a career-threatening disease, called University Burnout.

I guess the moral of this story is: Don't ruin your university years by not having any fun; the joie de vivre is much more important than homework done to perfection. As the French say, si tu n'est pas heureuse, que tu n'est pas vivant! (If you are not happy, then you are not living!)

It's Done!

What do I have to do tonight? F***, write my English essay. I could think of a million things I'd rather be doing. Oh well, it must be done, so I'd better sit down and prepare myself for the long and tedious task ahead of me. Wait, what time is it? Oh, it's only …

6:45 pm I still have the entire night to do it. Maybe I'll do something else for an hour to motivate myself. I know, I'll go to aerobics. Okay, it's …

8:05 pm … and I'm back from aerobics class and those blank sheets of paper are staring me right in the face. Ok, now I'll really sit down and write it. Oh, that's a great song they are playing down the hall. Maybe I'll just go down and listen, and then I'll come back and write. Well, now it's …

8:32 pm It was a really long song, but I've had enough procrastination; now it's time to get down to business. Oh s***, the phone. I wonder who that could be? Hello … oh hi Mom … I don't believe it, it's …

9:12 pm … and I haven't even started. This is ridiculous. No more fooling around. And this time I mean it!

1:16 am Ah, I'm finished!

I don't believe it, I feel so incredibly wonderful. Why did I take so long to start it when I knew I would feel this terrific when I was finished?

Accomplishing an essay or any other assignment in university has got to be one of the greatest feelings in the world. You feel so smart and so good about yourself because you know you can do it!

WEB: FAVORITE TIME-WASTING TECHNIQUES srvlgd.com/TWT
WEB: INTERNET: FRIEND OR FOE? srvlgd.com/IFF
WEB: FACEBOOK srvlgd.com/FB
WEB: TROUBLESHOOTING COMPUTERS srvlgd.com/TC

I Want my Mom

I've got the flu. For the last three days I've been sipping on juice and munching on Aspirin and vitamin C tablets ... but still no sign of relief from this headache, dizziness, and nausea!

Now, while I'm trying to overcome this misery, the rest of the university is out wildly celebrating the annual winter carnival. People are drinking enough alcohol to preserve an elephant while I'm in my small stuffy room feeling like they should. The only time I truly get to take part in all these festivities is when I stagger to the washroom and stand in line to puke!

It seems the only time I get relief from my dizziness and weakness is when I'm horizontal on my bed. I told a couple of my friends this, and they suggested with great enthusiasm that if I was only comfortable lying on my bed, they'd do their best to provide me with a couple of women to "help me recuperate." Thanks guys.

Now, I know that "I'm a big boy now," and "tough," and independent ... BUT I STILL WANT MY MOM!!! You see, she makes the best homemade chicken soup. If I were sick at home right now, I'd be lying in a double bed with a thermometer in my mouth, my dog lying at my feet, watching videos ... but here? Here, there's a bunch of noisy drunkards outside my window burning desk chairs in celebration of the seventeenth snowfall while chanting "Drink chugga-lugga-lugga!!!" It just doesn't have the same recuperative effect I'm afraid.

I've got the flu ... at university.

Panic Attacks

FOR A LONGER VERSION, WEB: PANIC ATTACKS srvlgd.com/PA

During my first year, I had a problem that I was at first hesitant to tell my family and friends about. Now, though, I realize that there was no reason to hide anything.

It began in the run-up to the Christmas exams; I'd wake up in the night in a panic – literally in a sweat. Sometimes I could go back to sleep but not always. Of course, the panic was always about the exams: had I forgotten to study something? Was I properly prepared for the various kinds of questions there would be, and so on?

On one level, I knew that these feelings were irrational and unrealistic, but they easily consumed me. They didn't help me study any better – in fact it was quite the opposite as I was often tired and dispirited. And when you are panicked, you cannot think straight. I ended up doing quite well in these exams, but it certainly was an unpleasant process.

When these exams were over, I thought that because the exam worry was gone, the panic attacks would dissipate. I went home for the holiday and settled down to enjoy the free time I hadn't had much of during the year. But I'd still wake up with the same panicky feeling, except that now it centered around other things, and not always the same thing. What if I had an accident that totaled my car? What if my mom lost her job? What if there was a terrorist attack that blew us all up?

Well, I'm exaggerating, but I think you get the point. No one could guarantee me that these disasters could never happen. But nothing in my situation was much different from what it ever had been, and none of this anxiety involved anything I could do anything about. Yet here it was. And it sucked. It was really the panic that attacked me, and it then started looking around for something to be panicked about. Of course, it could always find something.

Back at university, the frantic scramble to get everything done on time began again, and this time I wasn't coping well at all. I went to the Health Center to see a professional and was told that these panic attacks were in fact not uncommon at all, especially in university students because they are in such a state of chronic stress. She gave me a prescription and told me if things persisted, to return to the clinic.

At first I argued. I'm not a nut case! "Look," she said, "if you had diabetes, you'd wish you didn't have it, but you'd still take the insulin for it. This is a chemical imbalance in your brain, and the medication will probably deal with it." I was still hesitant about taking the meds, but I understood what she was trying to say. If it's a physical problem, it's not embarrassing. But if it's mental, it's a whole other story. After a few days, the attacks subsided, and I realized the pills were helping.

I'm still taking them. I learned there's no point in being ashamed of something you have no control over and that before you become involved in everything around you, you need to remember to take care of yourself first and foremost.

Breaking Out of my Prison

One of my biggest regrets about my freshman year was that I was in relationships for the entire time. Very quickly after I arrived, I got involved with a girl. While we had a good time and are still good friends, I ended up hanging out with her and her group of friends all the time. She went abroad second semester, and after only about a month I ended up dating another girl and spending most of my time with her.

As the year wound down, I realized that I hadn't had a chance to really branch out and make my own friends. I had joined a fraternity, but my social circles were limited to my Brothers and the friends of the girls I had dated. What I lacked was a chance to really figure out who I wanted to hang out with.

After returning to school for my second year, my girlfriend and I ended up breaking up. I was upset, but I took the opportunity to branch out. It was very liberating since for the

first time, I was single at college; I could go out and talk to other girls, date other girls and see what was out there.

Since then, I've made a lot more friends that I actually want to hang out with, not that I'm obliged to hang out with. I've also had the opportunity to meet other girls, and while I may not be ready to jump back into a relationship, finding out that people are attracted to you is certainly a nice confidence booster.

I felt constrained before, and now I have much more freedom. Sometimes I'll go out and it'll all be dull, or maybe wilder than I am comfortable with. But most times I enjoy myself.

I know a lot more people than I ever did before, and a much greater variety – age, nationality, background, interests: there are so many variables. I've also met people who I've really clicked with intellectually, and others who I expect will make good professional contacts in my future career. None of this would have been possible if I'd continued to spend all my spare time with my frat brothers and my ex-girlfriend's group of worthy but often rather boring friends. I figure this may be the only time in my life when there's this much variety and opportunity and choice available to me.

So if you find yourself constrained inside a virtual prison, even a pleasant and comfortable one like mine was, Rebel! Break Out!

Life in the Bubble

If you're a student at this university, chances are you will be familiar with the term "the University Bubble." Although you do become more independent and have more freedom in university, life as an undergrad is far from life in the real world. Sometimes you get so caught up in partying, clubbing, studying and classes that you tend to forget about the world around you. That's inevitable up to a point, but it's too easy to take it to an extreme so that for weeks at a time you forget that there are living beings at all outside the university.

The Bubble can get to the point of surrounding and consuming you before you realize that anything is happening. Then it can be too late: nothing outside your immediate life seems to have any interest or any meaning.

As I write this, a recession is in full swing, there are crowds in the street in a volatile and dangerous part of the world, and there's a ship carrying an apparently nuclear cargo to a country embargoed by the UN. A war could start this afternoon, and many of my friends have no idea of any of this; they would ignore you if you tried to tell them about it. No doubt as you read this, the specifics of the news from the rest of the world will be different. But it doesn't take much thinking to realize that this isolation is not a good thing.

For some, the program you're in can contribute to the Bubble effect. My own program is an example, in the sciences. It's all very specialized, esoteric, and all-consuming, and nothing in our daily grind has anything at all immediately to do with the world outside.

(In the end of course, it will. In the lecture halls and the labs, we're learning the things the rest of the world needs us to know and learning to do things the rest of the world needs us to do. Things that will only be possible because of what we're learning.)

But how to keep at least part of yourself outside the Bubble: even doing simple stuff like reading the newspaper regularly or listening to the news on the radio will keep you informed of important events in the rest of the world. If that seems to lose its interest and importance, you're on a downhill slide into the Bubble. (Mixed metaphors anyone?)

The university itself has lots of activities that have an outside focus. You might not think so, but as young adults we can change the future for the better, and this change can begin with what we do in university. Even getting involved in organizing or participating in a fundraiser such as a marathon, a relay, or a carwash or a barbecue for charity can broaden your Bubble-restricted vision – especially if you get involved in the organization and get

some idea of what the fundraiser is for. To date, this university's freshmen efforts have raised over two million dollars for local causes. It just goes to show how much goodness can be accomplished when we all band together.

University is more than residence and campus, believe it or not. Getting to know the city you're living in for eight months a year can be rewarding. Apart from taking in the sights, a tour around town is a nice break from college life. After blending into the downtown for an afternoon, you almost feel like a normal person.

Some local residents view the incoming students with trepidation, so getting involved with local activities boosts the reputation of the university. There's usually a variety of volunteer programs available, from day care, to working in a hospital or a senior citizens' home. There are lots of rewards in getting involved with something on the outside. It takes your mind away from your horrendous workload and the social pressures, and it gives you a great feeling of actually being useful to someone for a change.

For a broader perspective, I joined Unicef and the Cancer Society this year so I could help other communities and people. Your commitment can change people's lives. You can give your summers an outside focus too even if your circumstances are like mine, and you have no choice but to stay on campus because home is too far away or you don't have anywhere at all to go to. You've paid for your room for the whole year too. This summer, I'll be working at the medical research lab on campus.

So beware of the insidious Bubble. If you feel it coming on, Brainstorm, Investigate Possibilities for Remedial Activities, and Take Action!

Being Accused of Cheating

I had a horrible experience at the end of the first term. There was a statistics exam, and we weren't allowed to use calculators. I can see why; the calculators we usually use have the formulas in them, and some of them let you just input the data and do the calculation for you without your ever needing to know anything about how the math works.

But I didn't realize the rule also applied to other kinds of calculators which didn't have these functions in them. At the end of the exam, the assistant came round to collect the papers, and saw my calculator on the desk. It was in full view of everyone, a bright red children's calculator with big keys, a big display, and funny smiles all over it. But the TA brought it to the prof's attention, and he came to my desk and called me down big time.

He accused me of cheating. Actually, I hadn't used the calculator because the exam didn't have any questions that needed it. He knew that, of course, but it meant nothing to him. He just lost it. I said, "Sir, I didn't use the calculator and I'm one of your best students; I had 96% going into the exam – look it up." That made it worse. He implied that that made him think I'd got the 96% by cheating as well, and that I would probably get 0% in the exam or even the whole course; he'd have to ask the Dean. It was very scary. The guy was just yelling right into my face.

In the end, it turned out OK. He must have calmed down afterwards, or perhaps the dean talked sense into him. Nobody ever said anything but when my mark came out, it was as I'd originally expected, and not reduced by any cheating penalty. It was the worst experience I've had in my few months here, though, by a long way.

Everyone's Nightmare: Late for the Exam

Here's a piece of advice: Know when your exams are, and make sure you don't turn up late for them. I messed up with that once. Never again.

At the end of my first year, I faced the specter of university exams for the first time. All went by fairly unremarkably until my last one arrived. The day of the exam I woke up at 4 am

to study, and well before the 5 pm exam time rolled around, I was pumped and on my way out the door with sharpened pencils, erasers, and watch in hand.

On last thought, I checked the registrar's website to double-check the exam location. I was horrified to discover that the two-hour exam had begun at 3 pm. I didn't understand because I had the exam date written in big letters on the calendar on my desk. After an extended freak-out session, I discovered the reason for this catastrophe – I had mistaken the messy 3 on my calendar for a 5.

I panicked. After dashing off an email to my prof, I literally ran all the way to the exam room and found it nearly deserted. I ran back to residence and found that he had replied to my email that if I could catch him in his office in the next hour, which had already elapsed, I could attempt to write the exam but beyond that there was nothing he could do for me. I raced to his building only to discover that I had missed him. After a nervous bout of exhaustion-induced vomiting outside his building, I went back to my room stunned.

I can't even remember the hoops I had to jump through, but it was truly gruesome. They made it very clear that it was extremely serious. I had to be talked to by the Dean (not pleasant, I can assure you), and he contacted the prof on my behalf. I then had to stay on at the university for several days while they decided what to do with me. Everyone else had gone home, so there I was in my room sweating for the whole time, to say nothing of what everyone at home thought when I had to explain why I wasn't coming home for a while. I had to fill in forms with plausible-sounding bullshit.

I eventually was allowed to write a week later, another version of the exam, I think. Some of the questions were set up just slightly differently from the way the same kinds of questions had been written through the term; I never did find out for sure though.

It was a truly horrific experience that I hope never to relive, made a lot worse by its being 100% my own stupid fault. I have since adopted the habit of checking and rechecking my exam dates and times as well as developing contacts in most classes as a deadline safety net.

I Dropped a Course

In my first year, I constantly doubted whether I knew what I was doing, and I kept second-guessing myself. It was scary to think that I come this far by being accepted into a prestigious university with a scholarship, yet in most of my courses I didn't understand what my profs were saying. Feeling so completely unprepared was a shock. I had taken extra classes and programs in high school and the summer after high school, but it's a different thing to hear about something than to experience it for yourself.

Around November, when things were getting down to the last assignments and studying for finals, I realized I was completely hopelessly lost. I had been reluctant to go to TAs for help earlier on; I felt intimidated because they seemed like geniuses. So I didn't go, and the result was that I got lost. I also could have called my dad for help since he is an engineer and good in sciences. But I didn't. I didn't admit what was happening to my parents or to friends. I felt sick to my stomach every day.

I remember that a prof wrote on one of my quizzes, "If you don't do better than this, you are going to fail this class." I couldn't understand why she wrote that on my quiz in red ink when I already knew it. Like duh.

I did poorly on my midterms and finally went to a TA. Unfortunately I got an unhelpful one who made it seem like I didn't need help at all and knew the material. But I did need help. I then spoke to an adviser who suggested that I withdraw from one of my courses even though it was past the drop out deadline. So I ended up withdrawing from a class that I needed for my major.

Even though I was having difficulty with a few of my courses, that was the worst one. I didn't really understand how the prof was teaching; his style wasn't conducive to my learning. He was distant, and from the first he seemed to have his favorites, almost like he knew them before. His quizzes were ridiculously hard. We didn't have a book because he was in the process of writing a new one, so he sent us the chapters over the summer for us to print out. The book was hard as it was at graduate student level, and I barely understood what he was saying. So I dropped the course.

After that, I felt even more like a loser. Whenever I walked by the building that the class was in, I felt sick. And I still didn't tell anyone.

Looking back, I know now that I wasn't alone. We have counseling on campus which I did during my second semester. The counselor told me that tons of students use their services each semester; I learned that most people feel the same way during their first year, even though they don't always show it. The counselor also indicated that there were some courses that got dropped by a lot more students than others. And actually, I had noticed that the number of people in those classes had gotten smaller; I'd thought at the time that it was just people skipping, but now I realized, maybe not.

Everyone is on the same level. If you got accepted to this university, then you deserve to be here and you will probably do fine. People doubt themselves all the time; it's a normal feeling, especially since the profs throw the really difficult stuff at you right from the beginning to weed people out. It helps to make friends; I normally keep my grades private so I didn't share how I was feeling or doing. Maybe if I had, I would have realized I wasn't alone.

I realized that one of my biggest mistakes in the first semester was not reviewing my notes daily. I would go to the lectures and when the lecture was over, I wouldn't look at the material unless I had an assignment or a test coming up. But usually it was too late by that time. So it is a matter of keeping current with what the prof is teaching so that if there is a question, you can go to a TA right away to get it cleared up before you get lost.

I learned that sometimes people do drop out of programs or courses and feel like failures at the time. But often they end up in a different program which suits them much better. There are so many options out there for you, so don't think that any one thing is all you want to do or can do.

My second semester turned around very well. One of the things I did was enroll in a class about study skills and time management to help you study in college. If I had known that class was there in the fall, I would have signed up for it. And if I had reached out and spoken with TAs or advisers or other students before it was too late, I would have found out about the course, and things might have been different for me.

So it was a really hard experience for me. Now I don't get too disappointed if I see a lower mark. I would still like it to be higher but as long as I see improvement, I am happy. I know I belong here.

Appearances can be Deceiving

During our first week, one of the senior girls would tell people, "You're not going to do well. You think you were good in high school? Well you're not going to do well here." I also had an adviser who told me I wasn't prepared after talking to me for about two minutes; all I had said to her was that in high school I was used to getting straight As and working hard and figured that the workload here would only be a little bit harder. So she concluded from that one conversation that I wasn't prepared and would probably fail.

These put-downs were hard on me because I felt fairly alone my first term. I had not participated in Frosh Week activities and as a result,

I felt that when I got here, others had already formed their cliques and their friends, and so I found it very hard to make my own friends. I felt that everyone else was adjusting well but me, even though we really weren't close enough for us to be talking about our personal issues. Everyone else seemed to be having fun, and they seemed generally satisfied. And I felt very alone, like I was this little fish in a big pond. I felt lost, and I think university is a place you can get lost at very easily because it's so huge.

Later, I found out that the girl who was putting everyone down during our first week was doing it because she hadn't done well. And the adviser who concluded that I would likely fail apparently puts everyone down because she was a biology major who had wanted to be a doctor but didn't make it. I learned that some people get off on trying to prove they are better than others, and usually the ones who do this are struggling as much as you are.

I also learned that sometimes the people who look the most well adjusted and the happiest are struggling the most but just not admitting it. There was this guy in one of my first-semester science classes who would be chatting with everyone when I came in; he seemed so happy. All I could think was, "Why is he so happy and confident and I am such a loser?" He ended up dropping out of university completely; it was all a front.

If I had known then what I do now, I would have felt less alone and enjoyed my first term much more.

WEB: LETTING FRIENDS PICK YOUR MAJOR srvlgd.com/LF

WEB: REGISTERING FOR CLASSES srvlgd.com/RFC

Smarts

*Editors' Note: In this book, there are many references to companion pages on **srvlgd.com**. However, we'd like to draw your especial attention to one in particular which deals with preparing and using a personal timetable. It's an entire chapter whose format fitted the web a lot better than the printed part of the book.*

WEB: TIME MANAGEMENT srvlgd.com/TM

No One Could Have Prepared Me; I Had to Go Through it Myself

Coming into university, I had many different views on what it was going to be like. People tried to tell me: family, friends and even my older siblings shared their stories and their experiences. Never once did I think that my experience would be any different from theirs.

When I got here, though, it was nothing at all like I expected. After my first day of classes, my whole view changed. It was almost as if I hadn't heard any of those stories.

First and most obviously, there's just so much more. It's not so much that the work is hard, just that most of it is new, it goes so much faster, and there's so much more material you have to know about. What would take you a month in high school would take less than a week here. There's never a sense that you've finished. It just comes at you and keeps coming. When you take a break, you feel guilty because there's always something you could be doing.

In high school, I knew what teachers wanted because they laid everything out for us. In university, nothing is laid out, so you either don't know what the prof wants or once you finally figure it out, you get confused because another prof teaching the exact same thing to

another section will want something different. And then you go to another class next term and the prof teaches and wants assignments done in a completely different style again. Nothing seems the same, so you have no idea what to expect anymore. If you don't figure out what the prof wants soon enough, it would be a severe handicap and would make it almost impossible to do well in the course.

When I studied in high school, I would start making study notes a couple of weeks before the exam. But here, there's not time for that. For one thing, it always seems that this is around the time that profs begin to realize they've fallen behind, so they go even faster than normal. And even if this didn't happen, the time would simply not be there. You have to make your study notes as soon after your lecture as you can to get them out of the way. It's easier to make condensed notes right away because you can remember what went on in the class itself. Also, you can incorporate things from the textbook that seem important, again easier if the material is fresher in your mind.

You have to learn the various meanings of the word "read." Sometimes it means that you must know pretty well every word, so it might take you a whole evening to read fifty pages. Other times, it couldn't possibly mean that because there is just too much of it there. So you have to be selective and be smart in deciding what you actually need to pay attention to.

Sometimes if you are writing a paper, you can just leaf through the book, find a few parts of it that interest you, and then use those in the paper. If you do this, you might be able to "read" the book in less than an hour. Other times, you can go even further. You can go through the book, find maybe four sentences that are relevant to what you are doing, and put them into a paper or discussion. The prof recognizes where they come from and concludes that you have read the book. Well, in a way I guess you have. But it is not the same as spending a whole evening on fifty pages. Somehow you have to know what the prof expects, and often he does not tell you what he expects. And even more often, he doesn't know what he expects.

It took a while, until after the first set of midterms, for me to get used to everything and to know how best to do the work. At that point, even though each class was different, I had a pretty good idea of what the profs wanted and what I needed to know – what was expected, what was important to do, and what was not important. It was easier to study for exams, and I felt a lot more confident about them. It's hard to describe how it happens. It takes a while, but you just seem to get to know how to handle things and to be confident that you'll be right most of the time.

I don't think you can find out from anyone how to prepare yourself for what it's going to be like. It's something you have to experience for yourself.

University is like a movie: you can't take anyone else's word for how it will seem to you. You have to go yourself and see it and do it.

Street Smarts

One of the most difficult things about university is knowing how much time you should spend on assignments. I can remember spending an exorbitant amount of time on an assignment which was only worth one and a half percent. Of course, I found this fact out later! It's really hard to get used to not being able to do assignments perfectly. In university you can't hand in an assignment that is written exactly the way you want it.

Another thing that is hard to get used to is professors giving you assignments a week before they are due but then actually only

teaching the concept at 4:30 the night before. This situation is exacerbated when you are faced with night classes. Even these assignments may be due at 8:30 the next morning.

What happens is that you are given the math assignment a week before the due date. Of course, you are not taught exactly how to do the assignment. To make matters worse, you are tested on it after you've handed it in, but before it is given back. Obviously it is hard to study things which you aren't sure are right.

It is really important to divide your time wisely. Don't spend a lot of time on the little things because when the big things come up, you won't have the time to spend on them and you'll be burned out.

More Productive Pattern of Work

Recently, I have made a big change in my study habits. Now I am finding that I tend to get more accomplished than I used to and in a smaller amount of time.

Before, my homework routine was rather monotonous, mundane, boring, night after night after night. I would always eat dinner at 5:30 pm, finish at approximately 6:30 and then by 7:00 I would be in the library doing homework. I would always leave the library when it closed at midnight, and then I would do even more homework once I got back to my room. That's how each evening went.

Nowadays, I am finding that I am working more efficiently. I guess some credit should go to my new boyfriend. He and I usually eat dinner together, and we try to eat at a different time each night. After dinner we have a coffee and talk for a while, then start homework. We decided we wouldn't go to the library every night but some nights work in the cafeteria or a classroom in an attempt to vary the working atmosphere.

I have also found that when I have someone working beside me, I tend to work harder, whereas when I used to work alone, I wasted time. I'd worry or daydream or ponder about different things on my mind. I especially used to spend time worrying about the amount of work I had instead of getting it done. Now we do homework until ten or eleven at the latest, and then go to the snack bar.

So now that I am able to get more accomplished in less time, I am doing my homework and studying in a much more relaxed and happy state of mind. More importantly, my marks also reflect favorably on my new study habits and time management techniques. I believe that by varying your routine every night, you tend to be more productive. I needed someone else to help me realize this.

Now I've passed the wisdom on to a few of my friends. Unfortunately for them, they don't have boyfriends or at least not ones who are here. But they too have found that when you vary your schedule and working atmosphere, you tend to work more efficiently.

Working Together

When I first got to college, my number one priority was making friends. But after orientation, we no longer had hours upon hours to hang out because we all had work to do. A simple solution was for us to all meet up in the lounge and do our homework together. However, every time we would sit down to work, someone would start up a conversation and no one would get anything done. The work started piling up, and we quickly realized that group study time was ineffective. Slowly the number of people doing homework together started dwindling. Some worked up in their rooms, and others went to the library to find a silent corner.

Every so often we forget why we no longer do homework together. Recently, I went to the library with a friend to write a paper. We were there for five hours and I got only one page done. Instead we talked and listened to music. Neither of us is disciplined enough to sit in the same room and not talk.

Sometimes you can be lucky to find someone that you are able to work with. I personally don't like working with people I don't know well. On one hand you probably won't be tempted to talk about your life since the only thing you share is the class. On the other hand I often feel uncomfortable – for one thing there seem to be a lot of awkward silences. But I have found a few friends who I can do homework with and actually get stuff done. Usually they are the type of people who are really focused and will ignore me until I get to work.

If you can find one or two people who you work well with, I think it is a great motivator to get things done. Going to the library is not so daunting if you have someone to go with. Even if they slow you down slightly, it makes the work less stressful.

Write it, Retain it, Plan it, Complete it

I love my dry-erase calendar.

Yep, I'm a dork. Go ahead and say it. It won't be the first time I've heard it (and probably not the last). But I can't survive without this thing. I don't just put my assignments on it. Quizzes, appointments, exams, practices, games; you name it. If I know about it in advance, I write it down on my monthly planner. It may sound anal-retentive and more than a little obsessive-compulsive, and to be honest, I am – I mean, it is – but if there's one thing I've learned since starting university, it's that if you don't plan ahead, then you can't expect to have very much success.

I know it sounds horribly cliché and you've probably heard it all before: "Plan ahead, do your work in steps, book things ahead of time, blah-blah-blah." But, big surprise, Mom was right – again. (Isn't that a horrible irony?) I remember being in high school, hearing teacher after teacher tell me to plan ahead, and thinking, "I've got my week lined up ahead of time. That's way more than most of these other kids – what have I got to worry about?"

And in high school, I got away with it – minimal planning, that is. Well, minimal for me. On the fridge at home, I had two letter-sized calendars (this month and next) with important dates and appointments, as well as a sports schedule and a list of key phone numbers.

I always kept my agenda up to date on that week's homework, and I allotted two hours or so a night at my desk for slogging through assignments. And up until Grade 12, this worked for me, and it worked well. If I knew I had a practice, I would work around it; if I knew I had a workout, I'd do my homework earlier. But high school was the easy stuff. Child's play, in fact.

MORE ABOUT THIS,
WEB: HIGH SCHOOL WAS CHILD'S PLAY srvlgd.com/HCP

It's the scale of things that makes the difference. In university, planning ahead isn't an option. It's a necessity, and it needs to start on the first day. If professors didn't hand out syllabi on the first day of class, I can almost guarantee you that not only would I stress myself to clinical insanity, but there would be no feasible way for me to get anything done on time. I mean, my final exams are a whole month away, and already I'm starting a mild (albeit probably unnecessary) panic. I've got a research paper (oops, make that two) due two weeks from now, and I've already got the sources chosen and the outlines finished. I've booked my flight home for winter break, I've got a preliminary study schedule lined up, and I'm nervously awaiting our practice schedule so I can write that down too.

People will tell you that university is an opportunity to expand your social horizons, meet new people, and explore – and it is – but my advice to you is, make good friends with a marker and a whiteboard because deadlines come quicker than you expect, and all-nighters are never fun.

So that's why it's only the second week of November, and I'm sitting at the little desk in my kitchen, writing. Writing outlines, writing rough drafts and good drafts of research papers; writing homework lists, to-do lists, grocery lists, and Christmas lists; writing notes, emails, messages and letters; and, of course, writing schedules.

In fact, by the time I'm finished writing this, I'll probably have something new to write about: another article summary, perhaps; or a cognitive science assignment; or maybe just a postcard home to Grandma. In fact, besides eating, sleeping and sports, I probably won't stop writing until I drive to our game this weekend (and that's only out of mechanical necessity). Writing and scheduling are two things I do well, and lucky for me because if I didn't, I'd be in a fair bit of trouble.

What can I say? I'm a kinesthetic learner: if I write it, I'll retain it, and if I plan it, I'll complete it.

Hey, I really like that: "Write it, retain it, plan it, complete it." Hold on a second – I'm going to write it down.

Playing to Your Strengths

You are about to check your first university exam grade … please please let me do well, you're thinking. Your palms are sweaty, your mouth is dry, and you're squinting your eyes in an effort to try and not look at your mark. The page is loading, inch by inch … here it is! WHAT … I got a 52%? The tears start streaming down your face. I studied sooo hard for this exam, and I've never gotten a mark so low in my entire life!

That was my first university mark experience. I was in shock and I didn't know what to do. Here is the thing: you can study hard and fail or study less but correctly and ace. That was my problem; I did not study correctly. The moment I changed my learning style, my grades went up to the A's … I kid you not.

There really is no right way to study … each person varies. But I have a few questions and some tips to help you ease into your learning style:

1. **Do you learn best when listening to people talk?**

- When attending a lecture, sit up front to avoid any distractions from people around you

- Record the lecture (ask permission of the professor)

- Listen to it again afterwards, fast-forwarding though the parts you're sure about

2. **Do you learn best by writing things down?**

- Use different colored pens and highlighters emphasizing different concepts

- Read a paragraph from your lecture notes, put the note aside, then type a paraphrased version, to print off … this way you are actively writing as opposed to passively typing (trust me – there is a difference)

- Use sticky notes to summarize (in point form) what is on a page

3. **Do you learn best by reading things?**

- Read your lecture notes before and after class

- Read the textbook to look at the same concept from a different teaching perspective and make notes

4. **Do you learn best by a combination or all of the above?** Or are you unsure?

I was unsure. Fortunately, I was in a psych class where these things were discussed. I learned that there were tests that can help people figure out their optimum learning style. We did some, and I discovered that I'm primarily an auditory learner. But I do need to write things down to get them organized in my brain. Your university's counseling office probably has these tests available. However you do it, though, you really have to find out what works best for you.

A New Way of Working

When I first came here, I was very nervous, very uncertain of how I would do academically. My family is not rich, and quite a few of them have made big sacrifices for me to be here. It adds to the pressure to do well, and so does the need to keep my marks up to retain my scholarship.

I'm in math and computers, and before I came here I always felt that I had to understand everything completely before I would be ready for a test or exam. Absolutely everything had to be completely clear. But I was in a couple of classes that forced me to change that attitude. No matter how hard I tried, some things just refused to come clear in the way I needed them to. But talking to other people, I realized that they were no better off than I was, except that it didn't seem to bother them much, if at all.

A friend of mine in physics explained to me that there are some things, like quantum mechanics, that actually can't be understood in a concrete or intuitive way at all. Like the electron spends a good portion of its time here, and here, but in a place halfway between, zero percent of its time. So how does it get from one place to the other? The answer is amazing: "The equations don't tell us anything about that." In other words, a cop out! And it's the best anyone can do. Likewise light and all other parts of the spectrum: all waves, but they're particles at the same time. Huh? Well, there's no one who can explain it, and no one even seems to want to try. Another cop-out!

Well, if they can do it, so can I. Instead of trying to understand things, I asked myself the question, "What are they going to need me to do?" Mostly it was solving a bunch of problems or learning a bunch of proofs. I looked at what was going to be on the exam and made sure I could do all the things that would be there. Understanding it: well, I'm not sure. But it makes me a lot less anxious. And guess what: my marks haven't suffered at all, in fact they're even a bit higher than before.

So it all came about because of that change in attitude. Ask yourself the question "What do I need to be able to do?" Then learn to do it. Understanding: well, that's secondary. I realize now that it was a matter of taking control of my own brain.

WEB: PLAGIARISM OR NOT? srvlgd.com/PN

Taking Sciences

MORE ABOUT THIS,
WEB: MORE WORK THAN THE OTHERS srvlgd.com/MWO

Any science-related course requires a lot of discipline: the discipline to sit down at your desk five nights a week and learn. Though I tried my hardest to do as little work as possible, I finally resigned myself to the fact that there was no way around it. Some people didn't have to work as long or as hard as I did, but they might have been more efficient or smarter than me. But eventually, though it often doesn't seem that way at the time, you do get to see that the mark you get is directly related to the amount of work you do. It's a sad fact of life, but after high school, you can't get by without doing your work.

Another thing I've learned is that for the first time in your life, you've got to think for yourself. Gone are the days when you can pull an equation out of your bag of tricks, plug in the numbers, and get the right answer. Soon, you'll find yourself actually having to picture in your mind the movements of multiple free bodies in relation to each other, or the actual change in the structure of the reactants in a chemical change as they form the products. You have to think almost completely on your own. Often an important part of a problem is deliberately left out, forcing you to make the correct assumption. It's a true test of your knowledge (especially in an exam), because only if you really do understand what's going on can you come up with the right answer. And to be blunt, there's only one way to learn how to do this: practice, practice, practice.

Normally, you'll have to do assignments or problem sets regularly. Mine never counted much towards my final mark, but they were the key to doing well. Since I wasn't used to doing problems that were challenging (high school doesn't feature this kind), I used my problem sets to get my feet on the ground at university. But don't expect the exam to look even remotely similar to your problem sets. All these really do is help you to think logically. And you do have to do that on the exam.

One final though important thought: make lots of friends. Even if your friends are just people you see in class, that's fine. Sometimes just "talking shop" – about your classes, your labs, your profs – can relieve a lot of stress since often you find that everyone else is just as lost as you.

A particular type of friend comes in very handy around exam time when you finally get around to tackling those last, toughest problems, and that's someone who's smarter than you. The smarter the better. When you need that one hint to get you going, friends like that come in handy. Buy him or her a beer after the exam. And if you're one of those smarter-than-thou types yourself, take time out to help. For one thing you'll increase your own understanding, and for another, what goes around comes around. And you can always use all that free beer after the exam.

WEB: HEAD ABOVE WATER srvlgd.com/HW

WEB: BRAINS ARE NOT ENOUGH srvlgd.com/BNE

Top Five Ways to Study for Exams

I've been getting back some of my midterms, and I did pretty well. Here are my top five study tips.

5. **Read the textbook over … and remember it.**

    If a biology exam covers chapters 14 and 54-56, reread them. Most textbooks bold important terms and usually have a good chapter summary at the end. If you've worked with the material before, it might be enough just to concentrate on these parts and make sure you still have a handle on the material itself. Don't just glance over it though. Think about it in your head as you read through it, and understand it rather than memorize it. Close the book, then try writing your own version of the summary. Although I personally don't need to, I know that lots of people need to make their own notes from the textbook so as not to let their attention wander away. See also #2.

4. **Make some Cue Cards.**

Though this doesn't work for every course, it's very useful in courses where memorization is key. For example, memorizing the derivatives of a logarithm or the definition of all the terms related to mitosis. I personally have two sets of cue cards: one for math and another for biology. I don't take too many courses where memorization is necessary, but if I needed to, I'd have cue cards for all my courses.

3. **Study Groups! ... even if you're a genius.**

Study Groups are excellent for pounding information into your head; they also make studying a little bit less tedious and more fun. Your friends can help you answer questions you may be puzzled about, and if you are a genius, teaching someone how to do a problem will only further improve your genius-ness.

2. **Make your own Note Summary from your Notes.**

Making my own notes is something I do for every class with the exception of English. I find summarizing and writing the information in my own words helps me understand what I wrote down. There's also something about writing with your hand. It makes an imprint on your brain of what you just wrote. It may take a while, but it will make a big difference. Another advantage is that leading up to the exam, you can review these notes. You're too late now for that massive textbook, and the notes you made at the actual lecture may or may not make sense to you.

1. **Do your Homework.**

Doing homework is the best possible way to study for anything. I find that if I keep up with math/physics/chem/bio homework, when it comes time to study for an exam, I think to myself, "I know this, so why am I even studying?" Doing this homework may seem like a hassle to do every day, but in the long run, it will save you loads of time.

0. **Keep your Cool.**

For all of the above, make sure you never get stressed or angry. Stress and mood swings are a big reason for people doing poorly in exams. I try to stay easy going. I go into exams with confidence, thinking in my head, "I'm going to rock this exam!," and I come out usually doing so.

All-nighters

All-nighters, the result of procrastination, become somewhat commonplace in university. Recently, I just completed one myself the night before a math and a chemistry exam. Luckily, I had gotten sleep the night before and was physically up to the challenge. I was also fortunate to have a study partner who helped with encouragement when required.

Having such experience with all-nighters, I have listed some tips:

- If possible, work with someone.
- If you feel tired, go for a walk, preferably outside.
- Consume beverages containing caffeine. Energy drinks have the most, but try them out before the crucial time comes.
- Never work lying down.
- Set the alarm for early morning (just in case).
- Organize your life so that you don't have to do it again. You pay for it for days afterwards.

Day or Night: Know the Difference

All-nighters: something all university students go through at least once in their university career.

My first occurred on purpose, because I actually thought it would be neat if I stayed up all night. So one evening I decided to leave my homework (a physics lab) to about 1 am. I frittered my evening away by playing squash and socializing. Then 1 am came round. I sat down to do my work but my mind was really easily distracted. All I could think about was food and sleep. After 1 am, it takes about four times the effort to do homework than doing the same work at about five in the evening. That's what I learned.

I also find that my work done in the early hours of the morning is poor quality stuff, full of dumb mistakes and often lacking in inspiration.

Another bad point about all-nighters: they screw up your next day. You walk around in a kind of unpleasant dream. Know how to tell the people who do all-nighters? Go to a lecture; they're the ones that are asleep.

Different people work best at different times. Some work really efficiently in the evenings. Maybe you do your best work in the middle of the night but based on my experience and that of my friends, I think that if you're like that, you're in a rather small minority. I know my best time to work is between 7 am and noon. I found that out by trying out various schedules and that's what everyone has to do, I guess.

Selective Wisdom

Some of the hardest lessons I ever learned at university were that a) no, I'm not perfect, and b) even Superman couldn't get all this reading done on time.

You have to pick and choose what's more important. Look at your course outline and figure out how the prof writes the exam. What is the layout? How much is each question worth? A perfect example of what I am talking about is my ancient history course. You want to try reading 50-100 pages of ancient texts for Monday's class, then 40 more for Thursday's class? Of course not.

My prof set the exam up so that we had to identify 3 historical readings out of 5. For each, we had to give the name of the author, the historical context, and the importance of the passage. I got away without doing the readings because I knew that the midterm would be OK with only Herodotus, Thucydides, and Plutarch. Plutarch only wrote biographies, so that was easy. Herodotus wrote everything up to the end of the Persian War, and Thucydides wrote about the Peloponnesian War. Each author only wrote about one topic. Knowing only this, it would be easy in the exam to identify the passage. I was able to pass up hundreds of pages of reading that I had no time for.

So take a good look through your course outlines, figure out how the exams are done, and see if there are shortcuts. For most of your courses you won't be able to do this, but if you can, I highly suggest it.

WEB: PRIORITIZING srvlgd.com/PRT

Five Lessons

After many months of (mostly) honest endeavor, I've learned five important lessons that weren't in any of the course outlines or profs' notes. I learned every one of these lessons the hard way.

I learned to relax. Possibly the most obvious one to start with. It's so easy to get totally immersed in the work you're doing. Particularly when it's late at night and deadlines are approaching, you will encounter problems. These can and do drive you insane as you can't see anything wrong with what you've done and yet it's not coming out right. Yeah, like the famous bacteria coming out of your calculation at 250000 tonnes each. You can save so much time and trouble if you realize you're stressed, stop, and take a step back from the problem. Look again at the bigger picture; ideally explain it to a friend, just to regain the overall focus of what you're doing. Coming back to the problem later can help.

I learned to never expect things to work the first time. If you don't expect it to work the first time, you can take steps to ensure that when it doesn't work, it's easy to fix. This can include things like lots of output LEDs telling you when certain processes are done. Or extra lines of code which print out logging information so you can find out where your system failed. Designing a system as a series of connected small modules can help too; always break the problem down into smaller ones. These, of course, are examples from a systems engineer but the principle applies to anything that has math or chemistry in it. I suspect it works for a literary criticism or a sociology essay too.

I learned to play with things. It might sound like the hardest thing to do but toying around with the systems you're learning about, in your own time, is a great way to get an understanding of the subject. This inevitably leads to more marks at the end of the day. Experiment. In history, read something from a different era than what your essay is going to be about, or discuss it with someone from a different course in a different year. Play with ideas.

I learned to get to know my classmates. While the people in your halls might be into the same music as you and party with you late into the night, don't pass up opportunities to get to know the people in your course. When things get tough, you'll rely on each other for support. A lot of the time your classmates will be able to explain ideas more clearly to you than any textbook. I have certainly received more than my fair share of help from my classmates. Of course you have to be ready to return the favor or after a while you'll run out of friends to help you. Another thing: it's amazing how your understanding of an idea can improve when you have to explain it to someone else. You will be sure to encounter a question that needs you to do some quick thinking in order to be able to answer it. Over and over in these situations, I've had the thought: "I've never thought about it from that angle, and I can see how it makes things harder, but yes, there's something good here too." Plenty of insights come by this route.

Perhaps you've noticed that none of what I've said up to now could possibly apply to the person beginning the lab or the essay or the system design at the last minute. That leads me to the last thing I've learned. Easy to say, hard to do; it's like keeping your weight under control. However well people have done in the past, they can blow it all from now onward if they don't remember it. People don't really learn it; they have to work at it anew every time. Anyway, here's that lesson:

I learned to begin every major task long before the deadline.

Tips and Tricks of the Student Trade

1. Bragging about how you went out to the bar on Halloween and then failing your stats midterm is not impressive. Accept that there is work to be done.

2. Don't feel sorry for yourself – there is always some other student with more work than you. Just suck it up, put in the time, and do it. If you work hard, your marks will reflect that.

3. Try to do your assignment on your own before working with friends. When you all work together, you generally end up getting the same answer which could be wrong, and no one would bother to check. If you do it alone first, whether you get the right or wrong answer, it allows you to explain how you've done it which helps you learn. If your answer was wrong, you can see where you went wrong for future problems. Take it from me, doing the problem with five people does not mean you get the right answer.

4. Don't add up the total percentage of what a week's assignments and exams are worth. You will end up with a number obscenely large, such as 120%, in any given week. This number will consume your every waking moment and you will dream of it at night. It will scare you more than any horror movie you've ever seen. Trust me on this one.

5. Buy a huge dry-erase calendar that shows two months at once. This way, you can keep track of what's due and when, even (maybe!) get ahead of the game. Actually viewing when things are due in jumbo fluorescent pink letters never allows you to forget due dates (even at midnight). You can still put something out of your mind when it's written right there in front of you, but it's a lot harder. Also, putting the percentages under what's due helps you prioritize your assignments and exams accordingly. However, whatever you do, do not allow yourself to give into the temptation of #4. It causes more stress than it's worth.

6. Go to your seminars! I cannot stress this one enough. Almost all of my seminars give marks for attendance which normally total 10% of the final grade. If you go to all of your seminars you are guaranteed the full 10%. Many people

do not go because they "don't have any questions," or they think seminars are "a waste of time." Questions or no questions, come final mark time you will be glad you went when you see a nice 80% instead of a 70% – or even a 50% instead of a 40%. You don't have to be a genius to see how much of a benefit those extra, and essentially free, marks can be. All you need to do is show up.

And you know, you might be surprised at the end of the term about what went on there that helped you learn the material. You might even get good hints about how to get a good mark on the assignments, or what kind of thing is most likely to come up on tests or exams. That's something I discovered in one of my most boring seminars in my most boring course. Quite by accident, he gave the game away: it was clear what the exam question on this topic would be. I saved hours of useless studying.

7. On the other hand, in classes, do not waste space for the sake of wasting space. I am talking about people who bring their laptops to class and do not take a single note. Instead they find online stuff to be more appealing. Don't get me wrong. I am a laptop user myself and I do have a bit of a wandering finger in lectures from time to time, but I never miss important information. If you are not intending to take even minimal notes, please don't come to the class. Often you just annoy and distract everyone behind you who can see everything you are doing.

8. That reminds me of another point – don't think that what you do on your laptop in class is private. No matter how well you position your body in front of the screen, I can personally guarantee that there are at least five people at any given time watching your every click.

9. Get to know your professors. I once had a prof who admitted that if she liked you, she would mark you better than people she didn't like. I have a hunch that many professors do this but just don't admit it to the students. Maybe some profs are just not aware of it – that's what the one I was talking to about it thought. I imagine it would be less true in math and science courses, but still it might sometimes happen. Moral of the story: get everything in on time, and talk to your professors. You will get on their good side and maybe even swing an extra few marks out of them!

10. Don't let extracurriculars rule your life. If you enjoy doing them, by all means continue. I'm talking about the students who let sports and various other voluntary school activities take priority over their schoolwork. I know people who say that they have "too much to do" and therefore don't have time to do their schoolwork. I think that, for many people, this is an acceptable excuse. "It's okay for me to fail anthropology – it was only an elective. Besides I got to go to another university to row for a week!"

I'm here to tell you that it's not okay. Not even by a long shot. Many students tend to lose sight of why they are at university or college – to learn! Not to row or to become the treasurer for a non-profit restaurant on campus. Those are great things to put on a resume for sure, but they are not the reason you are going to school (or at least I hope not). You are here to become educated. You are paying to be there to become educated. So my final piece of advice to any new student is to put school first – where it belongs. If you think you have time for a part-time job or for any extracurriculars, then by all means do them. Just don't sacrifice your goals in life – a.k.a a degree and a future career – just because you like to do a little something on the side.

Striking a Balance

Self-Discipline

One of the hardest parts of first year university is striking a new balance in your life. There's moving away from home, sharing a bedroom, having classes that are much more challenging and involve way more independent work than ever before, meeting all new friends, and finding your place in a totally new environment. First year presents enormous new experiences: good, bad, and a mixture of the two.

My residence floor stayed up the entire night after move-in day talking and getting to know each other. We became like a family almost instantly and bonded more throughout Frosh Week. And then, of course, there are all the random people you'll meet and grow to love over Frosh Week. That week is one of the only times, ever, where you'll be able to go up to anyone at all, introduce yourself, and instantly have a new friend. This was one of my favorite parts of university, and with the possible exception of the exams, the most intense.

The week ended with the Faculty of Music serenading the campus with "Frosh Week Forever." And it did seem like Frosh Week could go on forever, but then those dreaded classes started. Wasn't university supposed to be all about the social scene? My first round of midterms said otherwise. Fortunately, in most programs, you can redeem yourself as long as you don't leave it too late before taking action.

My favorite (and most academically destructive) part of first year was living with all of my new best friends. When I was tired of studying, tired of electronic socializing, or even just tired in general, I could walk next door and hang out for hours on end. Spending three hours in the dining hall for breakfast, lunch, and dinner (each, of course) seemed natural. And then

there was that "S" word that everyone seems to forget about when they come to university … sleep.

My first two months of university were amazing. There were so many things that were so enjoyable. I don't regret anything and wish I could relive every moment. But after that first midterm, I realized that if I was going to continue on to second year, I needed to strike a better balance. I had enjoyed partying as much as I wanted and eating as much as I wanted. But now payback time had arrived in the form of my low midterm marks (and tighter clothes from my extra pounds!). I realized that I needed to set boundaries and learn some sort of discipline. I could party every night and have fun, I could lock myself in the room and study, or I could find a happy medium. The key to my taking control was realizing the consequences.

I didn't find it at all easy to organize my life in a more efficient way. It was a real struggle to balance things. I began to schedule some library time into all my days. Instead of using that two-hour afternoon break in class to go back to residence and nap, I hit the library and got readings done. I was shocked that I could get almost all my pre-labs and reading done by just using the time I had between classes. I also started printing off my notes before every class, getting at least six hours of sleep every night, and studying on a weekly basis instead of cramming before exams.

Now that everyone reading this is probably snoozing, I need to point out that because of all this, I actually felt like I had more time to hang out with my friends. My evenings and weekends were basically free because of the way I scheduled my days, and I never had to feel guilty about all the work I should be doing when I was procrastinating and wasting time. I boosted my marks after midterms, ended up getting the marks I'd expected of myself, and still had a blast! And oh yes, I gave up fries and snacking. My clothes got looser again.

Frosh Week should be one of the best weeks of your life. So should the first month of school when life can go by in a more agreeable way than ever before. Enjoy it and make the most of it. But don't let it go on too long.

Partying

Every university seems to have a night of the week that is the "big night" to go out. This is aside from Friday and Saturday, which are also big nights. You may even find that there are different drink specials at different bars every night of the week. The key is to choose a few nights to go out to truly enjoy yourself as opposed to partying every night in fear that you might miss out on a great time.

I remember Halloween weekend I had some work to catch up on: readings and essays to write, not to mention a second set of midterms quickly approaching. I had already gone out one night that weekend and had a great time. But my friends insisted that I join them in some festivities again, and I gave in. I woke up late the next day and somewhat regretted going out. I had spent the morning sleeping and didn't have much energy to get back into homework mode.

There is always fun to be had and there is always work to be done. So I was confronted with similar situations several times throughout the year. My experience taught me that sometimes you have to say no and stay in. You have to start that paper tonight or get uncontrollably far behind. Then, when your friends come around again, you can say yes, go out, enjoy the evening, and end up with a good feeling about what you've done. You've earned a break, taken it, and enjoyed it.

Not Fun Anymore

Much of your first year of university is spent learning how to manage your time. It can be tough to balance schoolwork, friends, family and extracurricular activities.

I had a good friend who had always been a lot of fun to hang out with but things changed and she became no fun at all. And actually, as I look back, neither was I.

Our conversations deteriorated, and we became obsessed with only one topic: how much schoolwork we both had and how there was not enough time to do it.

She would often tell me how she didn't know where to start with her essays, how she felt overwhelmed with the amount of material to study, and how badly she wanted better grades. Sometimes we shared these feelings, but other times she talked about her work so much that it began to stress me out too, and it was definitely a downer for our friendship.

I learned later that what we were doing is called ruminating. It's going over all your miseries again and again to no effect; you just go round and round. Most ruminators do it on their own, but I think it's worse when two of you do it together.

I got to realize that everyone has a lot of work to do, but if you just get it done, there is much more time to do fun things. Having her around taught me that no one likes to hear your complaints all the time, even good friends. We both probably could have benefited from spending more time actually studying and less time talking about it.

Editors' Note: At the risk of appearing repetitive, we urge once again that you go to the extra chapter on our website:

WEB: TIME MANAGEMENT srvlgd.com/TM

Taking Control of My Time

CONTRASTING STORY,
WEB: ONE MORE WEEK OF INSANITY srvlgd.com/OMW

When I started attending this university, I was entranced with the number and the variety of activities available. I've always been interested in lots of things, so I signed up for lots of things: academic clubs, badminton, debating, volunteering, choir. You name it, I was signed up for it.

Of course I couldn't do it all. But the time came when I just got so stressed out that I almost gave up trying. What I hadn't realized was that when you do extracurriculars, there are other people who are depending on your showing up. Even if you have urgent schoolwork to do or if you badly need down-time or sleep, you have to show up because you don't want to let people down.

Anyway, it all came to a crisis point, and I realized I couldn't continue doing it all. I hadn't been doing any of the things well, and I'd turned myself into a wreck. I had to take control. I couldn't have done it without a good friend from down the hall, but that's another story, I guess.

Reluctantly, I had to wind down most of what I had started out finding the most rewarding and enjoyable. Time wasn't the only factor; there was also the consideration of how stressful the activity was or could become, like debating and choir, and how much you let people down if you missed it once or twice. I realized something about myself that I'd only slightly thought of previously: I need down-time. I need parties, hanging out for an hour with friends, and even time on my own when no demands of any kind are being made on me.

Well, maybe I'm lazier now. My marks have gone up though because I have more time for assignments and can concentrate on them better. And I'm also wiser and happier.

WEB: TIME OF TRANSITION srvlgd.com/TT

Keeping Up – Just

The last three weeks have been a whirlwind and I've had tests and assignments and essays to do on top of my readings. When this happens, it's only natural that you let one or two of your subjects slide. In geography I've been doing research for my term paper due this Friday, and in English I'm struggling to keep up with my reading. Monday I have a short anthropology essay due, Tuesday an accounting assignment, and Wednesday a big biology lab write-up.

So at this point I feel very loaded down. However, it doesn't bother me excessively or render me sleepless. I know I will get all the work done; it's just a matter of using my time wisely. I think it takes a while to get to know your own capabilities and come to the realization that you can't keep up with everything all the time. You have to give yourself some time for socializing and relaxing. For me, this comes in the form of a long hot bath, and watching a favorite TV show with friends.

I discipline myself to work at least one day on the weekend. But you can go crazy if you don't give yourself enough social time, and you end up worrying constantly about all your assignments. You have to try and take it one day, or assignment, at a time, and keep your working time and socializing time balanced so that you can at least attempt to keep up with your work. I've realized that worrying doesn't solve anything, although I do have a problem with feeling guilty. But maybe that's inevitable.

Perfectionism and Workload

In my program, historically, there has been a dropout rate of around 30% at the end of the first year, after which there are far fewer people who quit. The profs tell you this right at the beginning, but the program's reputation is such that everyone thinks they know how brutal the workload will be. But they just think they know. No one can really understand until they've actually experienced it.

I thought I was well prepared for the workload. In high school, I had deliberately made heavy demands on myself; I chose the most demanding courses, did some college classes in my last two years to get college credits, and participated in lots of sports and clubs. I knew that I needed a very competitive resume to get into this program so I wanted to show as much as I could that I was well rounded, and that I took my academics seriously. But another of my objectives was to acclimatize myself to the workload that I knew would be coming once I was here and in this program.

I also did a summer college program here to get a feel for what was to come. Although the work was as demanding as I thought I could handle, I told myself, "This is great. I am always able to work hard all the time so I will be okay. And now I have gotten a really good start." Then I came into the program and I couldn't believe the workload.

Before, I'd never really had to stay up past 1 or 2 in the morning to finish things. And I wasn't used to having to finish something before I was really done with it. I had always been something of a perfectionist and hated having to rush through things; so I would get behind by wanting to add one more thing in order to make it as good as it possibly could be. But now there wasn't time and I had to accept that this work just had to be good enough and finished with. Then I could begin the next thing which there was not enough time for either.

As a result, I have slowly and painfully come to the realization that not everything has to be perfect, and there are just some compromises that have to be made. At times I have had to pick and choose what must suffer at the expense of another assignment. Often, I want to perfect my work for another hour but that hour just isn't there. I hate having to finish doing something that I know I can improve on. However, it's even more terrible to get behind because there's no way of catching up. Accepting this has been hard for me, and I still don't like it. I don't like these sometimes unrealistic deadlines at all. But although my classmates and I must sometimes skip meals, sacrifice our social agendas, give up free time, or pull all-nighters for such deadlines, it is extremely rewarding to be pleased with the end result and finish alongside your friends.

I wrestled with it and now I think that I've worked it through.

You can make the assignment as good as it could possibly be, but then you probably won't have time for the next assignment. So you have to compromise: make it as good as it can possibly be consistent with leaving enough time for everything else that has to be done. Your top priority has to be managing your time such that you produce the highest quality you can in the allotted time.

WEB: COPING WITH WORKLOAD srvlgd.com/CW

Internetless

For the past two days, my computer has been without internet. During those two days, I felt so cut off from the world. Normally when I wake up, the first thing I do is stumble to my desk and check my email. And then I get my breakfast and check my email again. And then I wash my dishes and check my email again. By the end of the day, I probably check it around eighty times. Now, I had to catch a few computer minutes at the library if there was one available (a rare occurrence), or find someone in my residence whose computer wasn't in use – also rare.

To go from checking eighty times a day to around two is a drastic change. At the same time, it was nice to have a change from my normal routine. Instead of sitting in front of my computer, I was wandering around the house while eating my breakfast, visiting my friends who I normally wait for in my room. It was nice to be forced to go out to connect. Of course, I never received anything drastic or important during those two days. I realized that the time that I spend on the internet could definitely be better spent elsewhere.

So I decided: from now on, my monitor will spend most of its time turned off. I will live a real life instead of a virtual one.

WEB: FREEING YOURSELF srvlgd.com/FY

WEB: LIFE IS BUSY srvlgd.com/LB

WEB: NOSTALGIA srvlgd.com/NT

WEB: PRESSURE IS ON! srvlgd.com/PO

Learn and Live

This is less of an anecdote and more like some good advice. University is not just a place to get a degree; it's also a place to grow and learn (and I don't mean just algebra and organic chemistry). There are people who come to university whose sole reason for existence is to study. I pity these people because they are missing out on so much in life.

Now I'm not suggesting you come to university to drink your face off, smoke your brains out, and then get booted out after first semester. What I am trying to say is that university is the end of your childhood. When you graduate, you will get a job, a car, some kids, and more responsibility than you can imagine. While at university, you must take advantage of the carefree lifestyle. Meet new people, do things you've never done before, and most of all, have fun! Somewhere, in between all this, it is quite possible to do enough work to get by and then some.

I know when I graduate I never want to say, "I wish I had done this or that in university."

You Do Have Free Time – Find it and Use it

You do so have free time! Unless you were that kid who signed up for seventeen different clubs and became the president of each, you truly do have free time. I have a full and rigorous academic load, work part-time, am a member of two clubs, and volunteer. I still have plenty of free time. I know others who are involved in way more activities than I am and still find time for other important things.

"But I'm different! I really don't have the time!" If that's your response to this, sit down and take a good look at the time you're wasting. How long did you spend hanging out with friends and roommates last week, with no discernible result either in terms of achievement or enjoyment? How about the internet? I swear that's the undoing of most people.

When you sit down to do your work, probably in the evening, there's a barrier between you and actually getting to what needs to be done. Your brain has to jump out of relaxing mode and into achievement mode. You look for things that'll give you just a few seconds more of pleasant drift. Your friends are nearby. Your roommate is right there. So is your computer, with the internet just a click away.

Guilty? Repent. Tomorrow is a new day, the first one of your new more-efficiently-conducted life. One trick I've used is to take thirty seconds before I go to supper to get rid of everything from my computer screen, replacing it with the documents I'll need for my homework: the prof's instructions, references to the readings, the blank computer document. Then I get rid of all the accumulated crap on my desk, open the textbook at the appropriate place, and set it beside the keyboard. I tell all the people who might distract me that I'm going right to work when I get in, and I don't want to be disturbed.

And if your analysis truly reveals that you're innocent of time-wasting displacement activities, better look to your schedule. If you're truly stretched so thin, maybe it's time to scale back on a few activities. Really, of what benefit is the club if you can only put in the bare minimum? Pick those important to you, excel in them, and regain some sanity.

This last is true only for a minority. For most, the problem is displacement activities, aka procrastination. In your heart, you know that's your problem too. Fix it. You can. And you must.

Home, Residence,
or Off-Campus

I Could Have Lived at Home, But I Chose Residence

It was interesting for me when I came to university because I was given the option of staying in residence even though I lived in the same city as my university. It wouldn't cost me anything because I had a scholarship that would pay for it. I chose to stay in Res because I wanted to get involved with the university and meet people; staying in Res would make it much easier for me to achieve these goals. Everyone I knew who had lived at home in their first year regretted it. Many had tried to get into Res but couldn't because it was full.

I expected that living in residence would save me time because I wouldn't have to spend well over an hour each day commuting. However, I hadn't considered the social life which often used up a lot more time than that. On the other hand, commuting is wasted time; social life isn't. Another big advantage was that I didn't have to be totally organized for the entire day; forgetting some small but necessary item just meant a quick trip back to Res. And now that we have a bus strike going on, which looks like it will last for several months, I can't imagine how the off-campus kids manage.

As well, it is very convenient to be only five minutes from your classes, library, bank machine, or athletic complex. This allows you to return to your room throughout the day for work, sleep, or whatever you want to do. And having someone clean your room for you on a weekly basis, something that would otherwise be a great chore to do yourself, is a huge luxury. Along with this is the meal plan which provides you with nutritious and (most often) good food.

Most of all though, all the friends I now have are the result of being in Res; these friends provide mutual support for each other and make for a lot of fun on any Friday night.

On the academic side, I can't count the number of times there was something I didn't quite catch on to; it was very good to have someone just down the hall who'd be doing the same thing as me at about the same time. Often, my problem was solved in a few seconds. Other times, it took longer. And of course it worked the other way too, with me being the helper. Occasionally I really would have preferred not to be interrupted, but you can't send friends away without a good reason, especially when you need them about as often as they need you. Sometimes there were times we both turned out to have the same problem, and it was a lot easier and more interesting to discuss it together than to get frustrated alone. Other times, one would think he had the answer, but then when the other started asking questions, the first one realized he didn't know it as well as he thought. I'm really a person who prefers to work alone, but it's certainly good to have a couple of people handy as backup. Of course now, I can just go online with them, but if we hadn't gotten to know each other in Res, I'd have been too shy to do that.

One more thing: It's amazing how often there's just a bunch of people doing some of the same courses hanging out together in Res (yes, including the bathroom or the laundry), or in the caf, or out for a pizza at the end of a long evening's work, and someone will say, "Hey, I heard that what Prof X really gives marks for in that assignment is … " Important, and if you spend too long by yourself, you miss it.

But like most things in life, residence is not all a bowl of cherries. Of course, there are annoyances and frustrations. Most obviously, the noise. You find yourself trying to work when your neighbors' music is so loud that it is blowing plaster off the walls. In my first month, from Thursday night to Sunday night, it was often so loud that I could not fall asleep, so I ended up buying a fan to drown out the noise. I'm sure they would have turned it down had I asked, but I didn't want to look like a party pooper. However, I found that after the first set of midterms, people started to quiet down once they realized they had done worse than expected.

By then, of course, the whole place has become a slum. Everyone who visits notices that and when I've visited other friends in different places, I feel the same way. Odd though, even though I'm normally a bit of a neat freak, somehow after a while the slum aspect of things becomes less important, unless it gets too extreme – which it sometimes does. And I must say, it's annoying always to be one of the cleaner-uppers when I'm hardly ever the one that makes these messes. Hey, that's life. Take the ten minutes to clean up; then get on with it.

Another Res problem is the temptation just to hang out with people because they're there and fun to be with, while you really should be doing your work. Fortunately, that's not a problem for me because I'm organized and I know how to control my life. But for many, it's a huge problem. On the other hand, video games and electronic devices can be tempting in the same way, and they'll still be there wherever you're living.

Lack of privacy (sometimes it seems your neighbors know more about your life than you do!) and the ever-present dramas on the floor can be annoying too. They seem to be about everything: schoolwork, marks, needing to drop a course or change a timetable, problems at home, partners and ex-partners, sleeping with someone and regretting it afterwards, coming out as gay. All very interesting and intense, but these dramas aren't things you can

ever walk out on, and they do use up a lot of time. Still, in the grand scheme of things, the time spent is a lot less significant than what I learned about my fellow human beings. I could never have learned all this at home. At least I hope not.

I Could Have Been in Residence, But I Lived at Home

I live in the city that my university is in. I decided to save money by living at home, about 25 minutes away, 45 in rush hour. When other students heard that, they would ask, "Really? At home? Don't you feel like you are missing things?"

Well, at first I thought that I might be. But I soon realized that, no, I could be just as much a part of the university as anyone else. True, the transit system in this city can't get me to the university very quickly or conveniently, so most of the time I have to drive (yes, and park!), but if I stay until the evening, I don't get caught in the rush hour.

During Orientation Week there was a huge group of students in the same position as me. I had all the same programming as students in residence; I just had to take an extra step to get there. At the end of Orientation Week I felt confident that I was going to have an incredible university experience despite the fact that I was living at home.

There are students who don't do that. They come, attend classes, and then go home. They find that because they went home instead of participating fully in orientation, most people in their classes have already made their friends at the university, and they don't know anyone here. So most of their friends are the same ones they had before they came. They're not part of the campus community, and they seem totally disconnected from the university. I was determined not to be like that.

It is harder in some ways. For one thing, almost everyone else is in residence; that's where they form most of their friendships, and that's where they make decisions about where to go and what to do. Most things are spontaneous. And unless you've arranged to stay with someone overnight, you can't enjoy the parties the way others can; you still have to drive home.

These are all problems that can be dealt with. I was on a varsity sports team which provided me with a great social network, and the off-campus program put on lots of events that I wanted to go to. So I was on campus far more than I expected to be; I felt like I was living there. I stayed with friends in Res some nights to get a taste of what it was like, and I had a meal plan so I could eat on campus a lot. I didn't let where I lived affect how I ran my life. I took initiative, made the most of the opportunities the campus offers, and definitely do not feel like I missed out.

But I have to admit that living at home does have its advantages. I have friends with roommates who are very sleazy in a variety of ways (never clean up, loud music, drunkenness, drugs). I visit their rooms to do work or socialize, but when the unpleasant surroundings get too much for me, I can leave and go home to a clean, quiet, organized house.

Some students love being away because it's an escape from what they see as an excessively restricted social life. They're tired of things like curfews, the feeling that you're being checked up on, and judgments about friends. They just can't wait to get away. I'm lucky because, although I sometimes do get irritated with my mom, on the whole we do have a rather good relationship.

What I'd say to others who live near the school they want to attend would be this: The university experience is what you decide to make it, so don't let where you're living affect what you want to get out of it. Take the initiative yourself to get involved, take advantage of the opportunities presented to you, and enjoy the first-year experience that you create for yourself.

Living at Home

Living at home and going to university has its pros and cons.

Superficially, living at home is good because, if you're really lucky, you have someone who will help you do your laundry, clean your room, lend you the family car, etc. It is definitely cheap, even including bus, parking, or other transportation costs. You don't have to worry about moving and deciding which things you absolutely need and which can be left behind because all won't fit in the back of your Toyota! Also, if you live at home, you don't have to insult your digestive system with good ol' university cooking.

Staying at home offers all the comforts of familiar surroundings as well as the support that you've grown accustomed to. It's really nice to tell your family some of your true feelings about university as they develop from day to day, without having to worry about the whole university knowing about it. Gossip in residence seems to go in a complete circle. If you tell something to someone, no matter how trustworthy they seem to be, you can be guaranteed that it will get back to you – only ten times worse than it originally was!

Home is also a great place to study. If you live in residence and close your door to study, then every five minutes, everyone you know will come and knock on your door to ask you to go out. By the time you get rid of everyone, so much time has been wasted – you could have gone out and had fun!

Also, you can't beat the guidance, honesty, trust, and understanding that no one else but a family can offer. It feels good to leave a party to go back to a nice, clean, quiet home.

But there is another side to not living in residence. I have found that it is very difficult to make close friends with students who live there. The only way to develop strong ties is to live in Res day and night! Being off residence, I always make it a point to stay for dinner at least one night per week. However, this usually proves to be depressing. All everyone does is talk about things and people you don't know. Then everyone breaks into laughter and says "Private Joke." Talk about feeling like an outsider. As for parties, you always hear about them after the fact.

Here is an example of what I'm talking about: I live five minutes away from the campus by car. One night everyone decided to have a pizza party (which they talked about for the next two months – extensively). When I inquired jokingly as to why I wasn't invited, they explained "Oh, everything is spontaneous in residence. We never plan anything." Well, that may be true, but seeing as I live so close to campus, I could have arrived a half hour before the pizza! If you're not there, people usually don't think of including you.

Savoring Every Moment

Residence. You always hear stories about the loud, wild and crazy environment that college residences create. You hear horror stories about the noise levels, the horrible food, the room-mate from hell, the minuscule bedrooms, and the challenges of sharing a laundry room and bathroom with hundreds of other strangers.

That's exactly what I was expecting and trying to prepare myself for when I moved into my new home my first year of college. I was living in a suite style apartment, 6 girls living together in a confined space for 8 months? Let the drama begin!

But I went with an open mind. Regardless of the horror stories I had heard from other people, I was still looking forward to starting this new chapter in my life. What I found out was this: people were partying or in the common room watching movies until you got up for class the next morning; the cafeterias closed way too early, and the food tasted like the cardboard box it came in! There were endless fights with roommates about whose turn it was to do the dishes or to take out the garbage. Half the stuff that was brought to decorate and fill up the room didn't even fit, and there never seemed

to be an empty washing machine or dryer. Every story of the shortcomings of college that I had heard was coming true.

But the thing was … I loved every minute of it. You didn't mind that people were up until 5 in the morning because half the time you were out there with them, and the other half of the time you were so tired you would sleep right through the noise. It didn't matter about the food because you had fun experimenting on your roommates with new recipes. You still liked your roommates and even though you may have disagreed on dish/garbage duty, you recognized that they were in the same position you were in, so they became instant friends, quite possibly for life. That tiny bedroom became a haven as the perfect set-up and places for things were worked out, and it became apparent that either the middle of the day or the middle of the night were perfect times for getting a free laundry machine.

Starting college can be crazy and scary, but it doesn't have to be. An open mind is all you need. Learning the tricks to living in Res is only a small part of the whole experience; you will never be this age or in this spot again, so relax and just enjoy it. And don't let the horror stories get you down.

WEB: WHAT LIES AHEAD? srvlgd.com/WLA

WEB: ONCE YOU ADAPT, IT'S GREAT! srvlgd.com/OYA

WEB: GOSSIP srvlgd.com/GS

WEB: RESIDENCE: HOW DIFFERENT COULD IT BE? srvlgd.com/RHD

WEB: AGGRAVATIONS IN RESIDENCE srvlgd.com/AR

WEB: LAUNDRY WOES srvlgd.com/LW

I Need Time to Myself

The big city and first year university were two things I have always wanted to experience, but the city I have yet to discover. Since I lived in residence during my first year, there was not much time to do anything off campus. The college was a community within itself, housing its own center of activities.

Every week, meetings were held to discuss and organize future events: sports competitions, dinner parties, pub nights … you were expected to take part. If you did not participate, other students would question your intentions and to some degree accuse you of killing college spirit.

I had always tried to take part in these extracurricular activities, but I found it difficult to organize my time for both academics and entertainment. On some nights, after a heavy midterm or a long study period, I felt I needed to spend some time alone. To relieve some pressure, instead of fast-paced fun, I would curl up in an chair with a book not related to academics, listen to some mellow music, and sip some hot tea. Those nights were extremely rare though since it was almost impossible to find a quiet place. The college was always alive with all-night visitors and parties, and there was usually some sort of disturbance coming from the quad.

My first trip back home for the holiday weekend made me realize what I have always taken for granted: the warmth by the fire, the sound of silence, a tranquil atmosphere, and a true sense of security. I would savor every moment, for I knew that in just a short time, the academics and college life would again be upon me.

Residence is a Class in Social Living

In residence, you're living with people you've never met before, didn't choose to live with, and who might have very different habits from you. Yet you have to get along with them just the same.

I have three siblings, so I'm used to sharing space. But the hardest type of person for me to share space with is the very kind this university seems to attract: spoiled rich princesses. Their problem is that they're used to having parents or maids pick up after them. They do things like put dirty plates outside their door, thinking they will magically disappear by themselves. Really, who thinks this way? Spoiled rich princesses, that's who. Picture their lives: they brag about how big their house is, how much stuff and how much money they have, how many exotic places they've visited, and how much richer and better than everyone else they are. And then they behave like idiots because they expect things to be the same here, especially that others should do their dishes and pick up their garbage.

I'm sure it's hard for them. But I think it's even harder for the people who are used to sharing to live with these people who aren't.

Then there are the bizarre things some of these girls will say. We had a floor meeting once where a couple of them brought up the fact that they didn't think the quality of soap in the bathroom was good enough, and the toilet paper wasn't the proper type.

Ironically, one of the things I was most looking forward to at this university was living in residence. Contrary to the archetypical undergrad stereotype, it wasn't the late-night partying scene I was looking forward to but the independence and freedom. Don't get me wrong, I love my family, but a part of going to university is growing up. I looked forward to meeting new people from all walks of life and faculties.

At first, I was excited about it all: the energy and the friendliness of people in my residence. But soon I began to notice the many different personalities that took getting used to. While living in residence has given me the opportunity to meet so many interesting people, I've learned that you can't get along with everyone.

Again, don't get me wrong. University life is everything I expected and more. So mingle with others, and don't get too frustrated when you get home from a full day of classes and arrive at the next one: Your Class in Social Living.

WEB: DIFFERENT PEOPLE srvlgd.com/DP

WEB: A SCARE srvlgd.com/AS

Living Co-ed

Co-ed Residence! A scary thought for a shy high school graduate considering university. You think there will be people running around, sleeping around. Sex is commonplace, right? Wrong. Believe it or not, residence life is one based on mutuality and trust. From what I've seen, promiscuity and bed-hopping are minimal (or at least hush-hush).

The whole atmosphere in residence tends to be a mature one. Everyone respects each other's privacy, and most people act in a fairly adult fashion. There may be nights when a group of girls and guys stay up in someone's room, talking and having drinks all night. But we are a bunch of friends. The barrier between guys and girls has been lifted. Consequently the fun and excitement of "chasing" has been lifted as well. The guys become big brothers of a sort and girls their little sisters to protect. Or sometimes it's the other way around. It's a nice family atmosphere.

As well, I think the co-ed residence contributes a lot to the down-to-earth feeling in residence. Because you are living with members of the opposite sex day-in-day-out, there is less need to impress them. The result: people don't dress up or put on an act. People can simply be themselves. Besides, people have seen you at your worst both physically (in the morning before a shower) and emotionally (stressing out during exams). They know how you are and how you act. There is no need for masks.

To me a co-ed Res situation is not just bearable – it's better! Some of the best friends I have at school are guys, and I've shared just as much, if not more, with them than with my girlfriends. It's easy to have a wholehearted discussion with a guy. Unlike with girls, there is no competition or rivalry; you get a guy's point of view for a change, and especially when discussing guys, it's perfect!

The best thing about residence is that everyone cares about each other: not for the way they look or talk but for who they are. Ethnicity, religion and gender are secondary.

The Delights of Residence Food

Monday night: poached cod; Tuesday night: stuffed pork; Wednesday night: meatloaf; Thursday night: chicken; Friday night: Hawaiian casserole. What does this sound like to you? Residence Food.

In all my life, I have never had such bland, boring and blah food. Some of the concoctions they come up with are incredible. Monte Cristo sandwiches with processed ham and cheese slices on French toast. Gross! Tacos that have almost no meat and are so soggy that they have lost most of their crunch. Sick! Roast beef on a bun which you have to have razor sharp teeth to bite through. Ugh! Limp, brown, soggy lettuce that looks like it's been sitting around for days. Barf! Scalloped potatoes that are ten times more crunchy than the tacos will ever be. These items and many more are examples of really bad cafeteria food. I admit that I am a picky eater, but when I pay this much to be on the meal plan here, I expect a little better quality food.

I guess I'm being a little hard on them because occasionally there are things that I like very much. Their homemade bread, coleslaw, oven-baked potatoes, meatballs and desserts are usually quite appetizing. So I look forward to seeing what they have to eat just in case I'm pleasantly surprised – which happens only once in a while. But one of the best things about Residence Food is that it really makes you appreciate a nice home-cooked meal.

Getting Messy with Peanut Butter: Life on a Meal Plan

I have the kind of meal plan card that lets you eat in the residence cafeteria downstairs or in one of the other places farther away that also accept it. There are only a few things downstairs that I really like; very basic turkey sandwiches, honeydew melon, grapes, and peanut butter toast are pretty much it. I find that a lot of food tastes of the same kind of spice and just isn't my cup of tea. So I use my meal card as a chance to venture outside of my comfort bubble and as a way to get creative with my options to create new meals that I won't get bored with.

Peanut butter is food and your best friend. Though peanut butter toast is a "been there, done that" kind of breakfast dish, I challenged myself to go to the next level. I eat banana peanut butter sandwiches, peanut butter on blueberry bagels (which is absolutely tasty) and peanut butter on hot banana bread. A discovery I made in one of my lectures is that a snack of peanut butter and bananas really is an energy booster to keep you awake.

And now sushi. I moved from the east coast to the west coast to attend this university. Back home, we have a lot of water but not a lot of sushi. I can't say I'm a big fish person, but I still fell in love with sushi. I stick to vegetable rolls like my personal favorite, yam sushi. Like most people, I didn't know that yam sushi was an option. It makes some breaks in between class really special, and I now know how to use chopsticks. Trying something new when you are on a meal plan is a smart thing to do. It is the right time to take that risk.

How do you eat healthy? If your cafeteria offers a grill or a fast-food-type service, you should stay away as much as possible. Yes, hamburgers and fries are yummy in all of our tummies but will not make you feel good when you are trying to sit through a class, and you are falling asleep in front of your professor. Not cool. I frequent the wrap and sandwich bar almost every single day. I also spice up my oatmeal with banana chips and granola. For snacks, I grab some fresh fruit like bananas, melon, kiwi or an apple. But there are those occasions where I get my really big mug and fill it up half way with hot chocolate and then load the rest with whipped cream until it overflows. Those special and memorable treats are allowed. Infrequently.

WEB: FOOD FOR THOUGHT srvlgd.com/FFT
WEB: SURVIVING RESIDENCE LIFE srvlgd.com/SRL

Do Not Disturb

Lately, I've been feeling very frustrated due to the fact that residence atmosphere is preventing me from getting my work done to the best of my ability. It always seems that as soon as I am getting right into some schoolwork, someone comes into my room and wants to visit. The visit ends up lasting a lot longer than it should, and by the time it's over I realize how late it is and that I've got to get some sleep. As I've been encountering this situation more often, I continually try to find an appropriate way to prevent it from happening again.

One day I decided to keep my door completely shut, yet still, someone decided to knock. I think I need a *Do Not Disturb* sign. I've been trying to get up enough nerve to explain nicely that I am very busy and can't talk at the moment, but it seems a hard thing to do.

Many times, as people walk into my room and continue talking, I continue doing my work. This is not a very polite thing to do, yet it is an automatic reaction; I know that my work has to get done. Many people on my floor don't share my feelings towards school, and this, I guess, is the problem.

I feel school is very important. I do believe that hard work should be combined with some fun in order to keep your mind healthy. I've noticed that on my floor, I am doing quite a bit more work than most. Some don't seem to care about their education at all. They will stay awake all night, making noise and disturbing others during the middle of the week. Obviously, the next day they are in no shape to wake up for their 8:30 am class. Again and again these students miss their morning classes. They then end up borrowing my notes to get caught up. I've realized that giving them my notes is not a very wise thing to do. I lent my notes to one person who has now had them for over two weeks. I guess I have learned from that experience.

Many people take education for granted. These are the people who go to university just to have a good time. They aim to just get by with the minimum possible amount of work. It is already evident who these people are. They haven't even started to do any work yet, and school started over a month and a half ago. Will they ever decide to do any work? Or will they just continue getting assignment answers from everyone else?

WEB: HOUSE HUNTING srvlgd.com/HH

Housing Problems

My first year of university, there was an unprecedented number of students coming, so the university had to combine some single rooms into doubles. As well, many students didn't get into residence. I was fortunate enough to get in, and I think my disabilities helped since I had indicated on my forms my preference in residence. For example, I needed a single room. I think that was taken into consideration because I did get in and I did get a single room.

For my second year, I didn't start looking for housing until August. There were over 2000 new students who couldn't get into residence, which was insane. There were so many people looking for places to live that the school stepped in and started buying residences and renting them out to first-years. The housing situation was that bad. I joined a social networking site to look for roommates and was lucky to find a place.

This last summer, I had to pay for three places to live. My second-year lease went from September to August, but I wanted to live with certain friends my third year. The lease started in May and the only way I could secure a place with them was to start paying in May. So I had four months where I had to pay for two places. I could have stayed at my original place if I had wanted to and renewed the lease; then I wouldn't have had the four-month overlap. But I chose not to because I didn't like the guys I was living with and the girl from the basement was going back home because she hated it here. So my share of the rent would have increased.

To make it worse, I couldn't get a summer job here and had to return home. My parents had moved so I couldn't stay with them. So I ended up staying with friends and having to pay a third rent. Granted, it was a small amount, but it was still more than I could afford.

You are really stuck because leases start at different times and you can't get a place without signing a lease. But paying three rents in one summer was something I would not want to repeat ever again.

WEB: TOO BAD FOR ME srvlgd.com/TBM

One Year is Enough

Residence has been a lot of fun, and it is definitely true when people say that you meet most of your friends while living in residence. Besides my roommate, my other closest friends only live a few doors down the hall. But nothing is forever.

The other night one of the girls asked me if I planned to ask for the same room next year; and I played stupid and said, "Oh, can I do that?" Sure I love the friends in my hall, but next year I think I'd like a change of atmosphere.

My roommate and I are thinking about getting an apartment next year. I think it would be so much more fun – we'd cook our own meals, have our own living room, and be able to decorate to suit our own tastes. I just hope we can find an apartment with reasonable rent.

Maybe we could buy a really good tent.

Living on my Own

The school year passed; then summer passed; and now, I'm in second year, blissfully out of residence and living on my own in a one-bedroom apartment.

I'm glad my first year was in dorms, though – I think residence was an awesome experience for me, and in the grand scale of Rez Life it was pretty prime real estate. Nonetheless, now free of both dining halls and co-ed bathrooms, I'm loving my new location (and with it my newfound freedom). I can cook what I want, I can buy my own groceries, and I have my own bathroom with my own shower (and it's always clean). I have a sofa and a desk and a bed and near acres of space (well, compared to a dorm room, that is).

Thanksgiving is this weekend, though, and after two and a half months away, I'm finally heading home for a few days. I'll see my parents, my brother, my aunt and uncle and cousins, and my grandma; I'll see my dog for the first time since she had her hip replaced (they say she's doing well). I'll get to sleep in my bed, in my room, in my house again, and for a couple of relaxing days I'll just kick back and spend time with my family (with occasional bursts of homework, of course). And on top of that, it's Thanksgiving – which means my mom doing what she does best: spoiling me rotten with copious amounts of good-for-me-yet-delicious food. I'll get all the trappings of an autumn feast, and I can guarantee you that when I fly back on Monday, I'll do so with a suitcase laden with homemade pickles, jam, hummus, and pumpkin pie.

This short visit home will do wonders – it will give me the long-awaited break I need, and when I get back to my apartment, I know I'll tackle my to-do list with renewed vigor.

If nothing else, my mom is an excellent role model – she cooks (healthily); she cleans (immaculately); she works (and works out), and she still finds time for leisure. I try to keep the same mentality with my apartment, too – if it's dirty, clean it; if it needs fixing, repair it; if it's unhealthy, don't cook it; and budget your time effectively. And while I don't mean to brag, I think I'm doing a pretty good job so far. While not spotless, it's at the least very tidy, and while I'm still a far cry from my mom's caliber, I'd like to think I cook relatively well.

And at the same time, I'm managing to balance practice, workouts and homework, all the while keeping a (relatively) cool head. This weekend will be like a spa date of sorts: I'll leave university stressed, irritable and tired, and return with new energy and self-confidence and be exponentially more productive. I'm no Suzy Homemaker, but I'm doing all right, and I think going home for a bit will just help me to reaffirm that.

Of course, the glamor will eventually fade. At some point in the coming months, I'll arrive home at 6:30 pm, my coffee reserves finally drained. I'll stagger through the door, drop my fifty-pound backpack, and blunder my way to the fridge where I'll be greeted by only cottage cheese, sandwich meat, cucumber and sugar-free Jello. My clean laundry will be waiting, unfolded, on the drying rack; my vacuum will be staring me down from the corner; my homework list will glare at me from my paper-strewn table; my unmade bed will sulk quietly beneath a torrent of sheets and haphazard pillows. It'll just be another weekday, and somehow I'll manage to get it all done; but in the meantime, with caffeine withdrawal pounding a staccato behind my ears, I'll frown behind a spoonful of tonight's gourmet dish (Raisin Bran), grab a pair of Advil from the bathroom cabinet and think … geez, my mom must be a flippin' superhero.

Sports, Frats
and Stuff

A Complete College Experience

I decided to come here and have a complete college experience, to have independence, to break away. Choosing to live farther from home helped me to do that. So have team sports.

The big difference is that I can't go home every weekend because I have practice or games. So I mostly hang out with people on my team, partly because a lot of other students go home every weekend and partly because we spend at least three or four hours a day together practicing. In some ways, you could say that I am not mixing as much as I could with other students, but I think my teammates and I have more fun than students who go home every weekend.

With team sports, you get to know more people quickly and well. I find team friends are more intimate friends than others who might be just party friends. You are together during the game and the practices and know who you can trust the most. This spills over into the rest of your life. Your teammates are some of your best friends; my team is the biggest support group I have.

Team sports also give you balance in your life. You are forced to organize your time as you often have to discipline yourself more than those not on sports teams. And if you have trouble with that, your team members will help you. We have classes, lunch, maybe a nap, practice, then dinner, then hang out time, then work time. But the days I don't have practice or a game, I sit around all day. So we use each other as a support system to motivate each other to go to class even when we don't want to go. We get through this as a team.

Sometimes you are forced to be more creative than other students on campus. For example, we can't drink for three days before a game. So we can't party as much as others. So what do we do? We invent new things to have fun doing. It's great for bonding, and sometimes you strike gold and find something truly fun. Sometimes this means just going to a toy store and playing with all the toys or going to a local market and talking with the locals. Other times it means having a BBQ in front of our dorm and chatting with other students walking by.

So my advice for first-years would be not only to live in residence but to live far enough away from home so that you can't commute. It forces you to get more involved. It forces you to break away from your friends at home and experience more of the world. You should be involved in something other than academics because university has endless opportunities, most of which you will never have again.

Sports at University

While at university, I feel that it is very important to stay fit as well as work on your studies. Tension often results from academic work and what better than some form of physical activity to work off these tensions? The opportunities for recreation at university are wide and varied.

Here there is a good athletic complex, complete with gymnasium, weight-room, pool, and squash and racquetball courts. You can't do them all: you just have to decide which one to do, and then do it! I find it's a good idea to do this on a regular basis, say three times a week, as this will keep you in shape and help you avoid injury from too long a layoff. The feeling after completing five games of squash and a 2500-word essay is like no other.

Taking the time for vigorous exercise actually does put you in a better mood for schoolwork – you come to the essay or whatever refreshed and feeling good about yourself. You're in a better frame of mind for getting down to it, and ideas seem to come a bit easier as well. Perhaps the old saying "healthy body, healthy mind" has a lot more to it than we realize.

Devoted to my Sport

I came to this university because of my sport. I love the game, I'm good at it, and it is because I play it well that I got a scholarship here. In my case, the sport happens to be hockey, but everything I have to say would be just as true for people serious about any intercollegiate sport.

Being a serious student-athlete, I practice hockey for a few hours a day and play hockey most weekends. Practicing and playing takes up lots of my time, but I still find a way to get my schoolwork done during the season. Yet when hockey finishes, I can't keep up with my schoolwork. It is actually harder to get everything done.

Why is that, you ask? Simply because I have more time on my hands. I don't have practice. I don't have games. So why don't I get everything accomplished?

Here are my best answers:

1. When hockey is in season, you're always working against the clock. If work doesn't get done now, there's no way that it can be finished in time to get handed in. When there aren't rigid deadlines, you always feel you can put it off. You think, "Oh, I'll have plenty of time to do this later." But then before you know it, it's late at night, your day has been wasted, and it is too late to do anything about it. Does that make sense? Thought not. But it's the way things often go for me and many of my teammates. When I have hockey, I will do more during the day, I will organize my time better, and I will get better grades.

2. People come by and ask me to come to a party or the pub. Even though I intended to stay in and do the work, I say yes anyway. Then it goes downhill as in #1. But if I have hockey, I can't say yes. Or I will suffer the consequences.

3. During hockey season, you know you have to be focused, organized, disciplined, controlled. And you can be. You know for sure that there's no time for things that aren't absolutely essential and urgent. You can plan time to go out and have fun, but it has to be planned. It's a frame of mind you're in, and it governs your entire life.

Actually, on further thought, these are not three different things but just one with three different ways of looking at it. There should be a way to just move back and forth from the relaxed, hang-out-with-friends mode, to the disciplined, task-directed mode. Maybe some people can do that. But for me and most of my teammates, we can't. I guess the moral of the story is, time management is essential, and hockey forces me to do it. Without activities governing my time, I don't have a clue.

Student-Athlete Realities

I went to my school on a soccer scholarship. It was twenty hours away and my parents drove me down on a Friday and left that Sunday. I showed up at our training camp not knowing what to expect. We practiced three times a day and in between those practices we would either be sleeping or eating. I had never felt so exhausted in my life and classes and had not even begun.

Our soccer season runs from the end of August until the beginning of November. During that period of time, roughly every other week we would leave on a Thursday, play a game away on Friday and Sunday and come home that Sunday night, usually after midnight. I missed some of my very first classes. You learn very quickly how to plan ahead and make sure you know what is going on in all of your classes and what assignments are due.

In my first year, on one of our very first road trips, I remember someone in one of my classes asking me if I had done one of the assignments. I remembered the prof talking about it but never really mentioning it again. I figured it would get brought up again closer to the due date. Someone else on my team laughed at me and informed me that this doesn't happen anymore; profs no longer remind you of everything. You get a syllabus at the beginning of the year and that's the set schedule.

This particular assignment was due that Friday night, and we were going to be on the bus until about 4 pm on Friday. I started writing stuff down on paper, and as soon as we got to the hotel I emailed the assignment to the prof just a couple of minutes before the deadline. From that day on, I wrote everything from the syllabus in my planner and kept it up to date. To the normal student body, this may seem like a burden, but to you and your team, these types of situations become second nature.

Being a student-athlete is definitely not easy, but it is one of the most rewarding experiences. My advice: on the days when you feel like you can't handle it anymore and you would rather just be a "regular" student, don't give up!

Here are a few things that I came to understand during my first year as a student-athlete:

- You might have been the best player on your old team but no longer. Everything is now at a higher level. You are competing for positions against people who are sometimes more than four years older than you.

- You will question yourself more than once a week as to why you are doing this. (For me, these thoughts occurred mostly during 6 am practices or fitness practices.)

- You need to show up to practice every time, and you need to make sure that all your assignments are handed in on time. You will very often feel like it is physically impossible to fit everything in.

- You will become very familiar with the phrase: "If you're early, you are on time; if you're on time, you are late; and if you are late, don't even bother showing up." You will find yourself showing up to everything at least thirty minutes early.

- You will learn to write everything down in your planner in order to stay on top of things. At the end of any activity, you will look into the planner to see what's next. Then you will learn: know what's next all the time. That way, when one thing goes overtime and the other one is just beginning, you will be able to make a choice.

- You will realize that somehow, although you have very little time to yourself, you are managing and getting through it.

- You will realize that no matter what, your team is behind you to support you.

- You will eventually realize that your team is your new family.

People do combine being an athlete with being a student. The rest of your team is doing it; if you're organized, so can you.

Branching Out

Here, the university makes quite an effort at the beginning of the first term to make students comfortable with being here and to connect them as quickly as possible with others. That makes it easier to develop a range of new acquaintances and new friends, unified under some banner or another. I chose to do sports which served the same purpose.

For many people, the friendships made in these first few days and weeks form the basis for their social life for the entire time they are at the university. Sports team, subject group, residence floor, society or club, fraternity or sorority: it really doesn't matter. All serve the essential purpose of kick-starting your social life and making you comfortable in this new stage of your life.

That first year, you are often missing home and your friends. I even had thoughts of transferring to another school in the first few weeks. Joining a team made me feel better. I also participated in other things that were specifically designed to bring us first-years together. But later I opted to branch out from what I now perceived as a kind of cage. I deliberately moved to a different floor, got involved in different activities, and went to different parties.

One advantage of branching out is that everywhere you go on campus, you meet people that you know. But the most important thing for me has been that even though I feel I have a lot of connections on campus and many different friends that I hang out with, I have met a few people with whom I have been able to make a much deeper and more complete connection. Not that we agree on all topics, but these are friends who are truly congruent with me.

The people who were on my team and on my original floor still seem to cling together. Next year they will share a house together, they still go on trips together, they party together. Together, together, together. But they are not branching out.

So strongly did I feel about this that I started a group. The purpose is to look at the mixes on campus, the cliques that have formed; we try to push people beyond their social boundaries. Because when you get down to it, we all share pretty much common interests by just coming to this school in the first place.

A friend of mine found the same thing. He played basketball in his freshman year and found that his entire life revolved around his basketball and the people he played basketball with. He joined the team to get to know people and to bond with them and it did serve that purpose. But it also limited the kinds of people he spent time with and what he did. He even went so far as to quit basketball after his freshman year so that he could branch out to get away from that team and that limiting mind-set.

The question you have to ask is: are you hanging out with these people because circumstances have placed you together or because they are truly the types of people who you would really want to become friends with?

Something was Missing

Editors' Note: For those who aren't familiar with the ideas of Fraternities/Sororities, here's a brief outline: partway through the first (Freshman) year, students decide if they want to join a Fraternity or a Sorority. Usually, these organizations are named by Greek letters, such as Omega Alpha Theta, and each has a building, or House, on campus. The process of choosing which Fraternity/Sorority you want to join, and which wants you, is called "Rush." About halfway through the second term, the decision is made on both sides; there's a weekend during which the "Pledge" is made involving an initiation ritual of greater or lesser intensity, humiliation, and secrecy. Then you belong, and your social life revolves to a greater or lesser extent around the Fraternity/Sorority, often on a lifetime basis. People in the House feel a great sense of community and loyalty to each other.

I go to a school with a very big Greek-life (fraternity and sorority) system, and I knew nothing about it when I first got here.

My first semester started out great: I had all the freedom in the world and met so many new friends, but by the end of the semester I was bored. Once the snow hit, nobody wanted to go out anymore, and the weekends were dull. As well – and maybe this will be surprising – I found that it was a lot harder to get down to the work that needed to be done for classes.

In previous years, I'd always done division I track, but now I'd decided that it just wasn't what made me happy. I knew that without track I would have tons of time on my hands. I needed a way of not wasting my days away sleeping and eating and a way to meet more people on campus without having to take the bus or tramp long distances through the snow and slush.

One day, someone in my bio class told me all about Rush and convinced me to just try it; even if I didn't join, it would be a great experience alone. So I registered and went through Rush, and I ended up getting a bid to my first choice House. I stuck with it and pledged for the six weeks.

The whole idea of pledging made me very hesitant to join one of these Houses, but during Rush, I made sure I asked each one about the process and if it was anything like in the movies. They all assured me that it was nothing like that, and I soon learned that they were right. Contrary to popular belief, I didn't have alcohol shoved down my throat or frat guys making me do dangerous stuff.

The first day of Rush was completely overwhelming. Going to every House on campus and having to talk to so many people was the hardest thing I had ever done. But in a way there was something exciting about it, seeing how there was something different about each House and thinking that I could soon possibly be a part of one of them. I always looked forward to the next day and finding out if I was getting closer to where I wanted to be.

Bid Day was definitely one of the best days of my college experience. I knew my life was about to completely change. It was a very fun and at times draining, process. Pledging was like taking one or two extra classes, but it was a very good teacher for time management.

I'm glad I decided to quit track and do Rush because it really opened my eyes to college. The weekends are no longer dull, I couldn't ask for better friends, and I know I have many shoulders there to lean on. I participate in way more community service. I have close bonds with over a hundred new but firm friends. I'm constantly meeting new people. And I have a place that I can call home while away from home.

I encourage everyone to at least try Rush; you learn a lot during the process, and you can see for yourself if it is or isn't for you. Each House is different, so there is a variety of options for you, and if it's not something that's for you, you will know.

WEB: AN OUTSIDER'S VIEW srvlgd.com/AOV

WEB: A POSITIVE VIEW OF GREEK LIFE srvlgd.com/PVG

Greek Life and Time Management

Although fraternities and sororities are a great social outlet, they can also be really good for time management.

The whole pledging and initiation process in itself is a huge time-management learning experience. You have to learn how to make the right decisions. If you have a big paper that's due on Monday and it's Saturday night and a pledging activity comes up, you have to decide if you are going to go out or if you are going to stay in to write the paper. If you do go out, you have to have a plan for how the paper is going to be done. If Sunday night is the only available time, well then, prepare for an all-nighter because that's what it might take.

Once you're initiated, it gets more complicated. Now you have more flexibility about your choices; the frantic pledging process is over so you have more time. But there are events all the time, and it's easy to forget the real reason why you are in school. You won't be able to participate in everything and still keep your marks up, and it's no longer a choice of yes or no. It has changed to one of selecting which activities you'll do and which you'll pass up. I've found that in order to do that, I need to make myself a timetable that extends at least a week ahead, and sometimes longer than that.

One good thing about my fraternity, and I think others too, is that your grades can only go so far down the drain. Then you begin to risk losing your membership. So there are bad consequences for you before the time comes that you have actually fallen so far that you can't recover. The fraternity is so much more immediate and intense than your future grades; thus this threat can be what brings you back to sanity. I've known that to happen to quite a few people. So really, the fraternity is giving you a cushion. A hard one, true, but a cushion just the same. I've known more than one person who's needed that.

So, as I said at the beginning, my fraternity has helped make me better at managing my time.

Fraternities and Sororities: Stupid Ones and Worthwhile Ones

I am in a co-ed community service fraternity which I joined for the sense of belonging and because I wanted to serve. 99% of my friends are in it and it is my entire life; I do nothing else. So I am not knocking sororities or fraternities. But …

I essentially lost my best friend last semester for eight weeks while she was pledging. For those who, impossible as it sounds, do not know about sororities and fraternities, let me explain a bit.

35% of the kids at this university are involved in some form of sorority or fraternity. There are social ones, there are community-based ones (which is what I am in) and there are professional ones.

To apply for sororities, they send the freshmen around to each sorority House on campus in packs like animals, where they get interviewed by all these girls. They have to run the gamut of all the Sisters in the House who take notes on what they are wearing, what they say, what accent they have, what religion they are. It's very judgmental. And essentially, you have to paste a happy face on yourself the whole time if you want to get in. It's ridiculous because all the girls are trying to impress the same types of people, so they all dress the same.

The pledging class is designed to create a sense of community which is why people call themselves Sisters and Brothers. Because you spend day after day and hour after hour in special experiences together, you get that feeling of Brotherhood or Sisterhood. So pledges are taken away from everything; it's very restrictive. The pressure on them is awful, ridiculous. On my floor, there are a bunch of girls pledging now, and they are not allowed to go out on the weekends. It's horrendous as these girls are used to going out every single weekend, even weekdays, so being forced to sit inside makes them all depressed because they can't go out and party.

Most of what they have to do when they are pledging is secretive, but I have heard horror stories about numerous students being sent to the hospital from overdosing on certain things. But this is not always the case: my best friend doesn't drink, and her Big Sister didn't force her to. Some are respectful of that. Others are very much into mind-control stuff.

My friend told me that last weekend they had a competition in which, in teams of eight, they had to smoke eight ounces of weed, finish two large cases of beer, four pizzas and a bottle of vodka, and whoever did it the fastest won. My friend didn't remember anything after 6 pm.

At the end of your pledging process, you get initiated into the Brotherhood or Sisterhood. Hazing is drinking, tying someone up and leaving him at the side of the road 200 miles away in his underwear to find his way back.

Here on campus, there are sorority stereotypes. One is for the Jewish girls; one is for the hippies; one is for the druggies; one is for the, how shall I say it, promiscuous girls; one is for the social rejects, and one is referred to as the one for the overweight girls. Don't get me wrong – there are some nice ones too with many upstanding respectable girls. My friend is in a social sorority, but she has a really good group of friends. She has a good head on her shoulders, great GPA, doesn't drink to excess or sleep around. But then she is in one of the respectable sororities. And she is nothing like a typical sorority girl. Or at least, as I see them.

The frats have their own stereotype. One is for sketchy guys, another for really trashy guys, another for the Jewish boys, and another for the social rejects. Another one is kind of a fake fraternity if you can't even get into the social reject one. But again, there are some really nice ones too with great respectable guys.

So why would you want to do it? Other than all the cons that I've already mentioned, it is very time-consuming. Rushing takes two to three weeks, and then there is six to eight weeks of pledging. It's an entire semester.

But on the up side, it's a sense of belonging. In my fraternity, the sense of community isn't as strong as in the social ones because they are forced to do everything together. They, from what I've seen, mostly hang out with each other. But many of us in this frat are involved with a lot of other things and have many other friends outside the fraternity.

Bottom line is: if you are gonna do it, think about it carefully and make sure that you know enough about it before you do it. And be aware that if you get accepted and then want to leave, people won't want to touch you. You're a reject; you've failed. But if you get in and make it through the pledging, you won't want to leave by that point.

I Don't Like Frats!

My experience with frats has been very negative. In my first year, I wanted to see what frat parties were like so I went to a lot of them. They were lame but I kept hoping they would get better. They didn't. Just a bunch of drunk college kids bumping around in a crowded basement to incredibly loud and bad music. It seemed that everyone's goal at these parties was to get as drunk as they could. Now I like having fun, but this just wasn't my scene.

At this university, frats are big; students find it exciting to be a member because there are lots of other frats to compete with which many say can be fun. But at other universities, frats can be a dying culture. My best friend attends one of these universities and says there is no competition and their frat parties are boring, maybe five guys sitting in the basement in their togas. What is it about frat parties and basements anyway?

Belonging to a frat is undesirable to me because it is just not my scene. It is undesirable to my friend because there is just nothing to do.

Not all fraternities are the same. Each one has a little bit of a different reputation, and people tend to gravitate towards the one that suits them. Some are decent and more social; some are seedy, and you wouldn't ever go to parties there. In my sister's freshman year here, she was given an introduction she never forgot. She was told which frats to avoid and why: over there is the date rape frat, that one is for coke-heads, and so on. People learn very quickly what happens where. And frats do tend to be labeled because each of them tends to have a specific reputation associated with it.

The process of joining a frat is supposed to be secret. Many don't help themselves by what they do to their pledges, ranging from pouring human waste on them to promoting underage and binge drinking and drugs. Some even get shut down because of their hazing; just last year, one was closed because of coke use in the hazing process.

I have often found frat members irresponsible and not considerate of others. Some of these frat Houses are quite nice, yet you often see garbage lying around outside and hear of them getting trashed inside quite frequently. And during our finals, we often were forced to study late into the night, but it was really hard to focus because some of the frats would blare their music very loud despite us asking them many times to turn it down.

I believe that you can have fun and party without seeking out a reputation such as this. It's a lifestyle choice. In our second year, we came up with an alternative when we had our own house. We began to host our own parties, and we were careful to keep the numbers low, the music level reasonable, and to keep an eye on the drinking. We even had activities. We had something called board games and booze, or we would do things like play Checkers, Monopoly and Scrabble. And then after people had a few drinks, we would bring out the Twister. I said we kept an eye on the drinking, but I didn't say that we didn't do it at all.

Maybe others have had positive experiences with respect to fraternities. But I am glad I chose not to be a part of it. To each his own, I guess.

Fraternities are Worth It

I've had the opportunity to read the frat-trashing story, and I disagree completely. The problem is that you hear all these stories about only the negative things that happen at a small proportion of existing fraternities. It makes me angry.

You hear about irresponsible and harmful hazing rituals, yet many former and current pledges will tell you that even though the hazing was tough, they appreciated the close relationships that they formed because of it. They say that they wouldn't have bonded as well as they did had they not gone through these tough rituals together. Some say it's like in the military. But I bet you none of them like to hear of hazing that gets out of hand.

You hear about parties where booze and drugs are everywhere, but you show me a dorm of first-years where you won't find a bunch of drunk kids "bumping around to bad music" whose goal is to get wasted. C'mon. These issues are not unique to frats. It's not the frats that are at fault – it's the guys who act like idiots and do dumb, irresponsible, and inconsiderate things. Those guys are always going to be around regardless of whether frats exist or not. Hazing, drugs and alcohol abuse exist in sports teams, in clubs, and in many organizations. So hey, why don't we ban them all? And we'll get rid of dorms too while we are at it.

Frats can do many good things. They collect money for charities. They organize various community service projects. They provide leadership experiences; look up all the great leaders who were members of frats during their college days.

Frats provide a unique experience for young women and men seeking fellowship and support. They provide a family away from your family back home. In my frat, it doesn't matter what ethnic or sexual orientation you are – we treat each other with respect and we offer each other our friendship.

The stories you hear about are tragic. But they are isolated occurrences and not the norm. The positive outweighs the negative.

Placements

When you attend university, there are many programs that offer placement opportunities: co-op programs, summer placements, and so on. It all depends on the program and the university. I had the chance to participate in two placements, and they were amazing learning opportunities.

The problem with attending a conventional post-secondary program is that you get the education, and then when you go for an interview after you graduate, you don't have the required experience. With a placement you can get both.

I had friends who didn't know where they wanted to work, and when they picked their placements, they didn't give it much thought; they just wanted something easy. I spent a lot of time thinking about where I wanted to work and did placements that were within my top two choices. I figured they would give me an edge when I went to get a job. During my last term, I did a placement and was hired by my current employer immediately afterwards. I was stunned, amazed, delighted.

Two friends of mine took courses where there were no co-op placements available but achieved the same result in a different way. They both applied for summer positions suggested by their prof; she even wrote letters of recommendation for them. So now, when they finish and the time comes to apply for a permanent job, they'll have good experience and another recommendation: one from an employer to add to the prof's. The only trouble was that they made minimum wage all summer, so both were even more short of money than they could have been. Well, for the one person, it didn't really matter because his parents are well off. But for the other, he's putting himself through school with work and loans; he gave up the high-paying road-crew job he'd had in previous summers. He'll survive, though, and will be in a much better position to apply for a job in his field when he graduates.

So if you do have the chance to do a placement, pick something related to where you might want to work afterwards. That way you are getting the experience to add to your education. Also, if there are no opportunities for placement at your school, try working or even volunteering for a related organization that interests you; this will give you experience that may set you apart from others when you start searching for a job.

WEB: REFLECTIONS OF A CO-OP STUDENT srvlgd.com/RCS

We Don't Have Time, but We'll Do it Anyway

Putting on theater takes a great deal of time and requires a commitment that's close to being absolute. The performance date is set, and absolutely everyone has to be ready. It might seem, therefore, that theater isn't something students in demanding programs like mine (architecture) can do where students have to work into the night and have very little free time. Two commitments that are close to absolute have to be one too many.

It might seem that way, but it isn't.

I've been involved in theater for many years, and when I came here, I missed it dearly. A close friend in my program was feeling the same way. One evening we were commiserating about the lack of theater in our lives. "Wouldn't it be great if … ": that kind of thing. Next thing I know, he says, "I figured it out, and I have a plan."

The trick to doing it would be scheduling all the rehearsals and other activities around our own timetable. Other people who got involved were going to have to fit in with that. We planned how it would all work, and we decided that yes, we really can do this. We had auditions, recruited people to do all the backstage stuff like costumes and makeup, and applied to the Student Association for funding. What fun it was to do this again. Our first production was modest, involving just eight of us, but we got such a good response that we decided to expand into a more ambitious production with more people involved and a bigger budget. Still, though, everything had to fit in with our academic commitments. It's a logistical challenge, involving late nights, early mornings, and weekends, but nobody complains.

Our target audience is busy students, and we do plays that people in our situation can relate to. The one we're doing now involves a group of kids in their twenties who haven't done much since high school. One night, one of their friends appears who has done something with his life: he's a rock star back in town on tour. He stops by to hang out with them, but the contrast between his success and the lives the others are living makes for a really interesting and volatile situation. It brings out people's fears about what is or is not happening in their lives, so it relates to the dread that shadows many students here, that they'll just go home after graduation to live on their parents' couch. It's about the fear of going out into the real world after the insulation of growing up. The fact that some contemporaries might be having great successes in their lives just makes things worse.

One surprise we're all agreed upon is that drama is another opportunity to "think outside the box." I believe students underestimate how multidisciplinary the world is, and the majority of people who succeed in creative professions don't just have one incredibly strong interest. They have several, and those passions interact constructively with each other. There are times during a rehearsal of a Harold Pinter play that I'd find myself thinking about the unconventional structure of the play, and suddenly I'm thinking about innovative ways to change the structure of my architectural design. Notes on acting also become general notes on presentation: how to be engaging and interesting to your audience. The process of writing a play is surprisingly similar to the design work we do in our program. The list goes on. Anyway, it's more than an escape for us: it's another pool to draw inspiration from.

One thing we pride ourselves on is that over half our audience is not related to the university. Given that we direct our productions to people in situations like ours, it may seem odd that it turns out that way. It's a good feeling that so many people from the city want to come and watch us perform.

We are proud of the vibrant and successful organization that resulted from our original modest efforts. Best of all, it hasn't had any negative impact at all on the work we do in our university program – quite the opposite in fact. The skills and insights we get from doing the productions actually enrich our schoolwork, and we return each day to our faculty with renewed enthusiasm that comes from having a short but complete break from it.

I Can't Do it All

I am the type of the person who in high school was involved in a ton of things from athletics to academics. Coming into university, I saw so many more things I could participate in. With the hundreds of clubs advertised during first week, there were lots of things that I really wanted to do. I joined things like debate club, a volunteer organization, badminton club, as well as some academic clubs.

All of these clubs allowed me to get involved in some issues that I felt passionate about. I also met a lot of really cool people I still talk to sometimes – even occasionally in my classes! Perhaps, I thought, I was making connections which just might pay off some time in the future. Some of our TAs have told us about this kind of connection being useful to them later on: introductions, advice on what to say in a letter or interview with a prof or an employer,

or occasionally, just whispered into the ear of an influential person, a complimentary few words.

Some of my friends regret not getting out more and being more involved. They look back at the first year and only remember going to class and partying. Not exactly something to write home about, in my opinion.

But soon I had a problem. I realized that there just weren't enough hours in the day for me to do everything. Work for my classes was beginning to suffer as well. In addition, the time for myself just wasn't there, and I was missing it badly – things like reading a magazine article, hanging out with friends for no particular reason. I know myself too well: that's a fix I need on a regular basis, and if I don't get it, I start having withdrawal symptoms.

Of course, the first thing to go had been my sleep because there were too many things that had to be done before the next day. Worse, I became so burnt out that for the first time in my life even when I did go to bed, I wasn't sleeping well; this made me tired in class which added more stress because I couldn't focus. It was a downhill spiral.

In the end, for my own sanity, I had to compromise. Sadly, some things had to go in favor of the ones I truly wanted to put in the time for. This meant I dropped two of the clubs I'd joined which immediately meant more sleep for me; that's what I needed the most. There's something called "sleep deficit" which took me several early nights to get over.

Now, near the end of my first year, I have learned that it is possible to be involved in the many things that I want to do. But I have to be sure that first, I can actually do them and second, given the 24 hours we have in a day, they are the things I want to do the most. So I shall see, and hopefully it will work out.

Sex, Drugs
and Stuff

Hard to Resist

Well, as I left my room after dinner, I truly intended to go to my psychology lecture ... I really did. I missed the morning lecture because of the drastic need to study for a chemistry test, so the evening session was my only chance to catch the visiting guest speaker.

Walking out of the residence, I was immediately hit by the biting cold, and my hands soon became numb. In retrospect, I shouldn't have made the slight detour that I did. I know I should have gone directly to the lecture, but I had to do a friend a favor, so I ended up turning left when I should have turned right. Now, if you had been a casual observer lying frozen in the snow, you probably would have gotten the wrong impression as I entered the all-girls' residence; but you must believe me when I say that I only had the best of intentions.

The warmth of the building as I entered was truly inviting. I walked through the carpeted hall, up the stairs, and as I passed through a group of women dressed in lingerie, I felt horribly conspicuous. I entered into yet another hallway and reached a door adorned with ribbon and cut-out snow flakes. I knocked, was pleasantly told to come in, and entered.

You must remember that when I arrived I did have the best of intentions, but as I stood there dumbfounded, even I had my doubts. She was lying on her bed reading a novel, her skirt shifted dangerously above her knees, her blouse leaving little to the imagination as it fit snugly around her ... well let's just say it fit.

"Hi, I didn't expect to see you tonight. How are you?" She sat up in bed, and her dark hair fell about her shoulders.

"Uh, er I'm feeling better all the time. I mean, I'm warm now ... quite warm actually. It's cold out, so I feel better now."

"That's good," she replied. "So, I thought you had a psych lecture tonight ... "

"Well, I do. I can't stay long. I just thought I'd drop by beforehand to give you back those notes I borrowed."

"Well thanks, you didn't have to do that. Are you sure you don't want to stay a little while? I can make some hot chocolate." She smiled ... and oh, what a smile!

You know, it never ceases to amaze me that the human brain can analyze information and reach monumental conclusions in such a short period of time. "Are you sure you can't stay?" After carefully weighing all the options and staring into her gorgeous brown eyes, it took me all of two seconds to reach my final decision.

"Sure, I can stay." I loosened my scarf, dropped my gym bag, and slumped into a chair. "Got any marshmallows to go with that hot chocolate?" I asked.

I didn't fully appreciate what effect that evening had on me – academically, that is – until I received my psychology midterm back. It was not a pretty sight ... I had learned my lesson. As I walked back from the lecture hall with the failed psych paper in hand, I resolved that I would never again jeopardize my academic studies for any social pursuits ...

... except with her.

Sex: it Happens

One thing about our dorm would surprise people (parents are not to read this section because they may be shocked): Sex happens all the time, all over. I have witnessed so many sexual activities I'm not a part of because I walk in on them. In the dorm rooms, in the washroom, in the laundry. Most of the time, people are drunk, but not always. It can be very awkward.

My first term here, I was continuing a long-distance relationship with someone I knew from high school, so whenever we got together here, I had to arrange it with my roommate. It was all about organizing things in advance which might sometimes be awkward if you have the wrong roommate. But you are thrown into this open environment, so you kind of become immune to it.

In high school, if someone heard you had sex with someone, you would think the world was ending. If one person knew, then everyone knew. In a small town when everyone knew, then you would be a bad person. So everyone was thinking of that, and not as much happened. But here it becomes like breathing, especially in the dorms. You can hear when someone above you or below you is doing something. Or in the room next to yours. I am good friends with my neighbors, so we would just laugh at each other and pound the floor or the wall or the ceiling.

Another thing that happens here is that you meet someone at a party who you don't know and have sex with them, but then the next week you realize they are in your class. It happens because our classes are so big. So you pretend you don't know it was them. Or that your phone is doing something that needs your urgent attention, like ringing.

You know you had sex with that person; you just go with it, and it never gets talked about. No one knows. It doesn't have to lead anywhere. It's beautiful on its own.

WEB: SEX srvlgd.com/SX

Getting Carried Away

I have recently been observing the effect of romance among students on their attitudes towards school. I'm trying to be objective. I don't have a steady girlfriend at the moment, but my buddy has recently acquired one. So I have seen him "with" and "without." I'm not sure whether he's a typical case or not, but here goes.

Before his girlfriend, he was in bed by ten and up by eight. He didn't miss a single lecture and his work was always completed on time. Lately ('with') he goes to bed about two and gets up about ten. He misses about four lectures a week and has handed two assignments in late during the last week.

Contrary to popular belief, I don't think it is the girl's fault. I feel it is his decision and he makes his own choices. The only benefit I have seen is that he is happier than ever. I hope he can find a happy medium soon before it's too late for his academic year. I am helping him by tutoring him in calculus, algebra, and chemistry, but I only have so much time.

(Later) There has been an update on this situation. My friend has since broken up with his girlfriend, and I have been seeing someone special to me. His work habits are back to normal now, and his marks reflect his change in attitude. On the other hand, he has no regrets about being with her and would even like to get back together with her.

In my case, the girl I have been seeing doesn't attend university and actually lives about an hour away. With the distance between us, I look forward to seeing her, but I can't see any adverse effects on my schoolwork.

I think this just goes to show that girlfriends or boyfriends do not necessarily have to hamper schoolwork and may even enhance a student's motivation towards school. There is a happy medium somewhere between "not at all" and "she's the only thing that matters."

It is of utmost importance to find this fine line before it's too late.

SEX, DRUGS AND STUFF

Chivalry: is it Dead?

Since I've managed so far to avoid what I call the "Every Night Pubbing Syndrome," I guess I just haven't been confronted as much with the question of "where should I spend the night tonight?" or perhaps more appropriately, "with whom?" … at least, not enough to make an issue of it.

I have however encountered a few intoxicated and somewhat horny "gentlemen." What a contradiction in terms! With a few drinks in them, they were anything but gentlemen! To my knowledge, I had done nothing to instigate or provoke such interest. Although I do realize that everything and everyone looks a little more appealing through bloodshot, blurred, and very drunk eyes, I certainly don't appreciate being "attacked," nor do I appreciate being in a position where I am expected to tactfully extricate myself from my amorous "friend's" arms. At the same time, without hurting his feelings, I have to politely explain that I'm not enjoying this.

To be blunt, with my workload, I just don't have the time for casual sex or "bedhopping." That's not what I'm here for; obviously, for some of us, it is. I just wish that those who feel that they just can't go without a nighttime companion (or companions) could control their selfish raging hormones long enough to realize: she really doesn't want me to do this. (If this ever does happen, I'll be sure to shake my pompoms and cry, "Chivalry is Not Dead!!")

I just wish too, that some of these guys would stop for a moment and think about how they're making the girl they're preying on feel like a piece of meat. The "gentlemen" of this university, to live up to such a title, should learn to appreciate the finer qualities of the female personality: wit, sincerity, warmth, honesty, and, just possibly, a sense of humor.

I hope they realize soon that their not-so-subtle advances produce exactly the opposite of the desired effect: they turn her off. Am I worshiping a dead god? I hope not.

Chivalry is Not Dead

I had the good fortune to read the thoughts of the woman who appeared to be quite distressed and repulsed by the male attitudes and actions at university. Let me take this opportunity to respond by saying: pick up your pompoms, baby!

I do not dispute the fact that there are a lot of men who continue to go out and get drunk, verbally and physically abuse women, and then do their best to take them home for some easy sex without taking any responsibility for the possible consequences. What I can't understand, though, is why these guys are successful. Are the women they pick up incapable of saying no? Are they so insecure that they need some companionship regardless of what form it takes? No, I give women more credit than that …

Nevertheless, I know one girl who we call the Gambler. We figure that she's got a slot machine in her room that holds numbers instead of hearts, lemons and strawberries. We've concluded that every night she pulls the lever, and the numbers that turn up are the rooms where she'll spend the night. Sound far-fetched? Well, it's quite possible when you take into account how often, with whom, and with how many she sleeps. Why did I relate this story to you? Well, it just goes to show that ladies, as well as gentlemen, are sometimes difficult to find.

And is a pub with its raunchy music, flying beer, and party atmosphere a place where men and women look for qualities such as delicate feelings, warmth, and honesty? I think not. No, they're looking for, how shall I say it, more primitive qualities. Men and women in such an environment are simply out for a "good time" and with all the stresses of university, justly so. I'm not trying to justify or excuse the rude and obnoxious behavior of drunken men. I'm just trying to point out with such an atmosphere and with so many women literally playing into the hands of such behavior, I don't think you should be surprised.

The gentlemen who are looking for sincerity, honesty, a sense of humor, and warmth in a woman are there at the pubs, eating dinner with you, and in your classes – they're just not as visible as the drunken, obnoxious, and belligerent guys who are made famous because of their immature antics.

WEB: BOYS WILL BE BOYS: RESPECT YOURSELF srvlgd.com/RY

WEB: TWO-TIMING GUY srvlgd.com/TTG

WEB: HOW TO FIND THE GUY OR GIRL OF YOUR DREAMS srvlgd.com/HFG

Wild Differences

There are big differences between people here, and a lot of the differences don't have much to do with the individual person; they're more to do with the group and the interactions within.

I was in a fairly wild group myself at one time; the parties were nuts. One time I went with two of my good girlfriends and we all got trashed. We played drinking games for hours, did things that no sane person would want to do, and it wasn't like we were the only ones. Everyone in the room was doing exactly the same thing!

Then someone pulled out some military body armor. That started a whole new round of shouting and drinking. People were putting it on and letting one of the guys beat them with a bat. I was the first girl to get "beaten," and they laughed. No one got hurt, but when I woke up in the morning, I realized how truly crazy it was and it scared me. Someone could have been seriously hurt. But we didn't care – we were just there to have fun. In a way, I'm glad I was there that one time; fortunately, no one came to any harm, and it certainly did teach me something about myself.

I try not to judge people or change them because I wouldn't succeed, and it's really not my place to even try. Drunks, potheads, sluts: I've partied with them all. Before, I might have been prejudiced against them, but it's hard to be prejudiced against someone you know as a person, who you can have fun with, and whose company you enjoy.

However, there are limits. In December I was dating a guy I knew from home. I would go up to his residence every weekend and party with all his roommates and friends. We always had a blast. But that's when I realized something. Even when I visited during the week, they were drinking. They never seemed to have books around or computers with anything other than infantile games on them. I don't think there was ever a time, even during the day, when I heard one of them say, "OK, bye, I have to go to class now."

I tried to reason with my friend, and he agreed, but then he carried on with the same group in the same way. I pointed out what he was doing, and he agreed with that too. I'm not going out with him now even though he's still fun and a really good person underneath. It hurts, but I think this group is going nowhere, and they could well end up there before they know it.

Even in my own residence, one Friday afternoon, around 3, I had just returned from class and there were girls running around the hallways being chased by boys. They were wearing thongs and that was it. Most of them I didn't even know, and I never did find out how my floor was chosen as the best place for their behavior. This was my house; my floor was my home. As I stepped over two humping bodies, all I could think was, I need to go into my room and lock the door. Fortunately, just like the party with the armor and the bat, it never happened again.

Through all this, I went to classes, did my work, and never did do anything that would do me any permanent harm or make me permanently ashamed of myself. It's harder to surprise me or shock me than it would have been before, and I think I'm coming through it as a more tolerant and a wiser person.

WEB: DOUBLE STANDARDS srvlgd.com/DS

WEB: BEWARE! srvlgd.com/BW

WEB: REVENGE srvlgd.com/RV

Squirtguns: a Residence Necessity

Anyone who has spent some time in a residence can attest to the need for proper water-fight equipment. The popularity of water-fights with their associated paraphernalia and survival gear has no boundaries. They can be found in almost every residence, dormitory, or other student accommodations. Hopefully, this article will highlight some ideas for the beginner who finds himself or herself in a waterfight with no defense!

The classic overkill situation is a bucket of water. Although very effective, this approach requires the target to be quite close and may result in the sacrifice of innocent bystanders. The bucket is usually a last resort.

From grade school, everyone remembers the water balloons and the hand-held squirt-guns. Anyone equipped with both is a force to be reckoned with. Combine the long-range "bomb" effect of the balloon with the close-range "surprise" effect of the squirt gun, and you have a potent offense/defense combination for some serious splashing.

Technological advances in aquatic weaponry have revolutionized the squirtgun. One weapon very popular in this city is the two-hand-operated watergun. It boasts a range of fifteen to twenty metres and comes in all colors. Unfortunately, it lacks in durability, but the cost is reasonable.

And don't throw that broken watergun away. The writer has seen customized versions where the water-clips from several guns were put together, increasing capacity by a factor of three. Another product is the oversized Magnum, which would be appropriate for any Dirty Harry fans.

Products on the market that are similar to the above two include the Jet Stream Water Machine Gun, the SuperJet, the Chief Squirter, and the Sound and Water Gun. Even for the public-schoolers of today, there is the He-Man Water Sword.

A final product which the writer has not yet seen boasts a battery-operated system which pumps water from a back-pack with a capacity of twenty liters. Imagine the possibilities with this!

Clothing is optional. Because most waterfights occur at the drop of a hat, preparation is necessarily minimal. For the planned raid, though, goggles and a Kiwi suit have proven effective. These types of raids can be carried out solo but are a lot more fun with a group of four or five.

That, in essence, is what waterfights should be: *Fun.* Whether you prefer buckets, balloons, or squirtguns, the main ingredient is fun. Remembering that, choose your weapon, and have a big splash!

A Really Scary Situation

I had a really scary situation my first night of my first year at university. The most likely reason for what happened was that something was put into my drink. There is a possibility that I just drank too much, but I don't think so. I ended up sleeping with someone unprotected and completely unaware of it. I assume it was unprotected as I don't remember. A really scary thing to happen your first night of university and first night away from home.

I woke up the next morning and I just didn't feel right. I was back upstairs in my room somehow and my insides were twisting. I had to go to the bathroom, and I felt like I was going to puke. I knew something was wrong, but I fell back asleep and started having flashbacks of the night before. Then I woke up and remembered some of it.

My parents and best friend were still in the city, so I called them to say I didn't really know what had happened but I needed to go to the hospital. By 9 am when they came to get me, they had to half drag me there. But it was too late to do any testing because I'd slept through the night and had showered. I was so scared, I was crying. I was petrified.

Later that day, I decided to try to talk to the guy about it. I knew what we had been drinking and who I was talking to before anything happened, but I didn't know who I had been with. So I went to their room to ask them what had happened the night before. I ended up speaking to the guy. He was very honest; he said that he had been very drunk. He had a girlfriend so he was very upset by this. I concluded that if something was put in my drink, it probably wasn't done by any of the people who lived there.

At that point, I began to feel better. My mom couldn't understand that. At first I was shocked, but then I thought to myself that there was no point in ruining my life over this incident. I had been cleared of anything that could go wrong such as STDs. The guy was nice and didn't have bad intentions. So I told myself that I was not going to dwell on it and let it destroy my life. There was no point.

Maybe I'm unusual but I feel I've recovered from this incident. Now, if I heard this happened to someone else, I would advise them to go for counseling. It would be hard but probably worthwhile. Perhaps – I can't really say because I didn't do it.

So, beware of how much you drink, and keep your drink with you at all times.

The Battle Against the Bottle

Being of sound mind and body at the present time (which, with the pubs here at university, is not always the case), and turning nineteen today, the issue of drinking is on my mind. Having successfully avoided the temptation throughout the majority of the first term, and now being confronted with it more strongly than ever before, I find myself weakening and giving in, drawn away by the "call of the wild," so to speak.

Not only the drinking but the dancing, socializing and general happy party atmosphere tempt me away from the drudgery, boredom and pressures of everyday university life and allow me a release from these daily frustrations. I find myself looking forward more and more to my nightly outings and caring less and less about my studies. Homework gets put on the back burner. It's scary. The influence of alcohol is frighteningly strong.

WEB: WEEKDAY DRINKING srvlgd.com/WD
WEB: NOT AT THE PUB srvlgd.com/NTP

An Addictive Substance, and I Started with my Eyes Open

Disclaimer: I would never suggest that anyone take up smoking just to meet friends. It is a terrible filthy habit and it is hard to quit.

But … I distinctly remember the first couple of days of university. I did not know anyone aside from my roommate, and neither of us really had many reasons to leave the room.

One day I noticed that there were a lot of people smoking outside and I started talking to them. Soon I was smoking. After that first encounter I felt like I really knew more people. When I went to lunch, I now had people to sit with and when I saw people on campus, I now would say hi. Eventually I started hanging out with my newfound smoking buddies.

Smoking was also really important for me in my freshman year because there are times that you really feel trapped in your tiny room with little to do. It was an excuse to go outside, relieve some stress, and talk to people. It's really interesting how the people you smoke with can end up being some of your better friends just because of those little special moments you spend with them that you don't have with other people. It becomes a sort of community – most people on campus can tell at every residence hall where people will gather to smoke. Doing something together, something that lots of people frown on, really does speed up the bonding. The alcoholics and the druggies must get that from their habits as well.

One day, my roommate said he was not going to smoke anymore (a good choice), and instead we came up with the idea of buying a football and a frisbee. We went outside to throw them around and surprisingly enough, other people started to get in on it. It could be a great alternative but I do feel that people are somewhat hesitant to ask to play. On the other hand, to be part of a group of smokers, you just have to come along and join in.

I don't regret it at all. It served a good purpose for me. But I'm glad I could give it up.

WEB: ENERGY DRINKS srvlgd.com/ED

I Used Stimulants

I had to use stimulants. I resisted it for a long time but eventually, there seemed to be no alternative. I always had fifty hours of work to do in the next two days, so here seemed to be the solution to my problem. I found that instead of working myself to the bone while constantly craving sleep, I was alert, happy and focused. I could maintain a full course load, participate in as many extracurriculars as I wanted, complete my homework in time and party 'til I dropped, or should have dropped, without wasting any time. I had squeezed every ounce of performance and productivity out of myself that was possible. And I was able to still have fun.

I told myself I needed the competitive advantage. I could still have been good without them. But with them, I was better.

I didn't think it was different than working under the influence of caffeine or nicotine. There's no disgrace in using those mood-altering substances to enhance your ability to concentrate, to achieve, and to enjoy. And I'm not even going to mention alcohol. So why the big deal about stimulants?

You might notice that all of what's written here is in the past tense. Have my attitude and my habits changed? Yes. But that's another story. And I'm not going to let you in on it.

Hacking your Brain

Quite a few people I know take drugs. None are druggies because they're rather careful about what they take. I haven't seen any of the addictive ones like coke or heroin – it's not hard to get them, of course, and some people have tried them, but nobody I know uses them regularly. The most common one I see and smell is weed. People use it to relax and to have a more enjoyable time on the weekend.

A good thing is that you never see anyone who's loud or violent because they smoke up; you can't say the same thing about drinking. Bad things are that you never know quite what you're getting, and that it's illegal. Cops swoop down on places where they know drugs are being used, and I sometimes wonder about what would happen if they sealed off the Res and searched everyone's stuff on a Friday night. A lot of people would be in a lot of trouble.

Other kinds of drugs that you often see are amphetamines. These have quite the opposite effect: they make it easy to keep plugging away at your schoolwork for hours longer than you normally would, so you can get that paper done or that exam studied for. These are not illegal drugs, and some people can fake ADHD and get a doctor to prescribe them. Taking them if you're a normal person is called "off-label." The companies who make them say they don't like this off-label use, but they probably don't work very hard to prevent it. They certainly make a lot of off-label money around here. Mostly, the people who take them haven't begun their work soon enough; they've partied and procrastinated for too long, and now the pills are the only way to get it done in time. Then the next time they have to get schoolwork done, they know what worked last time, so they think they can party more and leave the work until the last minute again, as long as they've got the pills.

But there are those who have a different attitude. They're serious about their work, and for some, their work is never good enough to satisfy them – the kinds of people who think of an A as not good enough because it should have been an A+. These people will tell you that they are actually smarter with the drugs: they can work a lot longer, focus better, and get things done that they wouldn't have been able to complete otherwise. I said to one of these people, "Hey, you're making yourself into a person you're really not." He agreed: "Self-enhancement," he called it. "I just want to be the best person I can be."

He told me that he could maintain a ten-hour a week part-time job in the cafeteria that otherwise he wouldn't have had the time for, and that without that money, he didn't think he'd be able to come back at all next year. He talked about people who are naturally depressed and negative about everything; they take antidepressants and then suddenly are different people from who they really are. That's true; I've seen it. I had an uncle who was bad-tempered and down on everything, and he suddenly became a changed and much-improved guy. Later, I heard it was because he'd started taking antidepressants. So what's the difference? Hard to answer that one.

But where will it end? If too many people have this attitude, everyone else will have to work longer and harder to compete with them. Profs will see what these people can do without necessarily knowing how they do it, so they'll increase their demands on all the others as well. That way, there will be pressure on everyone else to take these drugs. Or maybe they'll ban them and make us pee into a bottle before every exam. Another thing: The competition to get into this university is brutal, and I know some parents who get weekend and summer tutors for their perfectly normal kids at age fifteen and will do anything at all to make them get higher marks.

"Kid enhancement": it scares me to think of it.

WEB: AMPHETAMINES, THE COLLEGE WONDER DRUGS
srvlgd.com/CWD

More Drugs

I don't suggest taking Adderall. But if you don't have a prescription and it happens to fall in your hands and you happen to take it, you have to have work right in front of you. If you don't, it will do you no good.

I would clean my room from top to bottom, vacuum and dust, wash floors, and still have a twenty-page paper due. I would wonder where the time had gone and why I didn't do it? Once I took it to write a paper but got distracted by my computer. I spent the evening online, chatting to everyone I knew and completely forgot to do my work. I had these in-depth conversations about all sorts of deep issues, many with people I hardly knew. But my paper did not get done.

Adderall is very common around here. During finals, you will get thirty messages, all saying "Hey do you know where I can get Adderall for my friend?" And the price per pill doubles or triples during that week. I had a roommate last year who had ADD, so she had a prescription for Adderall. But she wouldn't take the pills; instead she would hoard them for finals because she knew she could sell them and make tons of money. Then she would message everyone she knew, "I have Adderall, come find me." She was already rich when she started but now …

Unfortunately, because this kind of thing happens so much, it makes it hard for kids who actually have ADD and need Adderall to focus. They often have to jump through hoops to get their scripts filled because of the abuse.

There are other kinds of drugs around here too: a fair amount of cocaine, weed, ecstasy, shrooms and acid. People have different attitudes about it all. I don't smoke, but sometimes I forget that weed is illegal because people often do it out in the open here. They smoke it at parties or in the bathroom or on the way to school. As I was coming here today, there was a group of kids sitting on the hill smoking a bowl. I bet they will still be there smoking another one when I am on my way out.

In the dorms, you are told that if they catch you smoking, you are out. But people towel the door and spray air freshener or fabric softener. Or they smoke into a cardboard tube or water bottle with the end cut off and dryer sheets stuffed into it so that it blows out a clean and nice smell. Eventually the kids who don't do anything but smoke or drink during first year will either drop out or get kicked out.

When you are a freshman, it is too easy to not go to class. Many get here and think "I love college, I sit in my dorm room and smoke and drink when I want. I party weekends and weeknights and I don't go to class. I cram during finals week. I love my life. I live in a residence with lots of friends around me and I don't pay bills, I don't pay utilities, I don't buy food. This is the life." But with no structure and drugs and alcohol readily available, you will slide if you don't learn to say no. If you do not go to your classes, you cannot make that up, no matter how much studying you do or how much Adderall you take.

I Had A Friend Who …

I know what you're thinking. "I Had a Friend Who … " doesn't mean what it says. It means it's me, but I don't want to tell you it's me. As in "I have a friend whose family is so hard on her that she's going to run away." Or "I have a friend who thinks she's pregnant." Rule of thumb: there's no friend.

Not true here. Full disclosure: I'm still here, it's April, my marks are not quite what I'd like, but they're OK, and I'm reasonably sure the exams will push them up some more because I've never worked as hard in my life as I'm doing now, and it shows. I'm pleased at how well I'm catching on to what needs to be done.

So it's not me. It's the friend who … got hooked on coke and quit school: Robert.

Yes, I'm gay. Yes, we did coke together. Yes, I did enjoy the coke; nobody who hasn't done it can have any idea of how amazing it is.

That's all I'm going to say about it that's good. It could have ruined my life. The feeling was s-o-o-o good; of course I wanted more. Next weekend. But after a couple of weekends, maybe on Thursday night as well. All my work was done … at least all that absolutely *had* to be done was done … kind of. So why not?

Then it wasn't feeling *quite* so good anymore. Disappointing.

So, a bit longer line; problem solved. Then, a distinct feeling of wanting it when I wasn't planning on taking it, didn't have any, and had plenty of work piled up. Then, giving in to the feeling; Robert always had some and would always do it with me.

Then, a couple of other friends, not knowing about it but mentioning they'd noticed a change in me. Not interested in being with them anymore? No. More to it than that.

Then, called down by a prof who I'd gotten to know quite well and liked. Missing classes, awful stuff handed in, some not handed in at all. Not like before. What's going on?

That night I woke up feeling terrible. Cold sweat, puke, guilt, the whole nine yards. And I resolved to quit while I still could – if I still could. At that moment though, I was determined. I sat down at the computer and told Robert: I'm going downhill fast. Faster and faster. I have to quit. So I have to quit being with you as well. That's why I'm walking the other way if I see you. And if I give in, and do it with you again, you'll know I've lost my resolve. Please respect my decision; thank you for a wonderful time while it lasted but goodbye. It was five am when I hit "send."

Later that morning, I went to the counseling office. No, of course I'm not the only one. The price has come down in the last few months, so the use has gone up. I haven't been doing it for long, so with their help, I could quit. It wouldn't be easy, but they'd had others further down the road who had successfully banished it from their lives.

They were right; not easy, but I'm pleased to say that so far, and with lots of help from them, it has worked. And I have worked hard to maintain myself drug-free of course and also to catch up on my schoolwork. The bad news is that I can't catch up completely because of my low marks (and zeroes) already there in my records and because there was just too little time and too much to catch up on. I've had to make some decisions about what to concentrate on and what to write off. I'll do just about OK in the end, I think. I feel a lot older and wiser now too, and next year will be better.

But him … all I know is that after my turn-around, he disappeared. He withdrew officially from the university, I learned. His parents had known for a while that he was an active gay (which they'd come around to) and what he was doing (which they quite rightly hadn't). They did not know that he'd dropped out. And they haven't heard from him for weeks. We agreed that if I found out where he was, I'd tell them, but if they found out, they wouldn't tell me.

Well, you can guess what has happened to him. So can I, but guessing is all I can do. He's a very attractive guy, so I know how he can make plenty of money to support his habit. I think his future will probably be pretty terrible

… and short.

Staying True to Yourself

While in first year, I was bombarded with many new things, mostly good, but some bad. Being quite a bit younger than everyone else, I had to put on my toughest skin and stay true to myself. I wasn't rigid; some of what I'd thought I'd decided turned out to be just unrealistic. It was OK to wear somewhat more revealing clothes than I had before or to drink a bit more than I'd previously thought suitable. Nothing important was being compromised.

However, certain things were pushed on me that I had to say no to. Yes you're right: Drunkenness, Drugs, Sex beyond a certain point, things like that. People were sometimes quite unrelenting at first, but eventually they did take the hint and stopped pressuring me. I stayed true to myself and didn't compromise certain things in first year. Later on, these same people would come up to me and say how they admired me for that and how they wished they were more like me.

As much as you try to make friends and try new things, sometimes you can be the only one who is unwilling to move on your values and your decisions about them. It might feel lonely at the time, but in the end you will not regret it, and others will have noticed as well.

After those years at university, you need to still be yourself. Whether or not you are happy with what you did in university will depend on the decisions you've made while you were there.

Not Your Typical Student

Students with Different Backgrounds

Students from the city, from affluent suburbs, and from rural areas seem a lot different when they first arrive. City people are more aggressive. They do everything faster. They talk and walk faster, and they seem a lot less friendly to others. I know that because I'm from the city myself. There, you just can't say hello to people you meet in the street, and your habit is to just focus on wherever you're going and whatever you're doing. Nobody looks sideways or acknowledges anyone else. Actually you just can't as sometimes if you look at the wrong person in the wrong way, it can be dangerous. As well, you don't have time to stop and be more friendly because everything is so fast.

People complain about us city kids and think we're arrogant, but it's not really arrogance; it's more a certain confidence. The fact is, in the city, you have to look confident. If you don't, there are always people who will instantly find ways to take advantage of you.

City people tend to look down on suburban people, and the other way around – especially people from wealthy suburbs who seem to expect the whole world to revolve around them. I guess if you have enough money, your world really does revolve around you most of the time. So you expect the rest of the world to do the same, and that shows in your attitude towards the rest of us. On the other hand, rural kids are often mistaken in assuming that all city kids are rich.

Here at university, you notice all this stuff at first. But everyone is in the same situation, and we're all close enough in background to make where we are from unimportant rather soon.

The university is big enough so that when going from one part of it to another, you don't see very many people or things that aren't part of it.

Our residence is in one place, and at the other end of the bus route are most of the classes, so you tend to meet mostly the same people every day. You don't know who most of them are, but you do recognize the same faces day after day. And it's strange: people nod their heads and smile at each other. For the ones who aren't from the city, it's the same way it's always been. Even for me, I didn't really notice the change until I went back home again at the end of the term and my friends told me I had changed. You do change (people at home told me I was talking slowly!), but it doesn't take long for you to just start behaving exactly the same way you had before: resuming the old habits in the old environment.

But back to the university: once you get to know someone and take the time to try to understand them, working with them or socializing with them, you often forget where they're from. It doesn't matter whether the other people are rich or poor, or African or Hispanic or Caucasian, or even male or female (except in a few cases!); they're just the people you're with at the time. They do come from different backgrounds, and they've had different experiences. So you can learn new things or new ways of looking at things by being with them. Instead of being a problem, the differences are now an asset and an enrichment for your life.

WEB: PRESTIGIOUS SCHOOLS srvlgd.com/PS

WEB: WHAT DO I WANT TO DO WITH MY LIFE? srvlgd.com/WML

WEB: A MATURE STUDENT'S PERSPECTIVE srvlgd.com/MSP

Better than I Ever Imagined

I'm a mature student, and the university courses I'm taking are to upgrade myself so that I can move up to the next level in my profession. Most of the students are in their late teens and although I often marvel at how young and callow they sometimes seem to be, I do find myself warming to them more than I'd expected. I can see my own children growing up in a few years to be just like some of them.

I'm fortunate to have excellent classes: lectures, seminars, reading, and writing about the topics that interest me more than anything else in the whole world. Working gives me an entirely new perspective on the same group of topics, and I often find my schoolwork is illuminated by what I see every day on the job.

Of course, there are dangers working in the same field as you are studying. Some of the profs haven't been outside the walls of the university for many years, and it shows. They can be quite sensitive to your contradicting them and using a recent first-hand experience to back up your point. You do have to bite your tongue sometimes.

But it's their perspective that makes these profs' classes so good. I find it amazing how often a topic comes up, and the discussion involves questions that ordinary people working in the field would never have thought to ask.

They blow me away, these profs. They really truly do.

Unusual Combinations of Courses

My academic career is rather unusual. Many of my friends are majoring in subjects that lead directly into a particular career, such as Engineering or Social Work. Most of them knew before they came here what they wanted to do with their lives afterwards, and then built their program around that. They have a vocational perspective on being here.

I've often envied them. I can't do what they're doing, though, because I'm not interested in any of these things, and I don't want to be spending my life doing these kinds of things. It's not wise, and maybe not possible, to try to do something that continually bores you. You have to listen to your brain and play to your strengths.

So what excites me? What does my brain latch on to? Well, it's English Literature. I've always devoured books. I'm excited by new literary movements and new techniques, and I love literary processes such as textual analysis. No way will I give these things up.

But I am stressed when I think about the future. I've been quite envious of people in Engineering, Architecture, and the like; people will pay them to do what they love doing – at least that's what they can justifiably hope and expect to happen. With one major, I could be a year closer to graduation; I'm not stressed about that because a degree in English by itself wouldn't lead me into any money-earning work I'd be interested in. University teaching: not my thing.

With these thoughts in mind, I decided to broaden my program and do a double major: English and Biology. It's not a combination that directly leads to a job, but it's one that I can at least hope will be marketable if I do well and can match myself up with a suitable career track.

I've been lucky, or maybe I chose the right university in the first place. I've found that I can take a wide variety of courses that will count towards my double major. I have a lot of bio, a lot of chem, and of course a lot of English. I'm also taking anthropology, psychology, and quite a bit of sociology.

The combination suits me extremely well. I'm continually noticing insights that come from one subject and pertain to another. I can discuss things from points of view that others can't have because they're too narrowly specialized. The insights from anthropology, for example, pertain surprisingly often to what I'm reading in literature. Another example: physiology, psychology, and sociology. All have insights they can offer the others.

You do have to have the kind of brain that notices these interactions or be able to train yourself so that you can see them. Two or three trees, sometimes of different species, but with branches that are intertwined with each other in lots of places: it's lateral thinking, thinking outside the box, and not everyone can do it. Even some profs can't do it and don't notice when I do it. Just seeing these things is rewarding on its own, though. But the times when someone you respect is impressed with something unusual that you've seen: they're truly exhilarating.

In the end, I'm banking on some of these abilities and skills being useful to other people – and that I can get paid for doing them! My track isn't simple like the architects or the social workers. But then I'm not one who ever goes with everyone else in a straight line from one place to the next. I have confidence in myself, though, that I'll look back in ten years or so and be able to say, "Yes, it hasn't been easy, but I chose my program well, and I've done well since."

Coming Back

I was away from studying for two years after the end of high school. I was a bit apprehensive about coming back to school, and getting into the swing of academics again is certainly quite difficult. Socially, though, it isn't too bad.

I get a lot of questions – what did you do in those years? Surprise: What I thought was a wasted two years turned out to be of some benefit. A few of the things which I described were less obvious to others than I would have expected. For example, people can work together on an entirely equal level despite an age difference of even forty years. It's just a bunch of people working together on the same or related tasks in the same place. And after a while, the age difference doesn't matter in the workplace cafeteria either.

Then I realized: Hey, that insight came from the time spent in the full-time work world. It turned out to be something useful for the eighteen year-olds to hear when they whined about being put into groups with mature students. Not only that: I found references to this phenomenon and put it into a project and was rewarded with a great big check mark and the comment, "Exceptional Insight!"

Transition from Community College to University

I decided two years after I finished community college that I would attend university. In college I took a Child and Youth Worker program and in university I planned to take a Bachelor of Social Work program. I'd loved my college experience and had a great time. But when I started university, I didn't know what I was getting into.

I thought I would be able to attend school full-time and work part-time just like I did in college. Man was I wrong! I was blown away by the difference between the two institutions.

I found university to be intense and very different from community college. In college I did a lot of hands-on, touchy-feely assignments and did very well without having to try very hard. In university, there is lots of reading, lots of writing, and lots of independent work. People who aren't self-controlled and task-oriented have a hard time staying ahead of the game.

Maybe because I was a couple of years older, I was able to prioritize my time well and manage many different things at once. I had to learn to do it though, and I was sorry for the younger kids who got themselves truly screwed up that first semester.

A big help was the seminars the university holds, the study groups, the tutors, the writing help centers. I attended everything. If nothing else, it helped keep the stress level down and made the transition a lot easier.

A Pause in my Plans

I dropped out of university a few months ago. I have to admit that more than one thing factored into the decision. It's really hard to be at one university and to have the person you care about the most at another. Chat, texts, free phoning and videoconferencing: nothing comes close to being together. But I was seemingly thriving and getting high marks, so it was all quite a shock to lots of people: parents, friends, profs.

High marks were part of the problem. I could have continued, but I reached the point around Christmas where I'd just lost academic steam and wouldn't be able to put out my maximum effort any longer to get the kind of marks that I was used to. The choice that I was facing was getting mediocre marks or accepting a pause in my studies. And I needed space from the academic world. Really needed it. Now.

I'd felt the problem coming on for a while – each semester seemed more uphill than the last. Actually, I'm quite proud that I lasted as long as I did. I do wish, though, that the university had offered some counseling or at least some information that would have made me think of the idea of taking time off so that I could have planned ahead, and made the decision and necessary arrangements in a leisurely, organized way. Then I could feel good about making a rational choice, as opposed to how I feel now – defeated and humiliated.

In other countries, I've learned, what's referred to as a "gap year" is rather common. It's an accepted and normal part of university life, most commonly just before people go, but also as part of what students sometimes do while they're there. There are some who never come back, of course. However, others make decisions while away that radically change their university program from what they'd originally intended and from what everyone else expected of them. Presumably, the new direction is one that suits them better than their original one.

I know I will go back to school and finish. I still have the same goals. I haven't changed direction. And I have begun to miss it. I miss learning things; even though I can always find other things to learn and fill that gap, it's not the same as being in a class I like. I feel now that when I am ready to go back to it, I will go back with new energy and focus and be able to graduate with honors.

The time away so far has been wonderful for me; I have had a chance to travel and do things that I wouldn't otherwise have been able to do. Maybe I'd never have had the chance to do them as I probably would have just gone straight into a job.

I'm far from the only person who could benefit from the course of action I'm taking. I think most people wouldn't know what was happening, but it would show in lower marks as their enthusiasm declined.

My advice to freshman students is this: be aware that this is something that might happen to you. If you see it coming on, consider your options well ahead of the time when you need to decide. Tell people what you're considering and benefit from their reaction to what you say. Then in the end, if time away seems to be what you need to regain your enthusiasm, go for it.

A Lifelong Process

I enrolled in a three-year Business Admin college program close to home because I didn't think I had the smarts for university; I also didn't have the marks but that was mostly as a result of the number of high school classes that I had skipped. I completed one semester of my program and hated it. The second semester, I switched to a certificate program, Automated Office techniques or something like that, just so the entire year wouldn't have been a complete waste of money.

After that year, I decided to switch colleges, go far away and enroll in a different three-year program. I didn't know anyone, but that was part of the appeal.

I found college easy and couldn't understand why others found it hard. I graduated when I was 23 and worked. But all I could get was contract job after contract job; nothing was ever permanent. Most of the contract jobs were shit work, pay and hours until I finally landed one that I really liked. Yet I still couldn't get hired full-time permanent because I didn't have a university degree. This was frustrating because I actually witnessed some recent university grads who got themselves hired full-time. None of them had a clue about how to handle anything; I felt my years of experience should count. So I decided to go to university and get my Bachelor's in the field I was working in.

I started full-time but later switched to part-time for two reasons: 1. I needed money which meant I needed to work and 2. I didn't fit in. I was working days and going to school at night, with both part-timers and full-timers. But I found the others in my classes to be much younger, often not taking things seriously, mostly socializing on their laptops, and likely only there because their parents paid. Truth be told, I resented them.

At this time, I continue to attend university part-time despite the challenges of managing school and work, and I have found the career I always wanted. I work full-time in a job I would have never gotten if I wasn't attending university for a degree. The point of my story is that education is extremely important and just because you may have made a wrong choice in the beginning, you can make better choices later on that will only help you out when searching for the perfect career for yourself.

Attending post-secondary education has not been a quick process for me. If you start to think of education as something lifelong, you won't be in such a rush to get finished and get that job. Sometimes that job won't come until you continue your education, but that is your choice to make.

Learning Disability?
Use What's There for You

I got early acceptance into a very prestigious university and thought, wow, this is awesome. I was so excited that I immediately said yes without even visiting the campus. Big mistake. And I didn't use the Center for Students with Disabilities at all. Another big mistake.

I was originally diagnosed with ADHD in Grade 6 and then later, panic and anxiety as well. When I first got to university, I didn't have trouble with anxiety at all because I was so excited. Of course, I knew about the Center for Students with Disabilities, but they didn't do much to introduce themselves. Here's where I made my big mistake: you have to initiate contact with the center yourself. And I didn't.

Here I was in my first midterm, a three-hour exam in a huge room crammed with students. Everything seemed to be moving around me. Everyone was fidgety, but I couldn't move. In high school, I could get extra time for tests and exams, could get up, take a walk around, stretch, relax a bit. But I never realized how important that was or even that I needed it. So I couldn't focus enough to sit there and finish this exam. As a result, I failed for my very first time; I had never done so poorly on an exam in my life.

After midterms, I was passing all my courses but not doing great. Mid 60s, high 60s, low 70s – nothing that I would have to run away from. But I really wasn't enjoying myself at all. The campus was too big: it took me forty minutes to walk to a class, and there were no buses on campus. So I walked everywhere which took a long time out of my day. There were other classes that I had to take the subway to, which also took up time. It was a big difference from living in my small town.

I realized I wasn't happy, and I discussed it with a few people. But when I came home at Christmas, it really sank in. Then I went back to the university after the break, and I thought to myself, "I don't want to do this anymore."

So I called my mom and told her that I didn't like this, didn't want to keep doing this and thought I needed to do something different.

My mom came down, and we went to a counselor at the Center for Students with Disabilities. That was the first and only time I ever went there. The lady suggested that I just do a clean drop – right out of the university. Then I would use my high school marks, mostly 90s, to get into a different university the next year. If I tried to transfer, my university marks wouldn't get me in because they were mostly 60s.

On one hand, I am not sure if the result would have been any different had I gone to the center earlier. The city was too big; I didn't like the atmosphere of the university; I didn't like the people. It was very competitive, very cut-throat. A lot of people were very rich, and many of them had extremely different life styles than what I had ever had. I hated my roommates as they were really untidy and dirty, but snobby too; one of them was a stripper by night, another didn't speak any English, and I never saw the other one because she was taking seven courses, which was unheard of. All of this combined made for an awful experience. It was just not my life and not what I wanted for myself.

On the other hand, if I had gone to the center, my marks might have been a little better, and I might have been able to transfer to another university rather than drop out. Maybe the whole process would have been less stressful and not as awful for me.

So my advice would be: If you have a disability, go straight to the center and talk to them. It is up to you. They won't know you have a disability unless you tell them. They won't know anything about you, so get permission from your doctor to send the university your paperwork, or they will not be aware of your situation. That's what I did when I started my first year again at a different university the next year. But that's another story.

Just Leave Me Alone

I am tired of people wanting to talk to me about my disability. I am inundated with email requests from people or organizations who want me to fill out some survey or attend some meeting. It annoys me.

Since I am registered with the Center for Students with Disabilities, they pass on emails and requests. I don't think the center expects us to follow up, but they are required to forward this stuff to us automatically. They send the emails individually so it's not like everyone sees other people's email addresses. It is all very private, and maybe there is nothing wrong with that. I just don't feel like responding.

I think that it's nice that people are curious enough to want to understand and learn about our disabilities, but I feel that if people are sending me an email, then they are not really that interested as opposed to someone standing there. If I want to talk to someone I don't know, they need to ask me in person. But then again, I don't really need to talk to them because I have already been speaking with counselors at the center. Why would I respond to someone I don't know when I can talk perfectly fine to somebody I do know?

When I receive dozens of emails from unknown people, how do I know if it's junk mail or not? At one time, many of us received emails in our university account pretending to be from the center and requesting our names and passwords. These emails weren't from the center at all, yet many people stupidly replied with their personal information and then people got into their accounts. You have to be really careful about and aware of stuff like this.

A New Beginning

After I dropped out of my first year of university, I came home. It was late January. I knew that I was planning on going to university again, so I applied as soon as I could to one of the ones I had liked and applied to the year before.

I had loved the campus and the city when I visited; it was a smaller university and a smaller city than the one I had left and more like where I come from, with nearby parks, people playing football and walking about. I never saw that at my other university, and I sure didn't see parks or greenery because it was right in the middle of a big city.

So I applied to this university and got early acceptance; this surprised me because a lot of other places, including two universities which had offered me scholarships the year before, wouldn't even consider my application since I had dropped out from a university already. This university was great; they accepted me, and they offered me the same amount of entrance scholarship that they had offered me the year before.

But this time, I went to visit the university before I started school and I went to the Center for Students with Disabilities to talk to a counselor. She gave me forms and advised me on what I would have to do once I registered for my classes. She told me to speak to my profs to inform them about my disability and to remain in contact with them since, often, I would need more time for tests and midterms than what was allotted.

It was helpful for the counselor to tell me all of this. But it was up to me to go. You have to ask because they are not going to help you if you don't want the help. It's not high school, and they are not going to chase after you. You have to be the one that recognizes that you need the help.

The center does post fliers, and my adviser did mention it during Frosh Week. They tell you to come see them either if you have a disability or if you suspect you have a disability. Because I hadn't been tested for my disability since Grade 6, the center arranged for me to be retested.

At this university, you have to register with the center every semester, and you have to register every course, exam and midterm. They make accommodations for you such as having time-and-a-half for exams, getting to write in a quiet place, being able to get up and walk around,

sometimes being able to take four courses instead of five; I took summer courses online to make up for this. I don't usually need the extra time-and-a-half for exams and have only used it once. But it's there if I need it which is comforting and reduces anxiety. It has also been very helpful for me to not have to write in a gym or large classroom.

It's surprising to lots of people how many students are registered with the Center for Students with Disabilities – maybe one or two in each classroom. We are different in ways that are hard for people (including us!) to understand. Our minds may work differently, and for us to achieve all that we're capable of, the difference has to be recognized and accommodated. We're less easy to recognize than people with wheelchairs or who are blind, but we're disabled too. When I think about it, I'm lucky to be a member of the first generation of students to get this kind of help. Previous generations didn't make it this far, or if they did, they dropped out.

My friend has dyslexia, and he received a great amount of support through the center. He needed a lot of time to write exams because putting words together was very difficult for him. Some people think it's stupid and silly and that we don't need the help. I used to think I didn't need it, but I have changed my mind. Support is there; we can benefit from it, and so we should take advantage of it.

Despite connecting with the center, anxiety was a problem for me. It started right after Orientation Week, and I began to have panic attacks. Internally, I was terrified that the same thing that happened at the other university was going to happen here – that I wouldn't be able to do it and would have to drop out again. And I was very scared because I knew financially I couldn't afford to do that again. My parents and I lost a lot of money from that first experience. When you realize that and know that this is your last chance to succeed, it is very scary.

The anxiety lasted about three or four weeks that first semester. I was throwing up every morning. Everyone else looked and acted so happy. I later learned that what people portray often isn't reality. But I didn't know that then.

I tried to spend lots of time with other people and not be by myself ruminating. This was good because I made lots of friends. I would call my mom as soon as I woke up, upset, and she would be there to listen to me, get me up and going, to get dressed and out the door to class. I was very lucky that I had very strong support from my parents; I could call them any time of the day or night. And I did.

It took about a month for the anxiety to go away. I continued to see the counselors at the center, and they were great. One in particular referred me to the doctor to find out if my medications needed to be adjusted or if I was suffering from depression, which I wasn't. I had been taking anti-anxiety medication for years, but this doctor also prescribed a relaxant. It made me tired but better to feel tired than anxious. I started taking it morning and night but wanted to be careful because it is an addictive medication. Then I reduced it to once a day. And then I was feeling well enough to stop. The counselor had told me that it would just take time for me; she was right. I started to relax and get used to things, and the anxiety slowly went away.

I got lots of support from the counselor, friends and my parents. Underneath it all, I knew I liked the university and the people and would get through it. And once I calmed down and adapted, I realized that I had met so many people and made so many friends because I wasn't hiding in my room even though I had felt like doing that when the anxiety was so bad. It's a truly awful feeling.

Getting involved in sports helped because it kept me occupied and not thinking about all my worries and fears. Even more valuable was the support I got from the Center for Students with Disabilities.

Subsequently, I did experience some anxiety again, had a lot of trouble at Christmas and debated quitting. But the period of anxiety was shorter this time just as the counselor had predicted.

When I came to this university, all I wanted to do was succeed. I wanted a fresh start. I had looked at my university dropout experience my previous year as a failure and wanted to barf every time I thought about it. But now I kind of look at it as a stepping stone. The facts haven't changed but my perspective on them has.

WEB: LOVE ME, LOVE MY OCD srvlgd.com/OC
WEB: TAKING STOCK srvlgd.com/TS

Stereotypes

I wish people wouldn't stereotype me. Some people think I am gay because I am on a women's hockey team, and some people think that since I am in a sorority, I must be rich, snobby, slutty, drunk, a cokehead, or maybe some combination. But I am none of those. I wasn't before and I am not now.

I am on a women's hockey team because I like playing hockey and I have a hockey scholarship, which means that I won't owe as much money when I'm done here. I am in my sorority because where else would you find such a large group of instant friends? (Well, they are instant once you are accepted and initiated.)

There are a lot of differences between sororities and there are also great differences within sororities including the extent to which your life revolves around the sorority.

Enough truth can be found in some of these stereotypes that I can see why people think that way. I am an exception to the rule on my hockey team: there are more lesbians on my team than I have ever seen in any group of the same number of girls. Yet my friend who plays hockey at another college says there is about an even split between gay and straight people. But the people on the team take you as you are. If you are not gay, that's OK. Nobody is going to try to persuade you. Same as if you are gay and in a group that's mostly straight. There is no pressure to be gay or straight. You learn to accept it. That's part of going to college and growing up. You meet people with very different lives from you, but you accept them.

Guys' team sports are different since not a lot of the team members will talk about guys on their team being gay, or at least I have never heard it mentioned. I think that the homophobia that's still out there would make it very difficult for a gay guy on the team to be honest; rather, he's probably in the closet because he knows his teammates might have a huge problem with his being gay.

But now here am I spouting out a stereotype of my own and shouldn't really do that. I am an individual, and anyone who I could call my friend knows me as an individual and not just as a member of some kind of group. Same with other kinds of stereotypes. Maybe there is a reason for the stereotype, maybe not.

Not all African-Americans are the same. Or Hispanics. Or Asians. Or tiny people. Or over-weight people. We are people, and we are individuals. Once you have gotten to know someone and long before they become a good friend, if they ever do, all of these things become unimportant. You just see the person there in front of you.

Ethnic Origins

There's one thing I see here that at first I didn't like. Most of the time, if you see Asian students, they're all hanging out together in a group. Part of the reason is language. I think some of them feel that their English is a lot worse than it actually is. Talking to one of them, you can understand everything, and as far as you can tell, they understand everything you say as well. OK, so there's an accent, but it doesn't get in the way of communication. They often think it does, but they're wrong. So you tend to see them most of the time in groups of their own people, speaking their own language.

I don't want to exaggerate this as a problem. People from one group don't dislike people from other groups, or look down on them – at least not as far as I can tell. Perhaps they do, but they know better than to say anything. But I really don't think so.

We're all in the same classes, and when you are in class, you don't care about someone's ethnic origin. Once in class, everyone is in the same situation as you are all here to learn. And sometimes we have to work with each other in groups chosen on a random basis. Once you start working with someone, both of you forget the differences and concentrate on the work you've got to get done together. While this is going on, it's no different from working with someone from the suburbs or the country. And it's usually not different working with someone from another country although there are exceptions.

A friend of mine was extremely disturbed for a while when she was working with an Asian student who contributed very little. When he did, she just didn't see how what he said could be fitted in with what was already there. A real cultural divide, but that's unusual. Most of the time, we can all work together with people from various backgrounds, and either everyone can gain from the different perspectives, or it at least makes very little or no difference.

But once the task is finished, you're less likely to socialize together outside of class with the person from the other country even though you could make the effort to do so. Next day, there she is, in the same group as before with the same people speaking together in their own language. Too bad in one way. But I guess the more ways people are like ourselves, the more comfortable and relaxed we tend to be. If you're familiar and comfortable with it, you will automatically connect with it.

In fact, one experience I've had gives me a bit of insight on exactly that. My family is from Romania, and even though I haven't been there since I was very small, I did grow up in a Romanian environment – our house is full of Romanian things, and we all speak Romanian together at home. Here in the university, for the first time in my life, I met another person my own age who is Romanian as well – from the same part of Romania even. In fact she's more Romanian than me; she goes there every summer and lives with her relatives (which I've never done).

Instantly, there was a bond between us, a connection different from what I've ever experienced with anyone else. It was wonderful because this was the first time I'd found someone my age who spoke Romanian. I just knew that she and I had so many things in common, more than we could ever talk about. We did talk about quite a few, and we laughed together a lot, especially about some of the things our parents do and say. We just felt s - o - o close to each other.

And that helped me realize how it is that all the Asian students from the same country can feel so much more comfortable in their own company than they are with people who've lived here all their lives. Because I could easily imagine myself going to university in an Asian country and seeking out anyone else from this country to hang out with. Very tempting. Almost irresistible.

To sum up some of what I've learned: first, the closer people are to you in background, the easier it is for you to socialize with them. In our social life, we tend not to look for challenges but rather go for comfort, reassurance, closeness, and easy relationships.

Second, it's all up to the individual. Once you get to know someone as a person, that's all that matters; the other things don't. And I'm told that, as a freshman, you see the differences between people according to where they come from but later, when you're a senior, you notice it less.

WEB: AN UNDERAGE INTERNATIONAL STUDENT'S PERSPECTIVE
srvlgd.com/ISP

Integration

This university prides itself on its diversity. As well as people of African and Hispanic origins, there are special programs for minorities, for refugees from dangerous countries, and a big international department. My major is in International Development, so for me, having all these different kinds of people around is a big asset.

I have to say, though, that the integration is only partly successful. There are lots of cliques, and they are mostly racially dependent. Asians, Middle Eastern kids, Puerto Ricans, Mexicans, city kids – they all stick together. The profs suggest coming together, but there is not enough dialogue. People don't want to go into others' zones. There are staff in the university whose job is to promote integration, and I can't help feeling that if that's what they want, they need to do something a bit more than what they're doing now.

I think that you can't prevent a lot of the segregation by teaching students about it while at college. It has to come before they get here. The university has to ask the right questions on the application form to get the right people to come and maybe do a bit more to prepare them before they get here. What actually could be done, I'm not sure. Perhaps it might also help if they did something to prepare the rest of us too, but again, I'm not sure what.

In class, it doesn't matter much. I'm in classes where having different kinds of people from different backgrounds all over the world is a big asset. Having someone explain their own life to you is a lot different from reading about it in a book. It's more personal, and it does make us all more tolerant of others and understanding of their points of view. Especially heart-warming is the friendship that has sprung up between some of the Muslim students and a couple of Jewish students in one of my classes. Heart-warming and sometimes eye-watering. Kudos to the wonderful prof who helped facilitate it.

But it's outside class, in the cafeteria and other places where people socialize, that you see people from the same ethnic group congregating together. I wish it didn't happen that way because I'd like to get to know better some of these people who I've met in classes and seminars. I guess the reason for it is that everyone feels more comfortable with other people with similar experiences. You know how someone will react to something you say, so you don't have to worry about offending someone or being taken in the wrong way. I know it's easy for me to complain because I'm part of the majority, and most of the time I don't need to pay much attention to these things anyway.

And I have noticed that the older people get, the more integrated the groups are that they form. Maybe my ideal of complete integration isn't hopeless; it's just harder than I'd thought and will take more time than I'd thought.

An Oriental Perspective

I'm from China. A few years ago, I spent a year on exchange in another American city, but the family I stayed with looked after me extremely carefully with the result that my contact with America was somewhat limited. So now, as well as being immersed into the university life-style, I'm also in a completely different culture. It shows in a lot of ways, like my not understanding a joke because it includes an allusion to a TV program I haven't seen.

The first thing I noticed when I came to America was that everything is really intense and moves very fast. There's a lot more freedom here and fewer regulations, political restrictions, and cultural taboos. That applies largely to the online world. Information flow is more abundant; there's more variety; it all runs faster; and it is more intense.

Take Facebook. It is huge everywhere right now! Every day, it seems it gets even more instant and crazy. I'm so paranoid that I have to check it several times an hour. We have websites just like Facebook in China. Just as it is here, it's very addicting, and young people are on it all the time. It's especially harsh for me because I have both the American and Chinese versions of Facebook to distract me from my work. But the advantage is that when I'm on that website, I feel like I never left China.

I've noticed that the ways people use Facebook are very different between these two countries. Here, people enjoy posting everything about their lives online. In this way, people have access to huge amounts of information every day. On the other hand, the internet is younger in China so people do not know how to make the most of it by sharing information. A contributing factor is that Chinese people are a lot more reticent about making their private lives public. The culture has not yet developed to that stage, I guess.

Another difference is that there's such a wide variety of information here in America. People are not afraid to voice their stands on current issues. The freedom of speech is also shown in news reporting. Here, there are five or six major TV news networks, newspapers and magazines everywhere, all with different points of view. Americans don't easily believe all that appears on the news, whereas in China, because media is thoroughly censored by government and there's only one point of view, it's hard to tell what the real truth is.

People from Asian countries probably wouldn't have too many studying problems in American colleges because they have been trained to work hard. The problem for us lies mostly in social life. Actually, all freshmen worry about whether they fit in with others in their first year. We're all far away from home, being exposed to an extremely new situation. We're all scared of being alone. We're all trying to make friends. However, it's especially difficult for an international student like myself, not to mention the fact that I'm the only Chinese person in my year, if not in the entire school.

People have commented that this school is quite reflective of the local rural and small town surroundings. I'm sure things are different in larger universities that draw on a more diverse population. At this university, I have been stressed out; I have been depressed; I have been confused. I have to accept that I speak more formally than most people and I often miss out on jokes.

It is easy to make acquaintances in America – people are outgoing and easy to talk to. But then, even though people ask, "How are you?" all the time, little do they really care about what you have to say about your life. In that sense, I found it hard to make really close friends. I do not understand how Americans are able to hang out in such big groups. I feel very strange being in a group and having somewhat trivial conversations with everyone. In China, people tend to stick together with three or four close friends most of the time.

Another confusion is the stereotype people have of college life. A phrase that I once heard comes to mind: "Kids! Drugs are bad. Alcohol is bad. Sex is bad. There's a time and place for all this, and it's called … College." So that's basically what's in most people's minds – we need to accomplish the craziness of a lifetime in college! So I guess college is also the period when people most likely go against their moral beliefs. Yep, that's just college; doesn't really count. Like if you bum a donut from someone else in a coffee shop, the calories don't count like they would if you bought it yourself.

There are definitely drugs, alcohol, and sex going on around me among people I know. And amazingly (for someone with my background), they talk about it too – I guess to show off how cool they are. On those occasions, I just listen and hold off on my opinions. I don't try to accept or oppose any of the life styles; I simply try to understand why such things happen. I mean, as long as I hold on to my own values and make the choices that are right for myself, nothing can harm me, right? Most of my friends (okay, acquaintances) respect my choices. So they don't really pressure me into anything. We still talk at the dinner table and sometimes hang out, but I'm very clear in my heart about who are the ones that I truly hold as my real friends.

Also surprisingly to me, when I come to think about things a bit more, I realize that I have in fact made several real friends who I can really relate to now. I guess things have been changing over time. Little by little and without noticing it, I am indeed making friends.

One more thing I've noticed that I really like about Americans is the "go-for-it" state of mind. I've always liked music, and in China, my friends and I would spend a lot of time singing, but just for ourselves. Sure, we'd have dreams, but here, it's more about fulfilling them. People write songs, form bands, and perform in musicals. Whatever the dream, it seems natural to try to achieve it. You can just start doing it, and make it become reality.

I think the most important thing to do as a freshman is to step out and try everything that's there. Fate won't come to you. You have to create your own. If I'd stayed in China for university, I doubt if I'd have learned that.

Race at University: Four Viewpoints

WEB: RACE AT UNIVERSITY (3) AND (4) srvlgd.com/RU

(1) I came here instead of a State university because of the financial aid. Even though tuition is more expensive, it was cheaper to come here because of the grants and loans I received. If you can meet the academic standard, this university will make it so that you can afford to come.

I feel it is different for me here than for a lot of other students because I am from a visible minority. Often minority students are more united because they feel they have to stick together. To have made it to a university of this caliber makes me feel I have to bring everything I have to it. I have to be on point academically, and I feel I have to do everything to the max. There is definitely a lot of pressure.

I come from a family that values education very much. We are from Trinidad, and there, people prefer to send their kids away to school if they are able to do so. It is all about education being the key to upward mobility in your socioeconomic status. Education is a gateway, so being able to achieve such a high level is exhilarating but frightening at the same time.

The minority students here are mostly either children of immigrants or immigrants themselves. You don't see many minority students from families who've been here for a long time.

I do tend to hang around with people like me. I like the fact that they can identify with what I go through and how I think. It's comforting, especially when you are so far away from home. People tend to stick with what they know and to go to a place where there are people who look like them. I always notice when I am the only black student in my class and if there is another black student, we tend to become friends quickly because we are the only ones in that class. We are still friends with others, but I find it's easier with each other. I also think it's important to keep our culture. You don't want cultures to be so diluted that you lose traditions and history.

It's different for dating because, if I want to date someone of the same minority, there are not a lot of options for me. I am either not attracted to them, or they are just a good friend so it probably won't work out. Or they already have a girlfriend. Maybe that will change. I hope so.

Here, there are black parties and there are white parties. A black party is going to be a dancing party where people might drink. A white party is where there is a whole bunch of drinking and maybe some dancing once people are drunk. Often people will pre-game, which means they go to a white party first to get tipsy and then to a black party to have fun. I have been to some good white parties, but often there are just beer cans and weird people everywhere, weird games, people making out with random people. It's just not what I am used to. I hate beer and that's what most of them like to drink. It smells gross, it's all over the floor and gets your shoes dirty. It's a completely different atmosphere. So when people ask me to a party, I tend to ask them which kind it is going to be.

Sometimes if a white person goes to a black party, people look at them funny, like they are at the wrong party. That must be stressful for them. I do feel it is easier for black people to go to white parties than for white people to go to black. Usually people are really friendly to us, but there is always going to be some ignorant person. One time, a white girl was walking past a party, and we were sitting outside. I heard some people call her "snow bunny" which was really disrespectful, I think.

I do have to say that I sometimes notice particular differences that bug me. For example, I have a white friend who used to do things when I was first getting to know her that annoyed me. She would change the way she talked which is a big pet peeve with me. Talk the way you talk; don't try to change it. Besides, I feel I don't talk like that, so I told her to stop it. She did, and I know she was embarrassed about it. We got over it, but she did have to be told.

It does make a difference that I am a member of a visible minority here. But I am okay with it.

. . . .

(2) I feel that this university sets us up for segregation and racism. They have a dorm for black kids which has a lot of programming about black or African things like celebrating the culture. There is also a Latino living center, an international living center, and quite a few other dorms for minorities. But it's hard to get to know people who live in these dorms if you don't live there too. Most of them don't come out and mix. If we see them around, we say hi, but they are not really friendly.

Once we tried to go to an Asian party, but they wouldn't let us in. They told us it was full but meanwhile, there were people walking in right by us with no problem. The difference was that we were a large group of whites, blacks and Latinos, and the people they were letting in were Asian.

I think the university puts us at a disadvantage by offering minority dorms and special programs. I grew up in a town where everyone is white, and it was a shock for me when I got here. I didn't know what I had gotten myself into. I chose to participate in this special summer program but when I got there, I found it was almost all minorities and hardly any white kids. That had never happened to me before. I'm fine with it now, but they just kind of throw things like that at people. Most people would refuse to go to things where there would be nobody like themselves there. I feel they should have just mixed people up instead.

I also feel that our university newspaper is racist. They say disrespectful things like how the program houses or dorms are like minority ghettos, and they compare them, often not in a good way.

People will always tend to gravitate towards people similar to themselves. Offering all these minority programs and putting minority kids together in dorms just makes it harder for people of different races and ethnic origins to get to know each other. The university just seems to make it worse.

Like I said, I wish the university would just mix people up so that we can all get to know each other.

Not Standing Out

One thing I really like about it here is that, for the first time in my life, I no longer feel that I stand out from everyone else. Here's why: I spent my whole elementary and high school time in a small town where almost everyone was white. I'm not. It's not that there was any hostility, or racism, or anything bad that was done to me or said to me. I fitted in well with the groups I belonged to, and I had lots of very close friends. Just as many, and just as close, as anyone else. But the difference was still there.

People I hadn't met before, especially older people, would look at me just a bit longer than anyone else or lower their eyes as I tried to meet

theirs. Perhaps I was exaggerating it in my mind, but it was always there. No matter what, I knew it was the first thing anyone noticed about me. Even if nothing actually occurred, I was always thinking that some small thing might happen at any time, and I would become self-conscious. I should make it clear that it didn't apply to people I knew well. But it was a feeling I was never able to get rid of.

But here, it doesn't apply. There are lots of people of all nationalities and all ethnic origins. So no one stands out, including me. At last I can feel that people I meet are seeing me just as another person, rather than as a representative of something, or someone with some characteristics they might not feel comfortable with. Stupid maybe. But it makes life a lot better for me.

And actually, I've had discussions about the topic with some people I've got to know since coming here: Caucasians. (Yes, they're still in the majority, although here not by much.) They have said something the same as I've felt. The watchword here is tolerance.

The most amazing example I've seen so far is one girl who used to be a Christian giving it up and becoming a Muslim because her best friend was a Muslim. No one thought that the reasoning behind it was any of their business unless she wanted to discuss it, which as far as I know she didn't. She looked a bit different, but it was the same person that everyone had liked before; they still did. Nothing had changed that had anything to do with them.

Here, there are so many different kinds of people (old, young, black, white, brown, gay, straight, Muslim, Jewish, Hindu, etc.) that no one can possibly pay attention to any of it. If people did, there would be fights all the time and life would be impossible for everyone.

You just have to see everyone you meet as a person.

Closing Reflection

If Only my Thirteen Year-Old Self Could See Me Now

If only my thirteen year-old self could see me now. If only there were some way to converse with my younger persona, to send her a letter, maybe, or give her a phone call. Or better yet, if only right now, she could be sitting here next to me – staring in awe at the strange person she has become and wondering how on earth such a transformation could be possible.

She'd be amazed by the hair color, for one. She'd be amazed at the size of me, too. She'd ask me questions, I'm sure – about university, about guys, about life, about herself – and I'd answer them, but vaguely, not wanting to spoil the present by meddling too deeply in the past. I'd tell her she'll be happy, for the most part; independent, self-sufficient, taken-care-of, well-loved. And I'd tell her that no, she hasn't yet figured out how to touch her toes both at once, or be any good at math, or do even a poor impression of a half-decent cartwheel.

And then I'd tell her about this. About here: about my house that I share with four other students, my university, my basketball team. I'd tell her all about first year, about living alone for the first time and how big and scary the world was, and how the friends I made at university were all there with me and helped me discover how to make the vast expanse somehow seem that much safer and smaller.

I'd tell her about lecture halls and residence and classes and profs and morning practices and mono, and just how exhilarating it is the first time you get an assignment back that you worked hard on and you get an A. I'd take her with me when I was called to the Dean's office – she'd feel the nervousness too – and then I'd share the feeling I had when he told me about the scholarship I'd won.

And then, I'd send her on her way – with a hug, maybe a tear, and good wishes for the future. I'd tell her to prepare for some hard times because there were going to be many of them. I'd tell her to always keep looking forward, never get too stuck in the short term, and to always take every endeavor one well-thought-out step at a time. Though I know it would fall on deaf ears, I would implore her to try to be patient – to wait things out and not rush right into them, and when she did make mistakes, to take time to sit and cry a little over them, but then use them as motivation for everything she wanted from then on.

I'd like to say these things to my thirteen year-old self. I'd like to prepare her for everything that's going to come her way, for the period in which she will grow from a wide-eyed and self-conscious little girl into what her now twenty year-old self would like to think is a capable woman. And I wish I could pass this knowledge on to her because I know it would have helped me immensely to hear it from the very person who experienced it. But, ultimately, that can't happen – unless I somehow master time travel – so I guess she'll just have to keep going without my help. But that's okay – because even though I can't help her, there are still so many wonderful people who can and will. And even though it's going to be hard for her, a ridiculously long and winding road that I know she'll have to traverse, I know she'll make it, and she'll succeed. And by doing so, even though I can't help her out, I know that she'll help me out instead.

But back here to the university. She'd be blown away.

Made in the USA
Middletown, DE
12 December 2019